HEI
FRO N

ᗞ Y
SMITH BURNHAM

PREFACE

AN interest in history and a love of historical reading will be most readily acquired by those children who approach this rich field of literature through the medium of stories of the great figures of the past. Such stories, if properly selected and told, give children those vivid concrete pictures of men and of events which are vitally essential to any real understanding of bygone days. At the same time such history stories may be so selected as to hold up right ideals of conduct and of character. Moreover, by their appeal to the emotions, which lie very near to the springs of conduct, they move to action. Tales of gentleness, of honor, of justice, of courage, of fortitude in suffering, of intrepidity in danger, of dauntless resolution, of iron will, inspire children to an emulation of those virtues. These "Hero Tales from History" have been written in the faith set forth in this paragraph. Through these stories the author aims to inculcate the fundamental virtues just named and at the same time to acquaint children with the names and achievements of some of those great men and women whose lives and characters are a part of our racial and national inheritance.

In the selection of the tales in this book the author has drawn upon all ages. Here are mighty men of the ancient world and makers of modern America. Some of the characters chosen as the heroes of these stories are great figures in world history, but the greater part of them were selected because they are among the foremost heroes of our own country and of our own culture. Of course in a book of this size {iv} many valuable stories had to be omitted. But it is believed that all the tales included are typical and representative.

These "Hero Tales" are not biographies of the men about whom they are told, neither has any attempt been made to join them into a connected historical narrative. They are just stories from the past told with constant thought of the stage of mental development of the children for whom they are intended. Each story has a hero, each is full of action, and the author has tried to tell each one in clear and simple language. The author has also tried to make each story teach its intended lesson without any moralizing on his part.

The history of the past can never become a vital thing to us until the men of the past are live, flesh and blood men. It is the author's hope that these "Hero Tales from History" will help to make threescore great figures from our past something more than names to the children who may enjoy this book.

Smith Burnham.

MIGHTY MEN OF LONG AGO

MOSES, THE GREATEST LAW-GIVER, AND THE MEEKEST MAN

LONG ago in the land of Egypt there lived as slaves to the Egyptians a race of white people called the Hebrews. There were so many of them that the Egyptians began to be afraid that they would over-run the land. So the cruel king, or the Pharaoh, as he was called, commanded that all the baby boys of the slave race should be thrown into the River Nile. But one little child escaped this fate, for his poor slave mother disobeyed the king and hid her baby in her hut. When he was three months old, his mother was afraid she could not keep him quiet any longer. So she made a basket, and plastered it inside with pitch, so that it would be water-tight and float like a boat. Into this basket-boat she put her baby.

The mother set the strange little boat on the edge of the River Nile, among the tall reeds called bulrushes, very near the place where she knew the king's daughter came every day to bathe. It was a cool spot, well guarded and safe from the terrible crocodiles that lived in the Nile. After making sure that the little boat would not sink, the mother went back to her work, leaving her daughter Miriam to see what became of her baby brother.

Just as the wise mother had planned, the princess soon came with her ladies-in-waiting, and spied the cradle basket rocking on the waves near the shore. She told one of her{2} maidens to bring it to her. The king's daughter knew too well of her father's command to drown or kill all the boy babies of the Hebrew slaves. So when she found a baby crying there, she pitied the poor mother who had obeyed the king by putting him in the river, still fondly hoping to save his life.

When the Pharaoh's daughter saw the babe, she said, "This is one of the Hebrews' children!" There was a pleading look in the face of the little child. He seemed to ask the princess to take him in her arms. The princess herself was married but she had no children. That baby, smiling through his tears, touched her mother-heart. How could she help saving his little life from her father's cruel law by claiming him as her own?

Just then Sister Miriam bowed before the princess and said, "Shall I go and call to thee a nurse of the Hebrew women, that she may nurse the child for thee?"

The king's daughter was, pleased and said, "Yes, go." So the happy sister ran and brought her mother to the great stone palace of the Pharaohs. Then the princess said, as if the mother were only a child's nurse, "Take this child away and nurse it for me, and I will give thee thy wages."

So, besides saving his life, that mother was royally paid for taking care of her own son instead of working as a slave out in the hot sun. Besides, she had a good chance to tell him, as he grew up, of the one true God. What if her boy should save his father's people from slavery, when he became a man in the palace of the Pharaohs?

In due time the daughter of the king adopted the young Hebrew as her own son, and named him Moses, which means "Saved," because she had rescued him out of the river. When Moses was old enough he went to live with{3} his royal mother, where he was educated in all the wisdom of the Egyptians, who at that time, nearly four thousand years ago, were the most learned people in the world. Although he studied in the college of the priests, who believed in the Sun, the Moon and many other gods, Moses never forgot what his mother had taught him about the true God.

Young Prince Moses had a great deal to do while he was growing to manhood. He is said to have become commander-in-chief of the Egyptian army that conquered the black and savage race living a thousand miles up the Nile.

In the Bible story are these words:

"And it came to pass in those days, when Moses was grown, that he went out unto his brethren, and looked on their burdens: and he spied an Egyptian smiting an Hebrew, one of his brethren.

"And he looked this way and that way, and when he saw there was no man, he slew the Egyptian, and hid him in the sand.

"Now when Pharaoh heard this, he sought to slay Moses. But Moses fled from the face of Pharaoh, and dwelt in the land of Midian."

This Pharaoh was not the father of Moses' foster mother, who was now dead. It is said that this king was afraid Moses would drive him from the throne and become Pharaoh himself.

For forty long years the exiled prince lived in Midian, studying, planning, and writing. It was during this time that he made the great decision of his life. He resolved to save his own people, the million Hebrews who were slaves to the Egyptians.

At last, Moses and his brother Aaron appeared before the Pharaoh, and announced that God had demanded that the king should let the children of Israel go free. It was a hard thing to ask, for the Egyptians still needed the great army of slave men to build great pyramids and temples.{4}

The king refused, and consented, and refused again, until plague after plague was sent upon the land of Egypt. At last, when the king's son, and the oldest child of every Egyptian family in the whole country had died in one night, the terrified and heartbroken king called for Moses and Aaron by night, and said, Rise up and get you forth from among my people, both ye and the children of Israel; and go."

"And the people took their dough before it was leavened, their kneading troughs being bound up in their clothes upon their shoulders."

This going out of the Hebrew people bound for the Promised Land, nearly four thousand years ago, is called "the Exodus." To this day it is celebrated by the Jews every year as the Passover.

When the Pharaoh realized that the great stone temples and pyramids of Egypt might never be finished, he was afraid because he had let the slave people go. So he ordered out his horses and chariots and drove hard after them till he caught them in camp beside the Red Sea. The frightened Hebrews began to cry and accuse Moses of deceiving them and leading them out into a great trap, to be killed like a million helpless sheep, by Pharaoh's army.

But Moses told the wailing crowds not to be afraid. Before the king's horses and men caught up with them a strong east wind came up and kept the tide from running in, thus leaving a bare sand bar right in front of them across that arm of the Red Sea. Moses commanded the people to march over as on dry land, an order which they lost no time in obeying. Then the Pharaoh and his horsemen came up behind and drove hard after them upon the{5} sand bar. But the heavy chariots stuck in the mud beneath the sand, and when the Egyptians reached the middle the wind changed, and the tide, which had been held back so long, rushed in and drowned Pharaoh and his army. Then Miriam and Moses and Aaron led these million freed slaves in a grand victory chorus of song about their hairbreadth escape.

Moses praying on Mount Sinai.

From an old print
Moses praying on Mount Sinai.
From an old print
But the people were always scolding and complaining against Moses, the dear, gentle leader who had saved them from their cruel bondage. It was his patient love for his thankless people, while through forty years they wandered in the wilderness, that gave Moses the name of being the meekest man that ever lived.{6}

At Mount Sinai Moses received from God and gave to the people the Ten Commandments, written on two tablets of stone. He spent his time during the long years of wandering in the wilderness in planning the laws and religion for his beloved people. He himself never entered the Promised Land, but died in the wilderness, somewhere on a mountain called Nebo. The Bible makes this statement of his death:

"So Moses the servant of the Lord died there. And he buried him in a valley, but no man knoweth of his sepulchre unto this day."

DAVID, THE GIANT-KILLER KING

NEARLY three thousand years ago a bright, handsome Hebrew lad was playing a harp while watching his father's sheep on the hills of Bethlehem.

One dark night there was a great stir among the sheep, and David saw a bear making off with one of the lambs. There were no guns in those days, but David had a sling, and he could fling a pebble almost as swift and straight as a boy can shoot a bullet to-day. So David ran and killed the bear by driving a stone through the big brute's eye into its brain. When he took the trembling lamb back to its mother, what should he see but a lion starting off with a sheep in his huge jaws. There was no time to gather pebbles. Grabbing a jagged rock in one hand, David seized the great beast by the mane with the other, and aimed quick blows at the lion's eyes, breaking his skull before the lion could drop his prey and fight back.{7}

That was a great night's work for one lone lad. After quieting his frightened flock, David took his harp and made up a song of thanks to the God of Israel for saving him alive from the jaws of the lion and the paws of the bear.

Not long after this, David's old father sent out to the hills for him. When the youth came down to the house, he found Samuel, Prophet of God and Judge of Israel, waiting for him. David's seven older brothers stood around eyeing him strangely, as the prophet said, "This is he," and baptized him by pouring oil on his head.

"What did the prophet anoint me for?" David asked his father.

"To be king of Israel instead of Saul."

"But I am only a boy, and King Saul is so big and strong—head and shoulders taller than other men. Why did not the prophet anoint our Eliab? He is almost as tall as the king himself."

"The Lord seeth not as man seeth; for man looketh on the outward appearance, but the Lord looketh on the heart."

After that David went back and herded his father's sheep, but his brothers were jealous of him because he had been anointed to be king.

As had often happened in the days of the Judges, the heathen Philistines came up and made war against the people of Israel, and the eldest three of David's brothers were in the king's army. Many weeks went by, but no word came from the camp. So the father sent David down with provisions for the brothers and a present for their captain.

The shepherd boy found the two armies in camps opposite each other, across a narrow valley. Every one was excited{8} over Goliath, a giant who came down every day into the valley from the army of the Philistines and challenged the king of Israel and all his men. Goliath was nearly eleven feet tall. He wore a bronze helmet about as big as a bushel measure, and his spear was like a weaver's beam. Even King Saul and David's tall brother Eliab were much too small to fight with the Philistine giant.

David could not bear to hear Goliath calling the king and his soldiers cowards and repeating wicked words about the God of Israel. So he went and told Saul he would like the chance to go down and fight the insulting giant.

The soldiers laughed at this, and Eliab told his young brother to go home and mind his "few sheep in the wilderness." But David would not be put off. He told how God had helped him kill a lion and a bear in one night. The lad was so earnest that the king consented to let him try.

The only weapons David took were his staff and his sling. On his way to meet the giant he stopped at the brook and picked up five smooth pebbles. Both armies looked on breathless at the strange combat. Great Goliath laughed at little David, as if the king of

Israel were playing a joke on him. He cursed David by all the gods of the Philistines, and yelled:

"Am I a dog, that thou shouldst come to fight me with a stick? For this I will feed thy little carcass to the birds."

Then David shouted back to Goliath, "I come in the name of the God of Israel whom thou hast defied."

All the Israelites and Philistines saw the boy make a quick motion with his sling, and heard a thud. The giant dropped his heavy spear, threw up his huge hands and fell, with a groan and a great clatter of armor, face downward on the ground.{9}

David's first pebble had done the work. It had gone swift and straight through the eye-hole in Goliath's brass helmet and sunk deep into his low, brutal forehead, killing him almost instantly.

"And when the Philistines saw their champion was dead they arose and fled. The children of Israel returned from chasing after the Philistines, and they spoiled (looted) their tents."

David playing his harp before King Saul.

From the painting by Schopin
David playing his harp before King Saul.
From the painting by Schopin
King Saul was so thankful that his own life had been saved, and that the people were spared from being slaves to the Philistines, that he made David come and live in his{10} palace as a younger brother to his son, Jonathan. This prince was not jealous like David's own brothers. David and Jonathan became such good friends that, though this happened nearly three thousand years ago, people say yet that two boys or men who are very friendly with each other are "like David and Jonathan."

After a time Saul and Jonathan were both killed in a battle with the Philistines. Then David became king of Israel. He proved to be one of the best of rulers. He wrote many of the Bible Psalms and played on his harp as he sang them. He planned to build a great house of worship for the God of Israel in Jerusalem, but, because he had been a man of war, he felt unworthy to do such sacred work. So he left the temple to be built by his son Solomon, the wisest king that ever ruled over Israel.

HOMER, THE HERO POET OF ANCIENT GREECE

LONG, long ago, when the world was young, and before men began to write books, a kind of men called "bards" used to wander about the land of Greece, from town to town and from court to court, playing the harp and singing of the deeds of the heroes of Greece. As years went on there came to be very many such tales sung by the bards, and handed down from father to son. At last, there came a day when men learned to write. Then the person whom we call Homer, the earliest and greatest poet in the history of the world, gathered together these hero tales and wrote them in beautiful poetry. This work of collecting these scattered stories of the exploits and adventures of the{11}

Homer, the blind poet, was led from place to place by a
young boy when he went to sing his songs and recite his wonderful poems
of ancient Greece.

5

Homer, the blind poet, was led from place to place by a young boy when he went to sing his songs and recite his wonderful poems of ancient Greece.

{12} Greek gods and heroes and making them into one great hero poem, called an "epic," was done nearly three thousand years ago.

Although nobody really knows anything surely about the life of this ancient Homer, the story goes that he was blind, and that he was very poor, as poets often are. After his death, when his two great poems had made him famous, seven different cities in Greece claimed each to have been his home. But the facts of his life matter very little when compared with the wonderful stories that he left for all the world to read. His epics were imitated by the greatest poets of Rome, Italy, and England, and have been translated many times into both poetry and prose.

There were two of these epics—the "Iliad," picturing the siege and downfall of ancient Ilium, or Troy; and the "Odyssey," describing the ten years' wanderings of Odysseus, or Ulysses, on his way back home after the destroying of Troy by the Greeks.

The war against Troy, which lasted ten years, was started because Paris, son of Priam, the old king of Troy, carried off from her home, Helen, the lovely wife of one of the Grecian kings. The "Iliad" tells of the bold deeds of many heroes on both sides. The strongest fighter in Troy was Hector, another son of King Priam. Achilles was the greatest hero on the side of the Greeks. One of the most beautiful scenes in art as well as in poetry is that of Hector saying good-bye to his wife and baby boy, and one of the best known examples of friendship is that of Achilles for his friend Patroclus.

The great gods and goddesses—for the early Greeks believed in many gods—all took sides in the struggle for Troy. Apollo, Minerva, and Juno helped the Greeks;{13} Mars and Venus helped the Trojans. They chose the side of the people who had especially served and worshiped them, using their mighty power to help and direct in the long war.

After nine years the Greeks pretended that they were going to give up the struggle and sail away to their homes. They built a huge wooden horse to leave as a peace offering, telling the Trojans that it was a gift for them to offer to their gods. The Trojans were only too willing to think that the Greeks were giving up the fight. They would not listen to the princess Cassandra, who warned them of danger, saying, "I fear the Greeks, even when they bring gifts." In spite of her words the city fathers accepted the strange present and trundled the big horse within their walls. That night some Greek soldiers who were hidden inside the hollow wooden figure jumped out of their hiding place, opened the six gates of Troy, and let in the Grecian army. The great warriors waiting outside swarmed in and soon captured the city.

Helen, the stolen queen, sailed back home and lived there in her little Grecian kingdom for many years after her rescue by her royal husband and his brother, another king, with the help of the Greek heroes and the gods who sided with them.

Among the Greeks who fought at Troy was Ulysses. His journeyings on the way from Troy to Ithaca, the rocky island where he was king, form a wonder story of ancient life and travel. Ulysses' ships were driven about to many strange places. First he came to the land of the lotus eaters, where some of his men ate the lotus flowers and forgot their homes and friends. The rest of them came next to the country of the Cyclops, giant monsters with{14} only one eye in the middle of their foreheads. The chief Cyclops caught the Greeks, shut them up in the cave where he kept his sheep, and ate two of them for his supper every day. Ulysses was clever enough to think of a way by which he and his men might escape. While the giant was out of the cave he sharpened a stake by burning it in the coals, and when the Cyclops fell asleep after his hearty supper, Ulysses and four of his men drove this sharp stake into his one eye, blinding him. Then the leader tied each of his men under one of the Cyclops' sheep, and himself clung to the long hair beneath the largest ram. When the sheep crowded out of the cave the giant did not know that they were carrying his prisoners with them. Before he discovered the trick the Greeks were safe on their ship.

After another voyage, Ulysses and his men landed on the island of Circe, a beautiful witch who turned the men all into swine and made them stay with her a long time. But Apollo and Minerva helped Ulysses undo the spell of the charmer. Circe warned Ulysses against the Sirens, who would tempt them by their singing only to destroy them all, and against Scylla and Charybdis—a risky place for a ship to pass, between a great rock and a dangerous whirlpool.

The wife of Ulysses also was beset with many trials and dangers. She was surrounded by neighboring princes, each of whom wished to marry her and become king of Ithaca. She kept on with her weaving, putting these suitors off by telling them she would give them her answer when she finished her weaving—but each night she unraveled all the weaving she had done in the daytime.

During the twenty long years of Ulysses' absence, Penelope's young son grew to manhood and started out to find his father. He reached home, after a vain search, just at{15} the time when Ulysses came back. The king of Ithaca was disguised by the goddess Minerva as an old beggar, so that no one recognized him but his good old dog.

Ulysses arrived at his palace at the very moment when, the suitors having become too urgent, Penelope brought out Ulysses' bow and agreed to marry the man who could bend it and shoot an arrow through six rings placed in a long line, as her heroic husband had been known to do. The feeble looking beggar was allowed to look on while the princes tried frantically to win the hand and the throne of the fair Penelope. One after another failed in the desperate attempt. Then the seemingly aged stranger asked them to let him try to bend the great, stiff bow and shoot the heavy arrow. They laughed at and insulted him, but he took the bow, bent it with ease, and shot the long arrow straight through all the rings, just as Ulysses used to do.

Penelope gave a cry of joy, for she knew then that the stranger was none other than her long-lost husband. Ulysses's disguise suddenly disappeared, and with his son's aid he shot the impudent suitors who had tormented his wife all those years.

SOCRATES, THE "GRAND OLD MAN" OF GREECE

SOCRATES was the son of a sculptor of Athens in the days of Pericles, a ruler who encouraged art and culture and made his city famous for its learning and beauty. As a boy, Socrates was taught by his father to carve statues. Nearly a thousand years afterward, a traveler in Greece described a group of figures, called "The Graces," carved{16} by the youthful Socrates. But the young man was not satisfied with being a sculptor. While he was working at his carving, his active mind kept trying to find out the reason for everything.

In Athens at this time there were not only many painters and sculptors, but numbers of men called philosophers, who gave all their time to thinking out the meaning of what they saw in the world around them, and trying to teach that meaning to such people as would listen to them. These philosophers differed widely from one another in their views. Some of the things they thought would seem very queer to us to-day, but they were doing their best to find out the truth.

A group of philosophers who held the same views was called a "school." The schools of philosophy were not like the schools of to-day. They were simply gathering

7

places, in some one's house, or on a street corner, or in a public porch, or in a grove, where men who liked to think came together for talk and debate. Instead of children sitting quietly at desks, a school was made up of grown men walking about and talking a great deal.

Socrates found that he was much more interested in listening to what the philosophers thought than he was in carving statues. So he gave up his work with his father and went out to visit the schools. But as he went from one school to another, he could see that no one of them was right in every way. He decided that he could not learn the real truth from them. So he resolved to walk the streets and ask questions of the people he met there. He was so anxious to know that he could learn from anyone he talked with, whether man, woman, or child. He met many men who thought they were philosophers when they{17} were not, for it was considered a great thing to be known as a famous thinker, and all men aimed at it.

When Socrates met a man who claimed to be wise, he would ask questions as if he himself did not know anything, and he would thus lead on from one thing to another till sometimes he made the man say the very opposite of what he had said before, making him ashamed of himself. This way of drawing out the truth by questions and proving the wrongness of some ways of reasoning is known to-day as the "Socratic method."

The Greeks were great believers in beauty. They thought whatever is beautiful must be right. But Socrates saw handsome men and beautiful women leading wrong lives, and he made such people angry by saying so. Socrates himself was far from handsome. He was short and thick-set. His head was bald and his eyes bulged out in a comical way. His nose was broad and flat; his lips were thick and his ears stood out, making him look like the clowns the Greeks laughed at in their great out-door theaters.

More than this, Socrates was poor. He had learned, while a young man, that those who had most of the so-called good things of life were the most unhappy. So he made up his mind that the best kind of wealth lay in not wanting much. He did not care for good things to eat. He went barefoot, and wore the same thin garment both summer and winter.

The Greeks were fond of art for the sake of art. But Socrates believed in right living, and loved art only for heart's sake—for the sake of doing good and making people happy. He also believed that to know is to live, and that in order to live right one must first know what is right. He claimed to have a certain force or voice within which{18} showed him what was right. He was the first of all the wise men of the heathen world to believe that this inner light should be a correct moral guide to right living.

Even the gods the Greeks worshiped did things of the worst kind; they were spiteful, cruel, and wicked. So the people did not think it wrong to act as their gods did. They did not understand what Socrates meant when he said he had a voice within himself which told him what he should or should not do. So they thought he was trying to make them believe in a strange god, when they had too many already.

Socrates takes the cup of poison from his judges.
Socrates takes the cup of poison from his judges.
Socrates was a great lover of his country. When the Greeks went to war he went in the ranks as a private soldier, and fought like a hero. In one battle he saved the life of a rich, handsome, brilliant young man who was very popular{19} in Athens. This youth soon learned to love the homely old philosopher and studied with him. Two other great men were pupils of Socrates. One of these became one of the greatest historians and the

other a great philosopher. They were both authors, and they wrote all that is known to-day about Socrates, who did not leave any writings to show what he believed and taught. Of course, most people failed to understand Socrates, and so they made him the laughing stock of the town. Yet many young men, led by the youth whose life Socrates had saved, came to him to learn how to live and be useful and happy.

But the people who were jealous of his influence over the young men of the city accused the old philosopher of teaching them of other gods and thus corrupting their minds. They had him arrested, but his students followed him to the prison, where he kept on teaching them the right way to live. Socrates was tried by a law-court of citizen judges and defended himself very ably. The story of his bold defense is told in a book called the "Apology of Socrates," by a famous Greek writer named Plato. He spoke of his aim to show people how little they knew so that they might learn more, and told his judges that he intended to go on in the same way if they spared his life. He was condemned to die, however, and thirty days after the trial they gave him a cup of poison called hemlock to drink. After he had taken this he went on talking to his students of the hope of a happier life beyond the grave. This was four hundred years before the birth of Christ. Socrates came nearer the Christian belief than any other philosopher of that ancient time who had no knowledge of the Bible and its teachings. {20}

ALEXANDER, THE BOY WHO CONQUERED THE WORLD

ALEXANDER was the son of Philip, king of Macedon, a country to the north of Greece. His father was a great general as well as a king. Young Alexander was a strong, active, handsome lad. A story is told of his "breaking" a wild horse which had been presented to Philip by a neighboring king. This horse was named Bucephalus—the Greek word for "Bullheaded." He reared, bit, snorted, and pawed the air, if any one tried to mount him. King Philip was indignant at being given such a present, and was about to send back the "bullheaded beast," as too dangerous to the life or limb of anyone who attempted to ride him. But Alexander noticed that the horse was frightened even at his own shadow. He begged his father to let him conquer such a splendid animal. The lad was so much in earnest that the king decided to let him try.

The young prince showed no fear as he walked up beside Bucephalus and patted him on the neck. He wanted to keep the horse from being frightened, as his fright was the cause of his wildness. By degrees the boy managed to turn the great brute's head toward the sun so that he could not see his shadow. Throwing off his velvet mantle, Alexander suddenly sprang on the horse's back. Instead of trying to restrain or guide the frightened steed, the boy let him go as fast as he would across the plain. When Bucephalus grew tired, the shrewd rider began to turn his head this way and that, while speaking kindly and patting him soothingly. When they returned from their long run, Bucephalus obeyed the prince's word and touch as a gentle, well-trained horse should. It is said that the huge beast{21} learned to kneel for Prince Alexander to mount, and that he carried his young master proudly through many a battle.

The king was so pleased with the courage and wisdom Alexander displayed in conquering Bucephalus that he said to his son, "You should have a larger kingdom than Macedon to rule."

As if to fulfill this wish, Philip went to war with several of the neighboring kings and left his sixteen-year-old son to rule over Macedon while he was absent. Then Alexander was allowed to command certain companies of the Macedonian army; in this he showed wonderful courage and wisdom.

9

Philip was murdered when Alexander was twenty. Then the kings whom the father had conquered tried to throw off the rule of Macedon. They said, "This new king is only a boy." But Alexander answered when he heard it, "They think I am a boy; I will show them that I am a man." And he did—not only by defeating the kings and armies his father had beaten, but by conquering the other states around Macedon whose kings had turned in to help Alexander's enemies.

At this time the greatest monarch in Asia was Darius, king of the Persians. He sent several nobles of his realm to seek the friendship of Alexander, king of Macedon. These men were surprised when they saw that the young ruler was not interested in their stories of the wealth and splendor of the vast countries of Darius. Instead, Alexander wished to hear about the extent of their kingdom, about its different peoples, and about the location of the rivers, roads, and cities. The men from Persia said to members of the court of Macedon, "Our old king is rich; but your young king is great."{22}

Alexander, both king and general, had a strange thirst for power. He left a true friend to control his kingdom in Europe and started east, with only a small army, to conquer the vast countries on the continent of Asia. King Darius laughed at the very idea of "a mere boy," with so few soldiers, coming to conquer him and the greatest and richest empire in the world. He came to meet the Macedonian army with an armed host about ten times as large as Alexander's. "That boy" soon routed and scattered the hosts of the Persians, and King Darius had to fly for his life, leaving his wife and her mother behind, as Alexander's prisoners. The young conqueror was kind to these and to all other prisoners of war. This was wholly different from the custom then; for ancient conquerors killed or made slaves of those whom they defeated in battle. Alexander gained two great victories over Darius and captured other kingdoms and walled cities after long sieges and hard-fought battles.

While in Asia he came to a temple where there was a puzzle which no one had solved. This was a strange knot in a long leather strip. This knot, it had been prophesied for centuries, could never be undone except by the one who was to conquer Asia. Alexander felt that he must unloose this terrible tangle in some way or other. So, when he was brought into the temple, which was at a place named Gordium, he took his sword and cut the strangely knotted thong in pieces! Ever since then when any one meets and solves in a surprising way what seems to be an impossible problem, he is said to have "cut the Gordian knot," as Alexander did in the temple at Gordium.

The young conqueror marched down into Africa, and not only took possession of Egypt, the greatest kingdom of{23}

Alexander the Great at one of his luxurious banquets.
Alexander the Great at one of his luxurious banquets.
{24}
that vast region, but built, near one of the mouths of the wide river Nile, a city to which he gave his own name. That city, Alexandria, is still one of the largest cities on the continent of Africa.

It became necessary for Alexander to lead his army farther eastward into Asia. After his great successes he began to indulge his appetites, in eating and drinking and in other harmful ways. Once, in a fit of drunken anger, he killed his best friend. This made him ashamed and sad when he came to himself and realized what he had done.

Because of his many victories Alexander is called "the Great." When he was only twenty-six, he had conquered all the important nations in the world of his day. It was because he had now nothing to strive after that he gave way to evil passions. He is said to have "wept because there were no more worlds to conquer." He became ill and died as a result of his excesses, leaving no child or relative to rule over the great kingdoms he had acquired.

Although Alexander the Great had conquered the world, he could not govern himself. Hundreds of years before his day, Solomon, the wise, rich king, wrote in his Proverbs:

"He that is slow to anger is better than the mighty; and he that ruleth his spirit than he that taketh a city."

FOUR FAMILIAR SAYINGS OF JULIUS CÆSAR

JULIUS CÆSAR was born at Rome more than two thousand years ago, about one hundred years before Christ. His family belonged to a noble clan of the patricians. The people of Rome were divided into three classes. Of these the patricians were highest in rank and fewest in {25} number. There were many more in the middle class, which at that time was largely made up of free men who could vote and hold office. The lowest class and by far the largest number were the slaves.

More than half of the Roman slaves were white, many having blonde hair and blue eyes. These had been brought as captives from the northern countries and sold in Rome. Some of the slaves, especially those who came from the Greek lands in the East, were more refined than the ignorant, brutal Roman masters for whom they had to do the hardest and dirtiest kinds of work. Worse than this, the Roman law allowed cruel masters to whip, torture, and even kill these educated men and women.

By right of the might of her wonderful armies, Rome made herself "Mistress of the World." So the patricians and the freemen looked with contempt upon other nations and said to themselves, "To be a Roman is greater than to be a king." The patricians were the proudest Romans, and the Cæsars were among the haughtiest patricians. Their family belonged to the rich, ruling class when little Julius was born.

Of course, there was no such thing as the Christian religion in Julius Cæsar's day. The only believers in the one true God were the Jews, who lived in the little, far-off country now called the Holy Land. The best educated Romans believed in Jupiter, Juno, Apollo, Venus, and many other deities who, they imagined, were ruling over them, and who were as selfish and cruel as the Romans themselves.

There were no public schools for children in Rome. Instead of millions of printed books, there were a few rolls of parchment on which Latin words were printed very slowly by {26} hand. Instead of using paper to write on, the Romans scratched their letters and messages on tablets of wax with large needles. As there were no newspapers then, the people learned what was going on in the world by word of mouth from speakers in the Forum, an open city square with a stone platform, around which crowded thousands of listeners.

The highest ambition of the youthful Julius Cæsar was to speak well to the people in the Forum and to win their friendship. He grew to be a tall, handsome, brilliant young man. He was not rich, and while his friends led lives of ease and pleasure, this young Cæsar studied hard. He learned to read and speak Greek, because then the greatest poems, orations, and plays were in that language. He traveled thousands of miles, to Greece and Asia Minor, to learn to be a good speaker and writer. And though he was a patrician, his real sympathy lay with the poor and the middle class, whose side he took almost from boyhood.

11

The Romans governed themselves, in some ways, as the people of the United States do to-day. That is, their consuls, or governors, were elected by the patricians and the free men. Sometimes the patricians were in power; at other times, the people of the middle class succeeded in electing their leaders. But in those cruel times the winning party sometimes killed the chiefs on the other side, and treated them all as if they were enemies at war. The uncle of Julius Cæsar had been one of the chiefs overthrown in such a civil war, and the young man inherited his uncle's love for the cause of the common people.

The first deed of Cæsar that brought him into public notice took place while he was traveling in the East. A crew of pirates, or sea robbers, captured him and held him{27} prisoner until a large sum of money, or a ransom, should be paid. Julius Cæsar succeeded in raising the amount and paid it to them to set him free. But before he left the pirates he told them that if he ever caught them he would have his revenge. Then he went and collected men and ships, caught his former captors, won back his ransom money, and ordered the ring-leaders crucified. Crucifixion was the Roman penalty for pirates and other thieves.

From the time Julius Cæsar was thirty years old, he was constantly in one office or another in the Roman republic. One early position was that of director of shows and sports. The Romans had theaters, with seats of stone rising one behind another from the central space, like the seats in a circus or college stadium. Here thousands of people could see and hear actors, poets, orators, and debaters. One of these theaters was so large that eighty thousand people could witness the games at one time. Instead of football and baseball, the Romans had running races and wrestling matches by athletes and fighters who came from all parts of the world. Most of them were slaves. Among them were men called gladiators, who fought each other with swords until one or the other was killed. The cruel Romans liked this part of the sport best.

Julius Cæsar provided such splendid shows and games that he made himself very popular with the people. He was elected to one office after another; and finally, after being sent as a kind of governor to Spain, was chosen one of the two consuls. The office of consul was the highest in Rome, and was somewhat similar to our president. When his term expired, Cæsar was made governor over the Gauls, a half savage people who lived in the country that is now northern Italy, Switzerland, and France.{28}

During the nine years while Cæsar was in Gaul, he had to fight many battles and conquer many dangerous tribes. Besides that, he crossed to the island of Britain, now called England. But Cæsar was kind to his enemies and prisoners. His "Journal," which tells of his wars in Gaul, is read to-day as one of the simplest and best books ever written.

The assassination of Cæsar.
The assassination of Cæsar.
His wonderful victories and great kindnesses made Cæsar the idol of the people. But he had enemies at home, and a rival, another great general named Pompey. The Senate were on the side of Pompey, and at last they decreed that if Cæsar did not give up his command and dismiss{29} his army by a certain day, he would be called an enemy of the country. Pompey and the Senate were against the poorer classes, and Cæsar knew that if he yielded to this command, the common people, whose friend he was, would lose their freedom. So instead of disbanding his army he marched it to the borders of Italy. He stopped on the bank of a little river called the Rubicon. Anyone who crossed that river with an army was considered an enemy of Rome. When Cæsar decided to cross the river and advance with his army against the city, he exclaimed, "The die is cast!" His words

meant that he could no more go back than a die, once thrown out of the dice-box, can be taken back. Nowadays, when a man decides to do something which may bring great loss to him if he does not win, and from which he cannot draw back, once he has begun, he is said to have "crossed the Rubicon."

Cæsar's fortunes, however, did not desert him, and he succeeded in driving Pompey away and finally conquering him. Within three years, after many victorious battles in Greece and Egypt and Asia Minor, he returned to Rome in triumph. By this time the Senate were willing to do anything for him that he wanted, and the adoring people chose him Dictator for ten years. That meant that although he was not called king he had almost the same power as a king.

Two of Cæsar's sayings are often quoted. Once, when he was pursuing Pompey, he started on a voyage when a storm seemed to be coming up. The sailors were afraid to cross the sea, but he said to them, "You carry Cæsar and his fortunes!" They set sail at once and reached the other side in safety. At another time he caught an escaping army in Asia. He announced this victory in three words:{30} "Veni, Vidi, Vici," the meaning of which was, "I came, I saw, I conquered."

By his policy of kindness to the people as dictator, Cæsar so won their love that they came even to worship him as one of their gods. The month in the year in which he was born was at this time named in his honor, for our word July is a shortened form of Julius. He governed Rome well and made many useful changes. One thing that he did was to arrange the calendar, which before this time was very clumsy. It was he who divided the year into months of so many days each, very much as it is divided now.

The climax of Cæsar's popularity was reached when he was offered a crown, to show that the people of Rome wished him to be their king. He refused this honor three times in public. But not all the men of Rome shared in this admiration of Cæsar, for one party, some of whom had been his friends, felt that his growing power was not good for Rome. They wanted their country to be a republic, and not to be ruled by a king. So they began to plot against Cæsar.

On the fifteenth of March, 44 B. C., just as Cæsar was about to take his seat in the presence of the Roman Senate, a group of men gathered round and began plunging their daggers into his body. Among them was Marcus Brutus, for whom Cæsar had done many kindnesses. When Cæsar saw Brutus with his dagger raised to stab him to the heart, he exclaimed with a sad smile, "And thou too, Brutus!" Then, covering his face with his mantle, he fell down and died. Of the twenty-three knife wounds that were found in Cæsar's body, Shakespeare wrote that the stab of Brutus was "the most unkindest cut of all."

Although Cæsar was murdered to keep him from bearing{31} the name of king, the mightiest monarchs of modern times took the name of Cæsar as the highest title a king could have—as the "Kaiser" of Germany and the "C-zar" of Russia. When these two recent Cæsars were put down, there remained no ruler in Europe who believed in governing by the cruel Roman law that "Might makes Right."{32}

HEROES OF THE MIDDLE AGES

THE CHRISTMAS CROWNING OF CHARLEMAGNE

ABOUT twelve hundred years ago, thousands of Saracens, who were among the followers of Mohammed, crossed the narrow strait from Africa into Spain. The world was then coming out of those centuries of ignorance and fear which are known as the Dark Ages. The dark-skinned people—Arabs and Africans—who followed Mohammed, went

13

about converting people by making them prostrate themselves with their faces turned toward the East and repeat the Mohammedan creed. Those who refused to bow down and repeat this creed were killed. Of course everyone was very much afraid of missionaries who used such methods as these, and large parts of Asia and Africa had come under Mohammedan control. When they reached the shores of Spain, they thought they were going to convert and conquer Europe, too.

The Saracens marched north through Spain and into the country of the Franks, whose great-great-great-grandchildren are the French people of to-day. Here the victory of the invaders ceased to be so easy, for they were met by a certain Duke Charles, who beat them in a great battle near Tours and drove them back. For his bravery in saving Europe from these dark-skinned enemies, Duke Charles was named Martel, the Franks' word for "hammer."

Charles the Hammer had a son, Pepin, who was called {33} the Short, because he was not a tall man. But though he was small, Pepin had a big, brave heart. He fought for his country against the Lombards, a savage people in North Italy, and he was rewarded for his valor and success by being made king of the Franks.

When Pepin was crowned by the Pope, he had a son Charles, twelve years old. This Charles was so ambitious that, even while a boy, he began to dream of conquering other nations, and becoming king not only of France but of other lands as well. All through his boyhood he dreamed of what he would do if he were king. It was not many years after his father's death, when he became king in fact, before Charles Martel's grandson had conquered so many nations in the south and so many savage tribes in the north of Europe that he became a king of kings, or emperor, and received the title of Charlemagne, which means Charles the Great.

Perhaps the best thing that Charlemagne ever did was to keep Alcuin, a scholar from Britain, at his court as a trusted friend and teacher. In those days such men in other kings' palaces were merely chaplains or religious teachers, but Alcuin taught the king, the queen, and the princes grammar, spelling, arithmetic, and other common branches. This Palace School proved to be such a good thing that the emperor ordered that not only any child of a nobleman, but even of the poorest peasant, could come to it if the boy showed talent for learning. The books in the Palace School were printed very slowly with a pen, sometimes in bright inks and gold. As there were no public libraries in those days, Alcuin searched the world for books for his pupils. These parchments were rare and very costly. Instead of Charles's children going to school, the {34} Palace School went with the children, as the emperor moved from place to place and from palace to palace.

Charlemagne's armies were led by brave knights called paladins. The foremost of these paladins were Roland and Oliver, who fought in combats and tournaments. They were both of heroic size, eight feet tall, and performed the same feats, so that one could not be distinguished from the other. A story is told of these two having fought five days on an island in the River Rhine without either of them gaining the least advantage over the other; so now, when two men are equal in some great struggle, people exclaim—"A Roland for an Oliver!"

Roland, also called Orlando, was the chief hero, and Oliver seems to have been his reflection or shadow. Roland was a nephew of Charlemagne. He is described in the "Song of Roland" as having a wonderful horse, a miraculous saber, and a magic horn, which he blew so that it could be heard thirty miles. The greatest story told of him is that he commanded the rear guard of Charlemagne's army as they were returning from Spain through a pass in the Pyrenees Mountains. Set upon by 100,000 Saracens, Roland blew his magic horn so that his uncle the emperor heard it eight miles away.

In the advancing guard with Charlemagne, however, lurked an evil genius, who told the anxious emperor that Roland's horn was not a signal of distress, but that his nephew was hunting stags in the mountains. Roland fought until the 100,000 Saracens were slain, and he had only fifty of his 20,000 soldiers left. Then 50,000 more Saracens came out of the mountains and killed the brave paladin and his fifty men. While Roland was dying of his wounds, this legend goes on, he threw his magic sword into{35}
{36}

Charlemagne is crowned Emperor of the Western World at Rome.

From an old print
Charlemagne is crowned Emperor of the Western World at Rome.

From an old print
a poisoned stream. Another version of the story is that Roland died of starvation while trying to find his way, wounded and alone, through the mountains to catch up with the army.

Charlemagne and his valiant paladins rode and fought in all parts of Europe, beating the savage Germans beyond the Rhine, and conquering tribes and peoples all over Europe almost as far as Constantinople, the great capital of the Eastern Empire. At last the dream of the twelve-year-old lad at his father's crowning came true, when Charlemagne himself was crowned at Rome, the city of the Cæsars, as Emperor of the Western World, on Christmas Day, in the year of our Lord 800.

It is written that the crowning of Charlemagne was prepared as a surprise to him by the Pope and his people in Rome. While Charles and his sons were kneeling before a shrine very early on that Christmas morning, Pope Leo appeared in the great church with a crown of gold set with many precious gems, and placed it on the head of the kneeling king, thus proclaiming him Emperor of the Western World. In an instant the Pope, the cardinals, the priests, and the people rose from their knees and chanted these words:

"To Charles the Augustus, crowned of God, the great and pacific emperor, long life and victory!"

Charlemagne was a wise and good emperor who did many things to help his people. He built a lighthouse at Boulogne to guide ships to port, encouraged farming and made wise laws. He was kind to scholars and his favorite recreation was talking to them. He spoke several languages very well and wrote a great deal. Among his writings were a grammar, poems in Latin and many letters.{37}

ALFRED, THE GREATEST OF THE SAXON KINGS

OVER one thousand years ago, the king of the West Saxons on the island of Britain, now England, had four sons. Alfred, the youngest of these, was his father's favorite. When this boy was only five, his royal father sent him to Rome to be confirmed by the Pope. After Alfred came back his queen-mother died, and the father made a pilgrimage, or religious journey, to Rome, taking young Prince Alfred, with many court gentlemen, soldiers, and servants.

On their way the king and his train were given a royal welcome by the king of France. Alfred's father fell in love with the beautiful young daughter of the French king,

15

and asked her hand in marriage. Her father consented, so the royal wedding took place on the Saxon king's return from Rome.

Alfred's new mother soon became very fond of him. Young as he was, he had learned to play the harp. But when he was twelve years old, Alfred had not been taught to read. Saxon kings and princes thought most kinds of learning were for priests and lawyers. When gentlemen made contracts or signed law papers, they did not write their names, but "set their signs and seals thereunto," as is done to-day in legal documents. All the books were written on parchments in Latin.

One day Alfred saw his French stepmother reading a roll of parchment on which Latin words were printed by hand in many colors. As the lad admired it, the queen told him she would make him a present of the scroll as soon as he learned to read and understand it. He went right out and coaxed a monk, or priest, to teach him Latin, and he soon became the happy owner of the beautiful parchment.{38}

Learning to read opened a new world to Prince Alfred. He wrote verses and songs for his harp, and began to compose both words and music of hymns to be sung in the cathedral near his father's palace.

When Alfred was fourteen his father died. Each of his three older brothers became king, one after another, and died within a few years.

Alfred was twenty-two when the last brother died and left him to be king. Some rough people, called Danes, from the north countries across the sea, had landed on the island of Britain, and the Saxons were compelled to give battle to them so as not to be killed or made slaves to those rough Northmen. So Alfred had to fight to keep on being king. When he began to reign, he ruled like all the other kings he had known. His father and brothers had treated the people as if they were made only to work and pay their way, like cattle; so Alfred did the same at first.

The fierce Danes kept coming over in larger numbers. In a hard-fought battle, Alfred was defeated and most of his army was slain. Flying for his life, the young king found a hiding place in the hut of a swineherd, a man who tends hogs. This man knew who Alfred was, but kept the king's secret from his wife, who thought the stranger was a poor soldier from the Saxon army.

Many stories are told of what the king did while he lived in the hut of this swineherd. These tales have changed so much, all the hundreds of years which have passed since Alfred's time, that they are called legends. The best known of these is the story of the king and the cakes. Once when the housewife was going out to do some work, she asked him, while he was fixing his bow and arrows, to mind the cakes she had left baking in the ashes of the fireplace. The{39} distracted king's mind was on higher things than coarse meal cakes. When the woman came in she found them burning. She was so angry that she called Alfred a good-for-nothing beggar, and added that if he could not pay for what she gave him to eat, he ought at least to look after her cakes a little while.

King Alfred divides his last loaf of bread with the poor
beggar.
King Alfred divides his last loaf of bread with the poor beggar.

Alfred had the good sense to see his own conduct through the poor woman's eyes. So, instead of being angry or telling her who he was, he said gently, "I am sorry I was so careless. I will try not to forget again."

"A soft answer turneth away wrath," Alfred had read in the roll of Proverbs in his Latin Bible. It may have been{40} during the long months he spent in the home of this shepherd that the humbled king decided to translate the best parts of the Bible into the Saxon language so that the people could read it.

Another story is that Alfred stayed in the hut alone while the family were away fishing. He had only a loaf of bread to last until their return. A beggar came and asked for bread. Alfred broke his little loaf in two, gave the man half, and ate his half with the beggar. The swineherd returned that day with fish enough for a family feast. In the night the beggar of the day before appeared, as an angel, to the captive king, and said that God had seen how Alfred had humbled his heart so that he was now fitted to rule his people wisely and well.

The Danish army was now encamped not far from the king's hiding place. Encouraged by the vision of the shining pilgrim, Alfred started out to see for himself how strong the enemy were and what they were going to do. So he disguised himself as a wandering musician, playing a harp. He played and sang for the Danish soldiers, and was soon taken before their fierce leader, like David, with his harp, before King Saul. The Danes were so pleased with him and his music that they asked him to stay with them. As soon as he had found out all he wanted to know, he took up his harp and left the camp of the enemy. The Danes invited him to come again.

Hurrying back to the swineherd's hut, Alfred sent word to the leaders among his people that he was alive and ready to go on with the war against the Danes. The people had been in despair, for they had believed that their brave young king was dead.

The Saxon chiefs came at once and knelt to King Alfred.{41} When the poor woman realized who her guest was, she fell on her knees and begged him to forgive all she had said to him. Alfred lifted her tenderly from the ground, and told her he would reward her and her loyal husband when he was safe on his throne again.

The Danish army was astonished, early one morning, to hear three trumpet blasts, and to see a great army of Saxon soldiers marching to meet them, led by that wandering minstrel! Of course, the Saxons gained the victory and made the Danes promise not to come and attack them again. They agreed, but did not keep their word long. After that, instead of waiting for the Danes to land in Britain, King Alfred fitted up a fleet of ships so that he could go out and fight them on the sea. This has been called "the beginning of the British navy."

Then Alfred improved the years of peace by making laws which allowed the people more rights and privileges. He invented a simple clock of candles, by which the people could tell the time of day. He rebuilt the towns that had been destroyed in the war and trained his people not only to fight but to till their farms. He made wise laws and did much to educate his subjects by having books translated from the Latin into Anglo-Saxon, the language of the Saxons. Best of all, he translated the Bible into the language of the people. Because of all the acts which taught the people how to make their lives better and happier he is known in history as Alfred the Great. In one of his histories, King Alfred wrote what he tried to do in his own life:

"My will was to live worthily as long as I lived and, after my life, to leave to them that should come after, my memory in good works."{42}

HOW WILLIAM OF NORMANDY CONQUERED A KINGDOM

WHEN the first son was born to Robert, Duke of Normandy, and Arlette, the daughter of a tanner, the nurse laid the day-old baby on the straw carpet of the castle. In those days most of the floors of the houses, whether huts or castles, were of earth or stone, covered with straw which could be cleared out, as from a modern stable, to allow fresh straw to be laid down. When placed on the floor in his little blanket, Baby William reached out and clutched some of the straws so tightly in his small pink fists that one of those who noticed smiled and said, "He will take fast hold on everything he lays his hands on when he grows up."

When William was seven, Duke Robert, his father, being about to make the voyage to the Holy Land, called some of his nobles together and said, "I am resolved to journey to the place where our Lord Christ died and was buried. But because I know this journey is full of dangers, I would have it settled who should be duke if I should die."

The nobles and knights took an oath that they would stand by his son William and not let any one keep him from being duke of Normandy. Then Duke Robert sailed away and died during the long voyage.

William was away hunting in a Norman forest when his faithful fool (as they called a sort of clown kept by a king to amuse the court) broke in where he lay asleep and shouted, "Fly, or you will never leave here a living man!" The young duke jumped up, dressed in haste, and mounted his horse, riding through the forest in the moonlight and fording rivers till he came to the castle of a friend who was {43} sure to be faithful to him. This knight and his three sons rode with William to his own castle.

It turned out that a number of the Norman lords who had taken the oath to satisfy Duke Robert were now declaring that they would not serve under the low-born grandson of a tanner. The fool had learned that they were plotting rebellion and the death of his young master.

William, who was now twenty years old, gathered an army of loyal knights and men, and waged fierce warfare against the traitors, who retreated within the walls of a Norman town. The young duke soon captured the town, and proved to these rebels, as well as to the men of the neighboring kingdom of France, that the grandson of a tanner might be a greater general than the son of a king. At the beginning of a great battle of brave knights against braver knights, a champion of heroic size came out from the ranks of the enemy and threw down his gauntlet, or glove, challenging any knight of Normandy to come and fight him with the sword. William himself took up the gauntlet, and drove his sword through an open place in the big knight's armor, so that he fell from his horse dead.

Then, like the Philistines of old when David slew their giant, the Duke's enemies fled in all directions. Many of them were slain in battle, others while running away were cut down by the battle-axes of Norman knights, and many more perished in the flooded river.

Those were brutal days, when people thought that whatever a great king or noble might do was all right if he only had the power to put it through. An example of such high-handed dealing is William's conquest of England. He had once paid a visit to Edward the Confessor, the priestly king of England. The duke claimed, on his return to {44} Normandy, that Edward had promised to leave the kingdom to him, as a relative. It happened that Harold, an English earl, was shipwrecked on the coast of Normandy. William seized Harold, shut him up in prison, and kept him there until he promised to do his best to make William King of England at the death of Edward.

Two years later, when Edward the Confessor died, it was found that in spite of his promise to William he had advised in his will that Harold be elected king by the witan, an assembly of English freemen. This body of men took the good old king's advice, chose Harold king, and saw that he was crowned at once. Harold excused himself for breaking his word to William because King Edward had decided in his favor instead of William's, and because the oath he had made had been forced from him while he was a prisoner.

18

William, however, was very angry when he heard that Harold had allowed himself to be crowned king of England. Getting together as large an army as he could in Normandy, he sailed across the Channel. In leaping ashore from his boat he tripped and fell forward with his hands upon the ground. Realizing that his soldiers would think this a bad sign, he clutched both hands full of earth, and rising he held them up, exclaiming, "See, I have taken possession of this land of England."

The Normans took position in the village of Hastings. Harold went into camp on top of Senlac hill, now called Battle, about six miles from Hastings, and dug trenches around. Here a great battle began at four o'clock in the morning of the 14th of October, 1066. In advance of the Norman lines rode a knight in armor, bearing the duke's colors, singing the Song of Roland, the great paladin in the army of Charlemagne, who had lived and fought nearly{45} three hundred years before. It was a brave combat, with many knights and nobles on each side. The Norman found the Englishman a foeman worthy of his steel.

The eldest son of King William rebelled against his father's authority and fled to the castle of Gerberoi. King William pursued him and besieged the castle. During the siege the king was wounded by his son in single combat, but they were afterwards reconciled.

The eldest son of King William rebelled against his father's authority and fled to the castle of Gerberoi. King William pursued him and besieged the castle. During the siege the king was wounded by his son in single combat, but they were afterwards reconciled.

The Saxons, entrenched on Battle Hill, held their ground so well that William saw he could not gain the day unless he drew them away from that point of vantage. So he ordered a retreat, and the honest Saxons chased the flying Normans, expecting to catch and slay them. But to their great surprise, the Normans turned and fought harder than before. Harold was killed by an arrow shot into his eyes. The Saxon army, without a commander, was thrown into confusion, and thus the day was won by strategy. William, Duke of Normandy, became William the Conqueror of England.

No one now had a better claim to the throne of England than William; so, in the new Westminster Abbey, on Christmas Day, 1066, he was crowned, and took his proud{46} place in history as William the First of England. He had to fight four years longer to break down all opposition from the northern counties. In rewarding the Norman knights and nobles who had helped him gain possession of England, the king gave them great estates scattered over the kingdom. William brought to the island many scholars and bishops, and did much to establish the Church of England. Though he had been rough and cruel, he was both shrewd and wise in proving his own rights and in strengthening his kingdom.

William ruled England with a strong hand for twenty-one years. He forbade the buying and selling of slaves; yet he reduced the Saxon farmers to serfs almost as low as slaves. He ordered a record like a census made, and a survey of the kingdom which was recorded in what is called the Domesday Book.

It was terribly hard for the good, honest Anglo-Saxon people to see the Normans move into their homes and force them to work like slaves on the very places they themselves had owned. But the Normans had the power and the Saxons could not help themselves. For hundreds of years the Normans spoke the French language, and the Saxons, the English. The very names of the meats on your table at home are signs of the

19

Norman Conquest, nearly nine hundred years ago. The animals in the pastures and stables of England were called by the names the Saxons gave them—as cow, calf, sheep, swine. But the meats of those animals when cooked and served upon the tables of the masters are still known by the Norman French names, as beef (Norman name for cow), veal (Norman for calf), mutton (Norman for sheep), pork (Norman for hog or swine). Milk is a Saxon word, but cream is from the {47} French, because the Saxons had to milk the cows and drink only milk, while they served their Norman lords the cream.

The Norman traits of keenness, tact, and worldly wisdom have been mingling for many centuries with the honest, sturdy integrity of the Anglo-Saxons. Little by little, as the races grew together, the nobles became less haughty and cruel and the poorer people were lifted out of their poverty. But it took many centuries for men to learn the lesson that

"Kind hearts are more than coronets,
And simple faith than Norman blood."

LION-HEARTED RICHARD AND WOLF-HEARTED JOHN

THE great-grandson of William the Conqueror was Henry the Second of England, a great and powerful king. At his death, in 1189, he left two sons, Richard and John. As Richard was the older he was at once proclaimed king and duly crowned in Westminster Abbey. He was also Duke of Normandy, and thought this a greater honor than to be king of England.

About a hundred years before the time of Richard, great armies had begun to sail from several of the countries of western Europe to the Holy Land in Syria. The rock-hewn tomb of Jesus, near Jerusalem, was in possession of the followers of Mohammed—Turks, Arabs, and Saracens—who controlled the country. The Christian people of Europe thought it very wrong that the Saracens owned the {48} Holy City of Jerusalem and could keep Christians from coming to worship at the tomb of their Lord. So throngs of soldiers went to the Holy Land to rescue the Holy Sepulchre, or tomb. The wars which they fought for this cause were known as the Crusades.

King Richard generously forgives Bertrand de Gurdun, who had attempted to assassinate him.

From the painting by John Cross
King Richard generously forgives Bertrand de Gurdun, who had attempted to assassinate him.

From the painting by John Cross
In the First Crusade, the Christian knights captured not only the Holy Sepulchre but also the city of Jerusalem. In the Second Crusade, about fifty years later, the crusaders were beaten back by the Saracens. Two years before Richard became king, the Mohammedans again captured Jerusalem and the sacred tomb. {49}

Young King Richard was fired with a holy zeal to win back the Holy City and the Sepulchre, and, if possible, to find the cross upon which Jesus of Nazareth was crucified. This relic was believed to have been hidden by the Saracens.

King Richard made many sacrifices to raise money for a Third Crusade. His brother John was glad to have Richard go away on such a distant and dangerous mission, leaving the younger brother to rule over England during the king's long absence. John was as cowardly as Richard was brave, and, down in his heart, he hoped the Turk would kill his brother so that he could have the throne. Because of the king's knightly courage he was given the title of Richard Lion-heart. If John had been named for the animal he was most like, he would have been called John Wolf-heart.

Richard was joined by King Philip of France, and the two kings, with their armies and those of the Archduke of Austria, reached the Holy Land in due time. They attacked the walled city of Acre—called Akka by the Arabs—and captured it after a long, hard fight and the loss of many thousands of soldiers.

But Richard was as overbearing as he was brave. He ordered other kings and dukes about, and his manner was so masterful that he made Philip and the Archduke of Austria very angry. After several bitter quarrels, the king of France left Richard to fight on without him. The French king sailed away home with most of his army, and plotted with Prince John to injure the absent brother and make John King of England while Richard was still alive.

Many tales are told of the struggle between Richard, king of England, and Saladin, the sultan of the Saracens. For hundreds of years after Richard Lion-heart's campaign in the Holy Land, Arab mothers would frighten their children{50} by warning them that Richard would get them if they were not good. Sir Walter Scott's great novels, "Ivanhoe" and "The Talisman," are stories of life in England at this time, and of knightly tournaments which took place between Richard and Saladin during this Crusade.

While the Crusaders were trying to capture Ascalon, it became necessary for them to work like stone masons in rebuilding certain walls. Richard went to work with a royal will, and most of the nobles and knights followed his example. But the Archduke of Austria said he was the son neither of a carpenter nor of a mason, and flatly refused to help. This made King Richard so angry that he struck the Archduke a blow with his mailed fist and gave him a resounding kick with his heavy iron boot. With all his holy zeal to take the Holy City, Richard Lion-heart had not learned that "he that ruleth his spirit is better than he that taketh a city." Then the Archduke and his Austrian army also left Richard to fight on alone with his few remaining soldiers.

What Richard had found hard enough with the help of the king of France and the Archduke of Austria was impossible without them. But Lion-heart was not only a very brave man but a fine general. He defeated the army of Saladin in a great battle at Arsuf and twice led the Christian forces within a few miles of Jerusalem. Quarrels among the crusaders however made it impossible to continue the war. King Richard also received bad news from home, that his brother John was plotting against him aided by King Philip of France. So he and Saladin made a truce to stop fighting for three years, three months, three weeks, and three days. Then the brave king of England started for home. Richard sent his army the long way round by water,{51} while he and a few knights, disguised as pilgrims, tried to go the short way by land, across Austria and Germany. In spite of his disguise, Richard was recognized by an Austrian soldier. When the Archduke heard that Richard was crossing his dukedom, he sent soldiers at once to capture the king who had insulted him.

Richard was a prisoner in a great castle for two years. A story is told of a young troubadour, or wandering minstrel, who started out to find his royal master by playing a lute and singing songs of love and hymns of the Crusaders. After months of wandering, he sang under a castle wall a favorite song of Richard's, and heard, to his great joy, a deep bass voice within the German fortress joining in the hymn. He well knew that the voice was none other than Richard Lion-heart's. Saying nothing, he hurried away and told some English friends where their lost king was. They rushed to Richard's rescue and paid the Emperor of Germany, who was over the Archduke in rank and power, a royal ransom to have their brave king set free.

When Philip of France heard that Richard was out of prison, he sent word to John, who had been making believe that his brother the king was dead, "Take care of yourself. The devil has broke loose!" When Richard reached London, John pretended to be very glad to receive his dear brother back as from the dead.

Richard reigned only a few years after that, for he was killed in one of his wars with Philip of France. While he was as brave as a lion, Richard was also as fierce and cruel as the king of beasts. He was not a good man as people to-day regard manhood, but he was much better than his cowardly brother John, who became king after Richard's death.{52}

JOAN OF ARC AND THE LILIES OF FRANCE

FIVE hundred years ago a little French peasant girl was working outside the stone hut where her father's large family lived, when she heard, or thought she heard, a voice saying to her, "Joan, be a good child; go often to church."

This Joan of Arc was so kind-hearted and so thoughtful for others that her friends made fun of her and said she was not like other girls; and her parents feared that she was growing too good to live. But Joan only wondered and smiled, said her prayers, and went often to church. When she was twelve or thirteen, she began to see visions and hear what she called "the Voices," saying over and over, "Joan, trust in God; for there is great sorrow in the kingdom of France."

"It must be St. Catherine and St. Margaret," Joan said to herself, as she sat spinning for hours at a time. What was the sorrow in France, and how could she make things better just by being good? She even doubted whether the visions she had seen and the Voices she had heard were anything but her own half-waking dreams.

One day she overheard the parish priest of Domremy, where she lived, telling of the troubles of France. For almost a hundred years the kings of England had claimed and fought for the right to rule over France, and lately, under their soldier king, Henry the Fifth, had defeated the French and driven their armies into the southern part of their own land. Henry the Fifth had died, but his son still claimed the French throne; and the French prince, or Dauphin, as he was called, had not been crowned king, because the English held the city of Rheims, where all{53} French kings were crowned. The English armies were pushing southward to lay siege to the French city of Orleans.

Joan heard the good priest and her father and mother sighing over the sad day that had come when foreigners were fighting to make slaves of the French people. And the dear Dauphin whom God had given them for their king was now flying from place to place before the armies of England.

After that day the Voices grew more earnest and definite. "Go to the governor," they urged her; "go and ask him to give you soldiers, and send you to the help of the king." Poor little Joan's heart sank within her, and she protested, "I am only a young girl. I don't know how to ride or to fight. They will only laugh at me." But the Voices kept on insisting, "Go! go! go! and we will help you save France."

Joan told her parents what the Voices were telling her to do. Her father laughed and threatened to punish her if he heard any more of such talk, and her mother was afraid her strange little daughter was going to die. Joan's brothers and sisters made fun of her and asked if she wished to marry the Dauphin and be Queen of France.

But Joan had a kind uncle who loved and sympathized with her. Her mother let her go to visit Uncle Durant, hoping her poor little girl might forget the Voices. When Joan told her uncle what she kept seeing and hearing, he promised to help her all he could. So he went with his anxious little niece to the governor of that part of France, and stood by her as she told the great man about the Voices, and repeated the latest command they had given her for him:

"Send and tell the Dauphin to wait, and not offer battle{54} to his enemies; because God will give him help before the middle of Lent. The kingdom belongs not to the Dauphin, but to my Lord; but my Lord wishes that the Dauphin shall be king and hold it in trust. In spite of his enemies he shall be king of France, and I will lead him to be crowned."

"And who is your lord?" demanded the governor with a sneer. "The King of Heaven," said Joan of Arc proudly. The governor, who was a rough military man, laughed loud and long at the faith of the little peasant girl in a white cap, red petticoat, and wooden shoes. Instead of doing as she asked, he told her uncle to give her a good whipping, to beat the foolishness out of her head, and send her home to her father.

Baffled and discouraged, Joan went home with her uncle. But the Voices kept saying in her ears, "Go! go!" Back to the governor she went, but he treated her as badly as before. Then they found another man to whom she told her story and added, "God in Heaven has told me to go to the Dauphin; with His help I must do it, even if I have to go on my knees." This friendly gentleman was deeply touched by her earnest words.

The people in the country who knew and believed in Joan of Arc pleaded with the men of influence in the neighborhood, and it was at last arranged that Joan should go and tell her story to the young king of France. To see if God were guiding her, as she claimed, the king changed places with a noble in his court; but instead of going up to the pretended king who sat in the seat of honor, Joan walked straight to the prince, where he stood behind some men of the court.

It is easy to believe what we will. The Dauphin listened to the burning words of the peasant girl with the pure,{55}

{56}

The victorious return of Joan of Arc to Orleans.

From the painting by J. J. Scherer
The victorious return of Joan of Arc to Orleans.
From the painting by J. J. Scherer
Madonna-like face. After she had won the king's approval it was not so hard for Joan to go on obeying the Voices. Dressed in a suit of armor which shone like silver, she led a French army to the relief of Orleans. She carried everywhere a beautiful white banner, embroidered with lilies.

The English laughed at that silly girl trying to be a man, and called her insulting names; but Joan did not mind, for she felt safe under the protection of the saints in heaven. One day, in an attack upon a fort held by the English, the Maid, as the French army now called her, was wounded in the foot; but she would not stop fighting. She mounted her horse again and led the charge as though nothing had happened. The English then thought she was a witch—that is, a woman working for the devil.

In another battle an arrow was shot clear through her shoulder so that the barb stuck out five inches. Then the enemy raised a shout of triumph. "The Maid can be wounded and killed," they yelled. "She is not a witch, so we are not afraid of her." But one of Joan's company pulled out the arrow and she led them fiercely in the assault. The English soldiers were frightened, for in those days every one believed in witches. Joan drove the enemy from one place to another until all the south country was cleared of the

23

English forces. Then the Maid of Orleans, as she was now called, led the king, with his court and the French army, to the old city of Rheims, where he was crowned, with great joy and splendor, as Charles the Seventh.

The Maid had put the lilies on her banner as the symbol of purity and of God's love and care over France. The French lily, or fleur-de-lys, has been the emblem of France through all the centuries since the days of Joan of Arc, the Maid of Orleans.{57}

Now the Maid, who had done all that the Voices had commanded, was ready to return home to spin and to tend the sheep on the hills of Domremy; but weak-hearted King Charles begged her to stay long enough to drive all the English out of France.

Against her wish, Joan yielded. While fighting outside the walls of a town not far from Paris, she was surrounded by armed men of the enemy. By mistake or through fear, some French people shut the gate in such haste that the Maid was left outside fighting a dozen soldiers single-handed. She was captured and put in a dark, damp prison. Here the poor girl, then only nineteen, was frightened and tortured to make her sign a paper confessing that she was a wicked witch, and that all she had done was by the help of the devil.

After waiting a long time in vain for the ungrateful prince, whom she had made king of France, to come and save her with his army, or to pay a large sum of money to ransom her, she was compelled to stand an unjust trial during which she was many times abused and insulted. This wicked trial was conducted by a false bishop, who condemned that sweet, heroic young girl to be burned at the stake in the market-place of Rouen on the 24th of May, 1431.

Twenty-five years after her death the Pope reversed the decision of the corrupt bishop. In 1920, nearly five hundred years after the Maid was burned to death, high and holy men in the ancient Church to which she belonged took the great step of declaring Joan of Arc, the peasant girl of Domremy, one of the noble army of martyrs in the communion of saints.{58}

FOUR LEADERS IN THE OLD WORLD

SHAKESPEARE, THE GREATEST MAKER OF PLAYS

PERHAPS there is no one who has done so much for the world, yet about whose life so little is known, as William Shakespeare. His father was a farmer and market man, and his mother was Mary Arden, a prosperous farmer's daughter. The father was so highly respected that he was made high bailiff, or mayor, of Stratford-upon-Avon, where the Shakespeare family lived.

It was one of the father's duties to give out licenses to players or actors who went from town to town performing their plays. Sometimes they gave their shows out of doors; and when theaters were built they were galleries around a space of ground. The people who paid the most stood or sat in the galleries and the poor people saw the play from the ground, called the pit. Strolling players were looked upon in those days almost as tramps are to-day. They had to have licenses like street bands nowadays. They often gave their shows in a town square and took up a collection for their pay.

John Shakespeare was fond of these shows, and there is no doubt that his son William was taken to see them before he went to the Stratford Grammar School when he was seven years old. Here the boy is said to have studied Latin, writing, and arithmetic. Judging from the specimens that are still to be seen of William Shakespeare's penmanship, it was not a great success. One of the great{59}

Shakespeare among his friends in London.

From the painting by John Ford
Shakespeare among his friends in London.

From the painting by John Ford
play-writers of Shakespeare's time wrote that Will had learned "small Latin and less Greek" at school. But Latin was the chief study in the schools of that time. It was sung and spoken in church, and it was thought necessary for even a farmer's son to study that language.

When William was thirteen his father was unfortunate in business, and the boy had to leave school to earn his living. There is a legend that he started in to learn the butcher's trade, but it seems more likely that he worked as a lawyer's boy and clerk. If all accounts are true, he must have been a mischievous lad, for the story goes that he was once taken up for poaching, or shooting a deer, in the park of one of the great men in the county.

When he was eighteen Will Shakespeare married a farmer's daughter eight years older than himself. By the time he was twenty-one the young father had three children. Two of these, Hamnet and Judith, were twins. Hamnet died before he grew to manhood, and about all that is known of Judith Shakespeare is that she, like her mother, never learned to read. It was not thought necessary then for farmers' wives and daughters to read and write.

A lawyer's clerk with five mouths to feed could hardly find enough to do in Stratford to earn a living, so William Shakespeare went to London to seek his fortune. It is said that he began life in the great city by holding horses in front of one of the theaters, as they did not have hitching-posts in Shakespeare's days. Then he was promoted to be prompter's boy. One of his duties was to tell the actors when it was time for them to go on the stage and play their parts.

Nothing is really known of what the young man from Stratford was doing for six or seven years. He made his{61} living in one way or another in connection with the theaters. At the end of that time a dying actor left some bitter lines about Will "Shake-scene." But another actor at this time called Shakespeare a good man, a graceful actor, and a witty writer of plays. Shakespeare seems not to have been a leading actor. It is said that he took the part of the Ghost in his own play of "Hamlet." He became so successful as a writer that he was "commanded" to bring his company and produce a play before Queen Elizabeth in one of her palaces.

It is recorded that Shakespeare was paid from thirty to seventy-five dollars for one of his plays. While it is true that thirty dollars would buy as much then as three hundred dollars to-day, yet that was a very small price to pay for the greatest dramas ever written. But the real value of the greatest things of the world cannot be measured by money.

Every one is said to have at least one great chance in life. Shakespeare's Door of Opportunity was the door of a theater. He did not wait for it to open; he opened it himself. Shakespeare's life showed that "poets are born, not made." He had the keenest insight into the human heart and life of all the writers who ever lived.

HOW CROMWELL CHANGED PLACES WITH THE KING

IN Shakespeare's day Queen Elizabeth came first in the thoughts of all the people of England. She was almost worshiped by the men of wealth and genius whom she gathered at her court, and by the people at large. By her cleverness and wisdom she kept England peaceful and{62} prosperous almost all through her reign. But she never married; so, when she died, her cousin, James Stuart, king of Scotland, became king of England.

James had been brought up to think that because he was king, everybody must bow to him as the Lord's anointed. It was he and his councilors who drove the Pilgrim Fathers out of England because they would not worship God, as James wished them to, in the Church of England, of which he was the head.

On his way down to London to be crowned, James stopped at the beautiful estate of Sir Oliver Cromwell. In the royal company was the king's eldest son, Charles, called by the Scottish people "the bonnie prince." The little Scotch boy, only six years old, already thought that the world was created for him and that no other boy had any rights which he, Prince Charles, was bound to respect.

The story goes that Sir Oliver Cromwell sent for his nephew, whose name was Oliver Cromwell also, to play with the prince. When little Noll, as they nicknamed Oliver, came in, his uncle presented him to the boy prince. Young Oliver tried to shake hands with Charles. Old Oliver, who wanted the boy to bow and kiss the prince's hand, said, "Pay your duty to Prince Charles."

"I owe him no duty," said Noll Cromwell. "Why should I kiss that boy's hand?"

King James only laughed at the Cromwell lad's spirit, and Charles and Noll were left to play together. The prince soon struck the other boy, as he was in the habit of doing, but naughty Noll struck back and sent "the bonnie prince" howling to the king with royal blood streaming from his little freckled nose.

Sir Oliver and the members of the royal party looked{63} with holy horror at the boy who had laid his hands on the Lord's anointed. Some of them thought young Oliver ought to be imprisoned in the Tower of London or even beheaded for his wickedness. But King James had sense enough to see that it was well for the prince to get "tit for tat" once in a while; so he only looked hard at little Oliver and said:

Oliver Cromwell visiting the poet Milton. Cromwell is
carrying the large hat affected by the Roundheads.

From the painting by David Neal
Oliver Cromwell visiting the poet Milton. Cromwell is carrying the large hat affected by the Roundheads.
From the painting by David Neal

"Thou art a bold lad; and if thou live to be a man, my son Charlie would do wisely to be friends with thee." Then he turned to Sir Oliver and the frightened friends standing{64} there, saying, "Harm not the lad. He has taught my son a good lesson, if heaven do but give him grace to profit by it. If he be tempted to play the tyrant over the stubborn English, let him remember little Oliver Cromwell."

Young Oliver went to Free School and then to a Puritan college in Cambridge University; but he had to leave school on account of the death of his father. Before he was thirty Cromwell was elected to Parliament, of which his cousin, John Hampden, was also a member.

Meanwhile King James died and his son, the prince with whom Oliver had quarreled when a boy, became King Charles the First. King James had been so sensible at times and so foolish at others that he has been called "the wisest fool in Europe." But Charles had even less sense than his royal father. He tried to abolish Parliament, thus setting up his own will against the will of the people of all England and Scotland.

Parliament, led by such men as Cromwell and Hampden, stood up for the rights of the people against tyranny. All lovers of liberty and human rights are greatly in debt to these two brave men who risked their lives to save their country from the selfish wilfulness of kings. Englishmen now were divided into two parties. The king's party were the Cavaliers, or Church of England men, who wore wigs or long curls and dressed in velvets, silks, and laces like grown-up Lord Fauntleroys. The parliamentary party were called Roundheads, so named because they cut their hair short, as men do to-day. Oliver Cromwell, who never saw an army until he was forty, was suddenly found to be a great general. Because of their stern, unyielding courage, Cromwell's soldiers were called "Ironsides." They often{65} went into battle with a prayer on their lips, or, in a grand chorus, sang a psalm of David while striking valiantly for the right.

At last it became necessary to sacrifice King Charles in order to secure the victory for Parliament, which stood for the freedom of Englishmen against the tyranny of kings. So a court set up by Parliament voted to put the king to death, and Oliver Cromwell was one of the signers of the death-warrant. As James, the king's father, had driven the Pilgrims out of the country, so now the Puritans in Parliament forced the king's sons to leave the country for their country's good.

During the few years in which Oliver Cromwell was Lord Protector of England, he did much to strengthen the nation and to repair the great harm brought upon it by the foolish whims of its extravagant kings. It was then that England learned the terrible lesson which Europe had to be taught almost three hundred years later—that no king has a divine right to do wrong to the people.

NAPOLEON, THE CORSICAN BOY WHO RULED EUROPE

THOUGH Napoleon Bonaparte was the greatest soldier of his time, he was small in body. His fullest height was a little above five feet. The story of his strange career shows how a poor, puny little lad made himself emperor of France and master of Europe, so that kings, generals, and prime ministers bowed, like so many servants, to his imperial will.

He began, while he wore petticoats, to wish to be a soldier.{66} He threw away his baby rattle for a brass cannon, and his first playthings were little iron soldiers. When he was old enough to play with other boys, he always chose to be a soldier and, small as he was, he was the one who told the bigger boys just what to do. Even then, if his mother gave him a piece of cake, he would go out to the edge of the little town and trade it to an old soldier for some coarse, black army bread. As he grew older, this soldier-longing became his ambition. His health was never very good. He was often nervous, wilful, and hard to manage. But he had a keen sense of honor, and always despised a coward.

Napoleon's home was the rugged island of Corsica. While he was still a little boy, he found, between some rocks, near the shore, a cave which he claimed for his own. This is still pointed out to thousands who come to visit the boy's birthplace, as "Napoleon's Grotto."

At that time there was a feud between the boys of the town and the shepherd lads on the hills around. Little Napoleon told the other town boys that if they would do as he said, he would make those big country boys stop throwing stones at them whenever they met. The town lads agreed to this; so Napoleon told them to gather stones and pile them in a row a little distance below the fortress which the shepherds had chosen behind some rocks on top of their hill.

The pale Bonaparte boy led his young army up till the country youths fired a volley of stones at them. Then he turned and ran down the hill followed by his company. The

27

enemy came out and gave chase, pell-mell. This was just what Napoleon expected. When the little leader got down to the piles of stones he shouted—"Halt!"

His soldiers obeyed.{67}

"Stones!"

Each boy gathered up as many as he could carry.

"About face!—FIRE!"

Before the astonished shepherds could stop they were met by a shower of rocks. The big fellows broke and scattered in all directions, and two of them were taken prisoner. Captain Bonaparte would not let them go till the other country boys pledged themselves not to touch his "men" again.

Thus eight-year-old Napoleon became the leader of the boys in his home town.

Before he was ten, he was sent to a military school in France, where sons of noblemen were educated. Some of those French boys were wayward, mean, and savagely cruel. They made fun of the shy country lad, for his rough Corsican ways and speech, and because he was small and sallow. Napoleon had entered the school on a scholarship, so they sneered at him as "the charity boy." He could not speak French at first, and pronounced his own name so that it sounded like the French words for "Nose of straw." As Napoleon's nose was long, straight, and thin, they laughed and shouted his nickname, "Mr. Straw Nose!"

All this made the proud, sensitive lad speechless with rage. He kept himself away from the rest. A garden plot was assigned for each cadet to tend. A few of the others were too idle to take care of theirs, so they gave them to Napoleon and he kept them in order as his own. In the center of his little kingdom he built an arbor where he could stay alone to study and plan as he had done in his little cave in Corsica, and woe to those who entered there without his permission. He had suffered this sort of life{68} nearly four years before his father and mother managed to visit their boy, who was almost a prisoner in military school. Napoleon wrote of the shock the visit gave his mother:

"When she came to see me at Brienne she was frightened at my thinness. I was indeed much changed, because I employed the hours of recreation in working, and often passed the nights in thinking about the days' lessons. My nature could not bear the idea of not being first in my class."

After finishing at this academy, Napoleon went to the military college at Paris. Father Bonaparte's death, about this time, left the family poorer than ever. Sometimes Napoleon did not have enough to eat. But that did not prevent him from studying hard. His great ambition kept him from starving. Some time after his graduation he was assigned to a small command in Paris. "Red" revolutionists were trying to destroy the city. Young Napoleon thought it high time to stop them. A mob gathered in a public square threatening to kill people and burn their houses. He opened fire on the mob and cleared that square in short order. It was said afterward, "Bonaparte stopped the French Revolution with a whiff of grapeshot!"

From being "the Man of the Hour" Napoleon went on until he became "the Man of Destiny." He was raised to the highest rank, and as General Bonaparte became commander-in-chief of the French army in Italy, where he gained brilliant victories over the Austrians. But the Austrians would not stay beaten, and while Napoleon was away in Egypt, Austria started in to win back its control of northern Italy.

When Napoleon returned to Paris he was the idol of the people. They elected him consul, a kind of president, of{69} the French republic. The Austrians were pleased at this, as it would keep "the Little Corporal," as the soldiers called Napoleon, in Paris. He

28

would have to send another commander to Italy, and the Austrians had gotten such a start that they could win the victory before the French forces could go around the Alps.

Austria was already crowing over its triumph and all Europe was laughing because General Bonaparte had been "caught napping," when one May morning Consul Napoleon and a great army came tobogganing down the mountain sides into the plains of Italy, as if they had fallen from the sky.

In a letter to his older brother, Napoleon wrote of this:

"We have dropped here like a thunderbolt; the enemy didn't expect it, and hardly believe it yet."

He had made his soldiers climb up the Alps Mountains in the highest, steepest place, dragging heavy cannon and army supplies after them. By his wonderful feat of crossing the Alps, Napoleon won by surprise the victory at Marengo, just as he had beaten the shepherd lads when he was a boy of eight.

The people now made their hero consul for life. After that it was easy for him to make himself Emperor of the French. At his coronation Napoleon snatched the crown out of the hands of the pope and placed it on his own head, to show that he was emperor by the right of his own might. Yet Emperor Napoleon kept on leading his armies in person. He still had to fight with other nations to hold his place as master of Europe. He gained even more brilliant victories, as Emperor Napoleon, than he had won as General Bonaparte. Not content with his record as a great conqueror, he gave the French people the Code Napoléon, a set of laws{70}

Emperor Napoleon at the Battle of Waterloo watching the downfall of his wonderful army.

From the painting by David Neal

Emperor Napoleon at the Battle of Waterloo watching the downfall of his wonderful army.

From the painting by David Neal

{71}

which proved him to be also a wise statesman and law-giver.

The kings and nobles of Europe always hated Napoleon. They said he was vulgar, and called him "the Corsican upstart." But the French people loved him as one of themselves. No general or emperor ever had more devoted followers than Napoleon Bonaparte. Millions of men gave their lives willingly to fight his battles. He waged war after war till there were but few fighting men left in France. Then the people began to think that Napoleon loved them because they could help him win victories to give him more power and fulfill his high ambition. They began to say among themselves, "He is sacrificing us for his own glory." While at the height of his power, Napoleon exclaimed, "What are a million lives to a man like me!"

When the people lost their faith in him, Napoleon began to lose instead of win his battles. Generals and nobles stopped flattering him and began to fight him. His own brothers and sisters, whom he had made kings and queens, deserted him. Even his wife forsook him, taking with her his only son, the idol of his heart.

Napoleon's last battle was at Waterloo, in Belgium. Because this loss brought ruin to him, the name of the place became a kind of proverb. When overwhelming defeat comes to a great man, people say, "He has met his Waterloo!"

The conquered conqueror was taken prisoner and sent thousands of miles away as a captive to the bleak island of St. Helena. He made the best of his hard lot as "the fortunes of war." But the years of loneliness endured by this friendless conqueror, who all his life had been selfish and merciless, are suggested by a well-known picture,{72} which shows Napoleon on the shore of that far-off rock in the southern sea, standing with hands clasped behind him, looking off across the ocean to where France lay.

NELSON, THE HERO OF TRAFALGAR

A SMALL English boy strayed away from his grandmother's house after she had warned him that gypsies encamped near by might carry him off. When the old lady found the little fellow sitting beside a stream too wide for him to cross, she exclaimed:

"Why did you run away, Horatio? I was half dead with fear—"

"Fear!" demanded the little lad, still in petticoats. "What is that? I never saw a fear."

The boy's father's name was Nelson. He was a clergyman of the Church of England. His wife had died when this boy was a baby, leaving eight children for the invalid father to care for. Once while the father was away for his health, young Horatio heard that his mother's brother had been appointed to the command of a British man-of-war. Horatio said to an older brother: "Do, William, write to my father and tell him that I should like to go to sea with Uncle Maurice."

Thinking the navy might be a good place for the boy and a benefit to his health, Doctor Nelson wrote to his brother-in-law. The bluff sea-captain wrote right back:

"What has poor Horatio done, who is so weak, that he, above all the rest, should be sent to rough it out at sea? But let him come, and the first time we go into action a cannon-ball may knock off his head and provide for him at once."

{73}

Thus young Horatio Nelson entered the Royal Navy. One of his first trips was as coxswain on a voyage to the Arctic regions. While dragging the ship's boats over the ice, the sailors had to fight with walruses and polar bears. Coxswain Nelson killed a big white bear and carried home the skin for his father.

When Horatio was fifteen he made a voyage on the warship Seahorse to the East Indies. A year and a half in that hot climate made the frail lad so ill that he had to go home. Of his thoughts while sailing home on sick leave he once said:

"After a long and gloomy revery in which I almost wished myself overboard, a sudden glow of patriotism was kindled within me and presented my king and country as my patrons. My mind exulted in the idea. 'Well then,' I exclaimed, 'I will be a hero, and trusting in God, I will brave every danger.' "

Young Nelson had too much pluck to be sick long. England was then at war with France and Spain, and he fought his country's enemies in malarial regions where hundreds of his fellows died from the poisoned air and serpent bites. When Horatio was twenty-two his health again failed, and he had to spend months in Brighton to recover it.

When peace was signed between England and France, in 1783, Nelson was twenty-five. He was presented at court in that year, as he was a favorite with the Duke of Clarence who afterward became King William the Fourth.

The next year Captain Nelson was placed in command of the battle-ship Boreas. He was very kind to the thirty midshipmen on board. When a boy was afraid to climb a mast, Nelson would say to him with a winning smile:{74}

"I am going to race to the masthead and beg that I may meet you there."

Once when he was invited to dinner with the governor of Barbadoes, Nelson said, "Your Excellency must excuse me for bringing one of my midshipmen. I make it a rule to

30

introduce them to all the good company I can, as they have few to look up to besides myself while they are at sea."

Nelson receiving the sword of the Spanish admiral surrendered after a naval battle in the war of 1797.

From the painting by David Neal

Nelson receiving the sword of the Spanish admiral surrendered after a naval battle in the war of 1797.

From the painting by David Neal

It is not surprising that men under his command exclaimed, in comparing him with other men, "Nelson was the man to love!"

The wars of Great Britain with Napoleon kept the young{75} navy officer in active service. During a siege a shell burst and destroyed the sight of his right eye. In another attack he was wounded in the arm. He shouted to those who wished to remove him from the fray,

"Let me alone; I have yet my legs and one arm. Tell the surgeon to make haste and get the instruments. I know I must lose my right arm; so the sooner it is off, the better."

In 1798, when Napoleon started out with the French fleet for an unknown port, to surprise and lay waste the countries of people friendly to Great Britain, these instructions were issued to Admiral Nelson: "Take, sink, burn, and destroy the French fleet." With his battleships Nelson set out to search the Mediterranean, but for a long time he was unable to find the French fleet. At last it was found at anchor in Aboukir Bay at the mouth of the Nile. The French were caught in a trap. Though Nelson had not eaten or slept much for many days and nights, he invited his officers to dinner on his flagship, the Vanguard, to discuss the coming battle. "If we succeed, what will the world say?" asked one of the officers.

"There is no 'if' in the case," replied the admiral sharply. "We are sure to succeed, but who may live to tell the story is a very different question."

Admiral Nelson had the colors flying from six different places on his flagship when they went into battle that very night. That engagement, now known as the battle of the Nile, was one of the greatest naval combats in history. The French flagship, L'Orient, on which Napoleon had sailed to carry war into Egypt, was blown up and the French admiral killed with all on board. The battle raged from seven in the evening until three in the morning.{76} Though the French had thousands more men than the British, most of them were killed. Nelson sent boats to rescue them from the burning French ships, but they preferred to go on fighting through the flames, amidst bursting shells and exploding powder magazines.

Napoleon's fleet was utterly destroyed. Nelson wrote of that night's work:

"Victory is not a name strong enough for such a scene; it is a conquest."

The whole world, which had suffered in dread of "that monster, Napoleon," went wild over the news. England made Nelson a baron and voted him a pension of ten thousand dollars a year. Other nations, rulers, and corporations showered upon him great sums of money, gold boxes filled with diamonds, jeweled swords, and gem-incrusted souvenirs. The Queen of Naples, a sister of Queen Marie Antoinette, who had lately been beheaded by the French people, was beside herself with joy. The poor people of Italy expressed their gratitude when Nelson's fleet was anchored in the bay of Naples. Bringing

31

cages of birds to the shore, they opened the doors and let the birds out to fly about the flagship and light on the beloved admiral's shoulders.

Three years later the conquering hero was called to strike another blow against Napoleon near Copenhagen, Denmark. Admiral Nelson opened the attack on the allied fleet, but the admiral higher in command, thinking it might be well to give Nelson a chance to withdraw a little, signaled him to retire to repair several disabled ships. Nelson, hearing of this, put his spyglass to his blind eye and winked as he said: "I really do not see the signal. Keep on flying mine for 'closer battle.' That's the way I answer such signals!"{77}

The men of both fleets fought with undaunted courage for five long, terrible hours. The enemy lost 1800 men and 6000 prisoners, but the British had only 250 killed, and 680 wounded. Of the Battle of Copenhagen, Nelson wrote:

"I have been in one hundred and five engagements, but this has been the most terrible of all."

For the victory at Copenhagen Nelson was made a viscount. But there was no time for celebrations after this, for Napoleon was now waging war to the death. Lord Nelson seemed to realize that the next fight must be the end either of France or of England. At last the great day came, off Cape Trafalgar, Spain, on the 21st of October, 1805. It is told of Admiral Lord Nelson that as he walked the deck of his flagship, Victory, that morning, his knees trembled more with excitement than fear. The one-eyed, one-armed hero looked down and shook his fist at his legs, saying: "Shake away, there! You would shake worse than that if you knew where I'm going to take you to-day." Then he gave the order for that immortal signal: "ENGLAND EXPECTS EVERY MAN TO DO HIS DUTY." Trafalgar was the greatest of all Nelson's victories. It broke the power of Napoleon and paved the way for Wellington at Waterloo.

At a shot from the mizzenmast of a French ship, the Lord Admiral fell. Captain Hardy of the Victory knelt beside him.

"They have done for me at last, Hardy," he gasped.

Nelson lived for hours, giving his last directions, then died in the moment of his greatest triumph.

"Now I am satisfied," were his last words. "Thank God, I have done my duty."{78}
DISCOVERERS AND EXPLORERS

COLUMBUS, THE MAP-MAKER WHO FOUND A NEW WORLD

IN a tall narrow house in the midst of a block on a narrow street in Genoa, Italy, lived a poor woolworker named Columbus. This slender house was only two windows wide and seven stories high. In the lowest story, in which there were a wide door and a grated window, Signor Columbus stored the bales of wool which he washed and carded, using a tool somewhat like the curry-comb for cleaning horses. He thus prepared the wool to be spun into yarn, which would later be woven and made up into clothing and blankets.

A small boy named Christopher went in and out of this foul-smelling place to play and work. Very little is known of the boyhood of Columbus. As Genoa was a large seaport town, it is supposed that he spent much of his time on the wharves watching the boats-galleys from Venice, with gay-colored sails, and strange-looking craft from Asia and Africa, with long, slim, lateen wings, veering about like swallows of the sea.

There were pirates, or highway-robbers of the sea, in those days. Little Christopher was sure to hear thrilling stories of how they fought hand-to-hand with sabers and axes,

and of how the wicked but powerful pirates murdered the men on merchant ships and carried off the women and{79} children to be slaves in distant lands. Young Columbus seems to have been fired with a boyish longing for—
"A life on the ocean wave,
A home on the rolling deep,"
for the next that is known of him is that he narrowly escaped from drowning in a shipwreck by swimming six miles to shore on a boat oar.

He landed near a town in Portugal and soon found work in a map-maker's shop. Here he had a chance to learn all the geography that was known four hundred years ago. Most of the maps he made were drawn as if the world were flat. But there were curious charts with lands and seas outlined on the six sides of a cube, and others drawn as if the world were shaped like a huge section of stovepipe. Young Columbus found the maps very interesting; but what seemed most wonderful of all was the idea that the world was round, as every child now knows.

In those days a man was not allowed to believe anything different from what every one else thought. So when young Columbus began to claim that the earth was round, people laughed at him. They thought he was crazy. Of course, a few astronomers and scientists knew how to prove the roundness of the earth by the shadow it casts on the moon in an eclipse, but most of the people could not understand such things. Columbus himself could notice that the surface of the ocean, within the short distance he could see, was slightly curved. He resolved to miss no chance to prove his theory, by learning all he could about newly-found lands; and he even began planning to sail around the earth to India and Far Cathay, as China was called in the old days.{80}

Travelers had been overland to the Far East and back. Daring sailors had sailed along the coast of Africa. But the great body of water to the west of Portugal was called the Sea of Darkness. People believed that terrible sea-monsters haunted its dark waters, and that if men were to sail far enough westward, their ship would go beyond the brink of the world, as over a giant waterfall, and fall down, down through space forever.

So when Christopher Columbus tried to persuade the king of Portugal and the princes of other countries to fit out a few ships and let him prove the roundness of the earth by sailing west to the Far East, no one would listen to him seriously. But the poor man could not give it up, though he spent many years wandering from country to country to persuade some one rich and powerful enough to supply the ships and men for such a dangerous voyage. Queen Isabella of Spain and her husband, King Ferdinand, listened to him, but when the matter was referred to the royal council, those grave men shook their heads and said such a thing was absurd and unfit for a queen even to think about.

Columbus was in despair. His wife was now dead and he had his little son Diego with him. The two were tramping across the country and came, about sunset, to a monastery on the border of Spain, where the boy asked for a drink just as the monk in charge happened to be passing. This monk spoke to Columbus and, seeing what an interesting man he was, invited the strangers in. Columbus told his strange, sad story. This monk had been a friend and adviser to Queen Isabella. Also he knew two sailors who might be a help in such an undertaking. He wrote at once to the queen, urging her to let Columbus come and talk{81}

Columbus pleading his cause before King Ferdinand and
Queen Isabella of Spain.
Columbus pleading his cause before King Ferdinand and Queen Isabella of Spain.

over the matter once more. She wrote back that she would like to hear what her friend the monk might have to say about it. He started the very night he received the queen's letter, and talked with her about converting to the Christian faith the people of the new lands Columbus might discover. As a result of this talk the good monk wrote to Columbus who, with his young son, was waiting at the monastery:

"Our Lord has heard his servants' prayers. My heart swims in a sea of comfort and my spirit leaps with joy. Start quickly, for the queen awaits you, and I yet more than she. Commend me to the prayers of my brethren and of the little Diego. The grace of God be with you."

The queen received Columbus this time with sympathy and kindness. She is said to have pledged her jewels to raise money enough to fit out three ships for his great voyage. Columbus was to command one of these and the monk's friends were to be captains of the other two. But after making the little fleet ready, they could not induce sailors to man the vessels for their ghastly voyage across the Sea of Outer Darkness. Sailors were always superstitious. Even to-day they will not start out on Friday, and many seafaring men will refuse to sail with a ship if the flag should happen to be raised "union down," or wrong side up, no matter how quickly it may be set right. At last Columbus had to take convicts out of prison and condemn them to hard labor as sailors for the terrible trial trip. Some of these men were desperate criminals.

The unknown western sea was far wider than Columbus had thought. This showed that the world must be much larger than he supposed. As they sailed on and on, day after day and week after week, across the untraveled sea, the superstitious convict-sailors were half-dead with fear.{83} They planned to murder the Admiral, as Columbus was now called, and his two captains, in order to turn the ship about and go back before they were engulfed in some great whirlpool of disaster. Columbus kept himself well guarded, and coaxed and flattered the frightened creatures, promising them all kinds of wealth and pleasures if they would only keep on a day or two longer. He offered an extra prize to the man who first caught sight of land.

On the night of the 11th of October, 1492, one of the sailors saw a glimmering light to the west. On the morning of the 12th, the Admiral was an early riser. There lay a tropical island, with "gardens of the most beautiful trees I ever saw," he said afterward. The sea was as deep blue as that along the shores of his native Italy. He and his two captains went ashore, with well-armed men in boats from all three ships. The water was clear and the bottom was white with sand and shells, while strange, bright fish darted about as they paddled along. On the island were parrots and other birds of gay plumage flitting from tree to tree as if startled by the coming of the first white men into their world. Columbus did not need his armed soldiers. After looking a long while he saw naked red men peering at them from behind the strange, tropical plants. After he made signs of friendship, the natives were no longer afraid.

Christopher Columbus was first to set foot on the new-found shore. Falling on his knees, his eyes filled with tears of joy, he bowed his face and kissed the sand of the new world. The happy company repeated prayers and sang a hymn of praise. The naked natives looked on with wonder to see the leader, who was dressed in rich red velvet, set up a red, white, and gold banner—the combined flag of Ferdinand and Isabella—and go through a long ceremony. They{84} did not know that those white strangers were claiming the country in the name of a king and queen far across the sea. Columbus named this island—one of the group now called Bahamas—San Salvador, or Holy Saviour. He still thought he had reached the Far East.

Admiral Columbus returned to Spain to report upon his reaching eastern India by sailing west. With him went ten of the red men he had found, whom he called Indians. He made several voyages after that—only once landing on the continent of South America. Some of his Spanish followers were jealous of their Italian Admiral, and Columbus died in a prison in Spain, after all he had done for that country, without even knowing that it was America, not India, that he had discovered.

MAGELLAN, THE MAN OF THE STRAITS

AMONG the lads in many lands who were thrilled by the stories of Columbus and his discoveries was twelve-year-old Ferdinand Magellan, a Portuguese boy. Like thousands of youths all over Europe, he then made up his mind to sail the seas and seek his fortune.

Portugal, though a small country, was the home of many men of great energy and daring. A Portuguese explorer, Vasco da Gama, had sailed around the Cape of Good Hope, at the southern point of Africa, and discovered that way to India and the Moluccas, or Spice Islands. On these voyages the Portuguese had landed, traded, and taken possession of important parts of Africa. Others had followed in the wake of Columbus, discovering and claiming vast regions in South America.{85}

So young Magellan formed a partnership with another adventurer and started out on voyages of discovery. For nearly ten years he journeyed to and fro between his little homeland and various points in East Africa, India, the Malay Peninsula, and the islands beyond. Frequently he had to fight battles with savage native tribes. In one battle he received a wound that made him lame for life.

Ferdinand Magellan.

Ferdinand Magellan.

When Magellan came home, he suggested to the king of Portugal that it would be a great thing for Portugal if a passage across or around America could be discovered, which would shorten the distance, time, and expense of going from Europe to the Spice Islands. He hoped the king would equip a fleet for such a voyage of discovery; but the king refused, and he set out for Spain to get help for his great undertaking.

At this time he received a letter from a friend who had settled in the Spice Islands, saying that he had "discovered{86} another new world, larger than that found by Vasco da Gama." Magellan wrote to this friend that he would soon be visiting those islands himself—"If not by way of Portugal, then by way of Spain."

After a long wait, the Spanish king consented to furnish five ships with two hundred and thirty-four officers and sailors, and to stock them with provisions to last through a two-year voyage. It was agreed also that Magellan and his partner should receive one-twentieth of the profits of their undertaking; and that they should be governors of the islands they discovered.

At last, after two long years of waiting, Magellan's fleet was ready to sail. Crossing the Atlantic seemed an easy matter then—twenty-seven years after the first voyage of Columbus. The first land they reached was the mainland of South America. The natives along the northern coast were friendly and ready to exchange enough fish for ten men for a looking-glass, a bushel of sweet potatoes for a bell, and several fowls (or even one of their own children) for a butcher-knife. Those people lived in huts and went almost naked, except for aprons of parrots' feathers. There were many birds of bright plumage and plenty of monkeys in those regions. Some of the natives were cannibals, cooking and eating the flesh of men they captured or killed in battle.

The little Spanish fleet coasted along toward the south. The wide mouth of the La Plata deceived them so that they sailed in until they found that it was only a river. As they drew nearer to the South Pole it grew intensely cold. The men on the ships begged Magellan to turn round and go home. Some of their number died of exposure and want, and the rest were afraid they could not live through{87} such a winter. Not only did they suffer from the bitter cold, but their ships had been damaged by storms on the way down the coast.

They stayed several weeks at a port in the country now called Patagonia without seeing a person. But one day an Indian giant strode in upon them. He was so tall that the white men's heads barely came up to his waist. His hair was dyed white, his face colored red, and he had painted wide yellow circles around his little, black eyes. When they let him see himself in a big steel mirror he was so astonished that he jumped backward and knocked down four of the Spaniards standing around him. When he understood that it was himself he saw in the looking-glass, he was pleased and they made him a present of a small metal mirror. They found the Patagonians to be savages of a very low and brutal type, who ate raw meat, and even rats, like beasts of prey. If they felt sick they stuck arrows down their throats, and gashed their foreheads with shell-knives when their heads ached.

Many of Magellan's men now turned against him, planning to murder him and those who stood by him, and then to sail back to Spain. Though they were the larger number the energetic ship master beat them at their own game. He executed one ringleader, and sailed away leaving another rebel on the shore, where he was, no doubt, soon killed and eaten by the cannibals.

As July and August are the coldest months near the South Pole, the weather began to moderate in October, which is a spring month. January and February are the hot season in that climate. On the 21st of October, 1520, they "saw an opening like unto a bay," and after sailing through its winding ways they found to their great joy,{88} that it led out at the other end into a vast expanse of water. At last they had discovered the only natural passage from sea to sea through the American continents.

Some of their ships had been lost and their provisions were eaten. Most of the men begged to turn back, now that they could report that they had found a great ocean beyond South America. "No one knows," they said, "how wide this open sea is, and we may all starve before we reach the Moluccas."

But Ferdinand Magellan would not turn back. He accused them of having faint hearts, and said that even if they had to eat the leather on the ships' yards he would still go on and discover what he had promised the King of Spain.

One dark night the commander of the largest ship deserted the others and went back to Spain with the greater part of their provisions. The other ships were thirty-eight days winding their way through the straits to which the great leader's name was afterward given, the Straits of Magellan. They saw so many fires in the land away to the south of them that they named it Terra del Fuego—Land of Fire.

Brave Magellan's threat had to be carried out. All their provisions had either been eaten or were wholly unfit to eat. So all they had to live on for a long time was the leather on the ships' yards. They hung it over the sides of the ship to soak several days in the salt water as they sailed along. Then they cooked it over a coal fire. The wide sea they were now crossing was so free from storms that Magellan named it the Pacific Ocean.

After three months of hunger and thirst, risking their lives in their devotion to leader and country, they discovered a group of islands now named the Marianne or Ladrone{89} Islands. Here they enjoyed the luscious fruits and reveled in plenty of fresh water to drink. From the Ladrones they sailed on and discovered the Philippines, where the natives were friendly and brought them coconuts, oranges, bananas, fowls, and palm wine, which they gladly exchanged for metal looking-glasses, red caps, beads, and trinkets.

Besides his wish to sail round the globe and take possession of new islands for Spain, Magellan's great desire was to make the savage people Christians. He had the happiness of seeing thousands of dusky islanders kneeling before the crosses he had set up. But in his zeal to show those heathen the power of the Christian's God, he led the warriors of one island in a fight against some unconverted savages and lost his life.

In three years, lacking twelve days from the time they started out, the ship Victoria returned to the Spanish port from which it had sailed, after making the first voyage around the world. This vessel was loaded with spices from the Moluccas, as Magellan had planned. A faithful lieutenant represented their departed leader at the court of King Charles of Spain, who rewarded the few survivors with high honors and liberal pensions.

CORTES, THE CONQUEROR

AMONG the millions of people who wondered at the strange stories of the new lands discovered by Columbus was Hernando, a seven-year-old son of a Spanish noble family named Cortes. His young mind was filled with longing for adventure. As soon as he was old enough{90} Hernando left home to seek his fortune on the island of Santo Domingo in the new world. The governor of this island was pleased with the manner, pluck, and energy of Cortes, and offered to sell him a large estate on easy terms. But the young Spaniard answered haughtily, "I did not come here to plough like a field laborer; I came to get gold."

It was not long before young Cortes saw a chance for adventure. He went with a Spanish governor to settle the island of Cuba. He soon became a favorite with this governor also. An adventurer returned from the part of the mainland now called Central America and Mexico with tales of the great wealth of the people called Aztecs, and of the gold mines there.

Hernando Cortes

From a painting by Peale, in Independence Hall, Phila.
Hernando Cortes
From a painting by Peale, in Independence Hall, Phila.

The governor of Cuba decided to send ships and men to conquer that country, and offered the command to Cortes, who worked like a hero to get ready for the campaign. He equipped eleven vessels with six hundred men. A hundred or more of these were sailors and workmen; and the rest, soldiers, some of whom were armed with muskets and some with crossbows. There were fourteen small cannon and sixteen horses in the outfit.

As Cortes was about to sail, the governor of Cuba changed his mind and sent an order to Havana giving the command of the expedition to another officer. But shrewd young Cortes got wind of this in time, and sailed away before the governor's messengers arrived.

The soldiers and other men of the expedition agreed to stand by the brave leader and capture the new country for{91} King Charles of Spain in their own name instead of the Cuban governor's. This was exactly what that governor feared Cortes would try to do.

When the Spaniards landed on the continent the natives were afraid. They had never seen a horse, and they thought the men on horseback were monster human beings with

37

four legs, half man and half horse. Yet they came bravely out of their hiding places to do battle with such frightful invaders. Then the Spaniards fired a cannon volley and shot off their muskets so that several of the Indians fell dead. "They are gods!" shouted the natives in deadly fear. "They have the lightning and thunder in their hands!" It did not take long for Cortes to make terms with these natives, some of whom became allies and interpreters for the Spaniards.

After founding a city at the coast, which he named Villa Rica de la Vera Cruz (Rich City of the True Cross), now called Vera Cruz, Cortes prepared to conquer the empire of the Aztecs with six hundred Spaniards and several thousand Mexican Indians. Montezuma, emperor of the Aztecs, heard of his coming, and tried to make him leave the country by sending rich presents from his capital in the mountains. But that did not stop Cortes.

In order to insure victory, the Spanish general committed a brave though desperate act. Choosing one ship from his fleet he manned it and sent a trusted officer back—to Spain, not Cuba—with some of Montezuma's rich presents. With these Cortes sent other proofs of the wealth of the country which he was about to conquer and add to the empire of King Charles of Spain. Then, after taking from the other ten ships everything the Spaniards could use in the new country, Cortes ordered those vessels burned and sunk.{92} Thus, having burned their bridges behind them, they had no way of escape but to go forward and fight for their fortunes, their country, and their very lives.

On the march of two hundred miles to Montezuma's capital, the Spaniards beat the Tlascalans in battle and made friends with those Indians against the Aztec tyrant, as the Indians called Emperor Montezuma.

The Indians of the hot countries of America were not so savage as those who lived in the northern parts of the continent. But they had a terrible religious rite which they had learned from the Aztecs. They offered human lives to appease the sun god. Though the Aztecs were a peaceable people otherwise, they often went to war to take prisoners for these horrible sacrifices.

Cortes broke into a temple at one place on the way and murdered the priests who were killing and offering human beings to the sun god. He set up a cross and invited the people to become Christians or be killed. In that way he gained many converts from among the frightened Indians.

But with Hernando Cortes this kind of conversion was but a step toward gaining gold and power for himself and for the king of Spain. After many terrible battles, in which he massacred the helpless natives by thousands, he and his few hundred white men, with thousands of Indian allies, reached the capital of Montezuma. Built of stone on an island in the midst of a beautiful lake, this civilized city was connected with the mainland by six long stone bridges or causeways. The splendid capital, with its palaces and temples of hewn stone, had much of the beauty of Venice. The city measured twelve miles around. It was then hundreds of years old, and proved that the ancient Aztecs knew how to build great stone houses and bridges.{93}

The capture of the City of Mexico by Cortes

{94}From the painting by Alonzo Chappel
The capture of the City of Mexico by Cortes
From the painting by Alonzo Chappel

Montezuma came out to meet Cortes, borne on a golden throne on the shoulders of Aztec nobles and officials. He wore priceless feathers and his garments were embroidered with many-colored gems. Even his shoes were gold. His courtiers carried carpets to lay down before him, so that his sacred feet should not touch the ground. How the eyes of those greedy Spaniards glittered when they beheld such signs of the great wealth of Montezuma and his people!

The white men were received with great honor. They were served in golden goblets with a strange, rich drink which the Aztecs named chocolatl. This delicious drink is now called chocolate or cocoa. Montezuma told the Spaniards that their coming had been foretold by the priests for hundreds of years, ever since the visit of a pure white man, a son of the Sun who had come down from the skies. This sun-god had told the Aztecs that he would come again with other sun-gods and reign over the empire forever.

Cortes pretended to be the long-expected "fair god" of the Aztecs, and persuaded Montezuma to visit him in the palace assigned to the Spanish leader and his officers during their stay in the city. The people, who had no reason to believe in the Spanish soldiers, crowded around the sedan chair of their king, crying out against him because he was placing himself in the wicked hands of the strangers. Montezuma told them not to fear, for their guests were honorable men and he was sure that all would be well with him. But he soon found that he was not a guest but a prisoner, betrayed by a pretense of friendship. The Mexicans came again and attacked the palace which Cortes and his men had now turned into a fortress. During the months when the Spaniards held Montezuma as a prisoner a fierce war was waged with the Mexicans.{95}

While Cortes and his army were in such desperate straits, word came that the governor of Cuba had sent ships and nearly a thousand men to bring the general and his followers back, to be punished as deserters. Cortes and a picked band crept out of the capital one dark night, marched hundreds of miles to the coast, and surprised and defeated the army the governor had sent. Then he returned, with all those armed men and many more cannon and horses, to relieve the small garrison he had left to hold the many thousands of Aztecs at bay, and capture the city of Mexico.

The Aztecs were frightened when they saw the thousand soldiers Cortes now brought up against them, for it looked as if the new troops had come down from the skies to the help of the Spaniards. When the battle was fiercest, the broken-spirited emperor went out to plead with the natives to stop their fighting. This made them so angry that they hurled stones at him and he died of a broken heart. The hatred of his own people was even harder to bear than Spanish cruelty.

After more fierce fighting, Cortes completed the conquest of Mexico. Years afterward he returned to his old home in Spain, where he was, for a time, treated as a great conqueror. But he suffered in later years from remorse for his treachery and cruelty. When he grew old he was imprisoned through the influence of Spanish enemies.

One day an old, broken man with shaggy gray locks pushed through the crowd around King Charles of Spain, now known as Emperor Charles the Fifth and the most powerful monarch in the world. When the emperor asked the old man who he was, he replied with indignant pride,

"I am Cortes, the man who has given you more provinces than your ancestors left you cities."{96}

DE SOTO, A GOLD HUNTER IN SOUTHERN SWAMPS

HERNANDO DE SOTO was the Spanish grandee, or noble, appointed governor of Cuba and "the Floridas" about twenty-five years after Florida was discovered. It was

Ponce de Leon who landed near the southern point of North America, on Easter Day, 1513, and named that lovely country Florida—Land of Flowers. De Leon had heard a beautiful story that far inland in the heart of the wilderness there was a magic spring that would make young forever all who drank of its sparkling waters. Though he searched long and eagerly, Ponce de Leon discovered no Fountain of Eternal Youth, but he did find endless swamps full of snakes and alligators.

De Soto, the new governor of Florida, made up his mind that Ponce de Leon was a very foolish old man. He ought to have known that there are no such things nowadays as springs of eternal youth. He, Hernando de Soto, was going to show his practical good sense by finding solid, yellow gold—for what good is youth without money to enjoy it with? De Soto was already a very rich man, for he had served under Pizarro, the cruel conqueror of Peru, and he had gone home to Spain one of the wealthiest of its grandees, in those days of wonderful discoveries and marvelous fortunes. Still Hernando de Soto was not satisfied. He wanted to be like Pizarro or Cortes—to conquer a great country and capture from its dusky people gold mines and vast wealth.

Therefore on a bright July day he left Cuba in charge of a high official and sailed away. He and his knights in armor stood on the decks of their nine ships, large and small, and waved farewells to the fair ladies who stood{97} on the castle tower at Havana weeping bitterly, fearing that they would never see their brave lords and knights again.

Governor de Soto and his fleet came to anchor in the harbor now known as Tampa Bay. During the night they were aroused by horrible yells and showers of arrows from the shore. In the morning the Spaniards made a landing, though the natives fought hard to keep them back. Before night they met a man who could be of great use to them. He was a member of a party that, after De Leon's discovery, had gone to Florida to find gold, but had been driven back. This young man, Juan Ortiz, had been captured and kept by the Indians as a slave. A member of De Soto's scouting party tells how they met this poor fellow:

"Towards sunset it pleased God that the soldiers descried at a distance some twenty Indians painted with a kind of red ointment that they put on when they go to war. They wore many feathers and had their bows and arrows. And when the Christians ran at them, the Indians fled to a hill, and one of them came forth into the path, lifting up his voice and saying in Spanish,

" 'Sirs, for the love of God, slay not me! For I am a Christian like yourselves. I was born in Seville, and my name is Juan Ortiz.' "

The Spanish governor received Ortiz as if he were his own long-lost son. He made himself very useful because he knew both the Spanish and the Indian language, and thus could help the Spaniards to talk to the natives.

De Soto now started inland leading a brilliant company of knights and private soldiers, all in bright armor. Over the shining helmets were waving plumes, and many a mailed fist held aloft a rich and beautiful banner. There were hundreds of horsemen and many more men marching on foot. No more richly dressed men and horses ever started out on a Crusade to regain possession of the Holy City.{98} But the object of this Spanish quest was gold. Spanish serving men drove along with this rich and gay procession four hundred fat hogs. De Soto had decided not to risk being starved to death as so many explorers had been. And gamekeepers held in leash, not falcons to catch and kill birds or beasts, but bloodhounds for hunting Indians.

Instead of mountains of rocks from which gold could be mined, De Soto's men found swamps. The weather was sultry and moist. Insects got inside their knightly armor and stung them to madness, and venomous serpents coiled around their armored legs.

Indians shot poisoned arrows at them from the bushes. Their coats of mail were so heavy that stout knights sank deep in the bogs. They advanced very slowly; they wallowed rather than marched, and their days and nights were spent in weariness and torture.

The fame of the white men went on ahead of them. As De Soto advanced he found the savages on the warpath ready to drive back the invaders. All along their line of march they could hear savage threats in the distance. Juan Ortiz told the Spaniards that the Indians were shouting:

"Keep on, robbers and murderers! In Apalachee you will get what you deserve. No mercy will be shown to captives, who will be hung on the highest trees along the trail."

After the Spaniards had marched through the lands of five different chiefs, they found a great chieftain who seemed to wish to make friends with the white men. De Soto gladly accepted, but Juan Ortiz warned him to look out for treachery. So the white men were secretly prepared; and when the traitor chief gave the signal to his men to attack, the Spaniards raised their battle cry, "Santiago!" and thousands of the savages were killed by a few hundred Spaniards.{99} Hundreds of Indians took refuge in a lake. There five good swimmers would lie side by side, on the surface like logs, forming a human raft on which the best archer would stand and shoot back at the white men. The fight lasted all day and nearly all night. Before morning all the Indians were killed or captured, put in chains, and divided among the Spaniards as slaves.

The Indians, who at first thought the white men were gods, were now sure they were devils. The boasted village of Apalachee was only a few straw huts on a knoll in the center of a great swamp. And the savages who defended it with bows and arrows were no match for armed Spaniards; the white men killed nearly all of them.

Cold weather came on, and the Spaniards went into winter quarters. A beautiful Indian girl-chief in that region came bringing pearls and gems to the Spanish chieftain. But he demanded gold. When she understood this she sent men to a far country for the yellow metal he desired so eagerly. De Soto and his men now rejoiced, for they thought they had found the object of their long and painful search. When the red messengers returned the stuff proved not to be gold. It must have been copper ore or "fool's gold."

During the second year of their long march, the Spaniards were led southward to Mabila, which is believed to have stood on the shore of Mobile Bay. This was a huge fortress, the greatest native town the white men had yet seen. Within an immense stockade or wall of tree trunks on end stood a number of houses each of which would hold hundreds of Indians.

Tuscaloosa, the Mabile chief, set a trap for the Spaniards. The battle which took place here was the worst of all. The{100}
{101}

De Soto on the bank of the Mississippi

{101}From the drawing by H. L. Stephens
De Soto on the bank of the Mississippi
From the drawing by H. L. Stephens
Spaniards lost seventy men and forty horses. Then they set fire to the Indians' houses, and the savages perished in the flames.

De Soto's men were heartily sick of fighting. They also despaired of finding gold in southern swamps. The governor heard here that they were plotting to desert him at Mabila and return by boat to Havana. So, instead of waiting for a ship to come from

41

Cuba, he ordered them to march farther into the wilderness. As the prospect of finding gold became more desperate, De Soto seemed to grow more cruel. Indians were beheaded for small offenses; friendly scouts were tortured and sent back with insulting messages to their chiefs.

The farther west the Spaniards went the more bitterly the natives fought and the more successful they were in battle. In one place the Indians burned nearly all the Spaniards' hogs, and feasted on roast pork for many days. After terrible wanderings, the few remaining Spaniards came to a wide stream at Chickasaw Bluff, a few miles above the present city of Vicksburg.

Though it is often stated that De Soto discovered the Mississippi, he was not the first Spaniard to see that wide and muddy stream. The Great River meant nothing to him. As he wandered up and down its banks he contracted malarial fever and died miserably. Faithful friends placed the body in his heavy armor and wrapped that in blankets weighted with sand. Then, on a dark night, they paddled out into the middle of the stream and sank it in a hundred feet of water, where the Indians could not find it and wreak their revenge upon De Soto's remains. His followers attempted to go farther west but became discouraged and descended the Mississippi to the Gulf of Mexico. {102}

SIR FRANCIS DRAKE, ENGLAND'S FIRST GREAT SAILOR

AMONG little Francis Drake's earliest memories was his home in the hulk of an old ship near a navy yard in the south of England. His father was a sort of chaplain to the fleets which kept coming and going there. Francis heard the wild tales of seafaring men about pirates and Spaniards, and seafights, and the wonderful wealth in distant lands.

Young Drake's soul was fired with a fervent longing for life and adventure on the high seas or the Spanish Main, as the region along the northern coast of South America was called, where wedges of gold and silver from Peru and pearls and precious stones were stored in treasure towns, waiting to be shipped to Spain. But Francis was the eldest of twelve children and his father was poor. So the lad was bound out till he was twenty-one to work for a skipper, or owner of a small trading vessel called a barque. In his work there was plenty of lifting and lugging to do—moving baskets and bales on and off his master's boat. He had to work long hours—often at night. His food was scarce and coarse and his pay was very small indeed, for his work was thought not worth much more than his learning the sailor trade.

Sometimes they sailed the barque across the Channel to France or Holland and brought back a cargo to England; but that was as far as such a small craft could be trusted to go. Francis often saw great ships riding high on their majestic way to foreign lands, and he felt sure that those lucky sailors would have thrilling times with pirates and Spaniards, and come home loaded down with gold and{103} silver, spices, precious gems, and thrilling stories. Much as he yearned to go on a long voyage, the faithful fellow stayed by his master, worked hard, and learned all the ins and outs of sailing a ship, whether large or small.

Just before Francis was old enough to be his own man the good skipper died. As he had never married and had no near relatives, he left his barque to his faithful apprentice. Young Drake continued the business, running from port to port and market to market for about a year, when he saw a chance to sail on a longer voyage and engage in a larger enterprise. He had a cousin, John Hawkins, who was captain of a vessel. This cousin now had a little fleet of five ships and was about to engage in the slave trade. As Francis had learned to manage a ship, Captain Hawkins offered to put the smallest vessel in his fleet under his young cousin's command. So Francis sold his barque and became captain of his cousin's ship Judith.

Now, at the age of twenty-two, Francis Drake was embarking on the voyage of life with the prospect of great adventures, as he had always dreamed of doing. Slave trading was not considered wrong four hundred years ago. The ships would go to Africa and buy or carry off negroes and take them to some foreign country to work in fields and mines. There the blacks would be sold for gold, silver, pearls and other things of great value. Sometimes the owner of a fleet would make a fortune in a single adventure. Of course, there was a great risk to run. Although England and Spain were not then at war, the English and Spanish treated each other as enemies when they met on the high seas.

For this voyage, Captain Hawkins got leave of Queen Elizabeth "to load negroes in Guinea and sell them in the{104} West Indies." As a sign that the hundred and seventy men on Hawkins's fleet saw nothing wrong in stealing black men from their homes and selling them to be slaves, here is a motto which that captain had written to govern his soldiers and sailors: "Serve God daily, love one another, preserve your victuals, beware of fire, and keep good company."

Hawkins and Drake seem to have had no trouble in seizing negroes on the coast of Africa, or in selling their human cargo in the Spanish ports of America. But as these slavers were starting back to England they were caught in a storm and had to go into a harbor in Mexico for safety and to repair damages. While they were there a Spanish fleet five times as large as theirs, loaded with gold and pearls, came in also for repairs. The English agreed to leave the Spaniards without touching their ships if the Spaniards would let them alone. But the Spanish captain did not keep his word and there was a fierce battle. Hawkins and Drake did great damage to the Spanish fleet. They reached England safely with two of their ships, though they had lost nearly all the treasure they had received as pay for the slaves.

Captain Drake complained to the queen of the way in which the Spaniards had deceived them, but she was afraid to go to war with a country which had such a powerful navy as Spain's was then. So the bold English captain took matters into his own hands. He made one voyage after another, attacking Spanish settlements where gold and silver were stored, boarding Spanish vessels, killing the men or taking them prisoners, and bringing their rich cargoes to England. Within a few years the Spaniards lived in terror of their lives when they heard that Francis{105} Drake was near, and the king of Spain appealed to Queen Elizabeth to stop those attacks, calling Drake "the master thief of the western world."

On one of these expeditions, Drake landed on the Isthmus of Panama, or Darien, as it was then called. Some of the natives showed him the way across to the South Sea, or the Pacific Ocean, as Magellan had named it, and when they had ascended a mountain about half-way across, Drake climbed a tall tree from which he gazed upon the broad, unexplored ocean.

"May God give me leave and life to sail that sea but once!" murmured Captain Drake to his companions.

But Queen Elizabeth had heard of the terror of the Spaniards and ordered him to stop, lest he plunge her kingdom into a Spanish war before England was ready. So for a while Francis Drake stayed at home and suffered because he was not allowed to fight with the Spaniards.

About five years after his first sight of the Pacific, Captain Drake sailed away from England in command of a fleet of five vessels of which the flagship was the Golden Hind.

43

The object of the voyage was a secret. This was about sixty years after Magellan, the Portuguese master-sailor, had discovered and passed through the straits named for him.

It took five months for the fleet to reach the eastern coast of South America. In due time they found and passed through the Straits of Magellan; but the ocean beyond was more terrific than Pacific, for a fierce storm drove the Golden Hind even farther south than Tierra del Fuego, so that Drake was first to land at Cape Horn, the southern-most point of South America. At the place where the waters of the Atlantic meet those of the Pacific, Drake lay{106} down and embraced the sharp point of rock and exclaimed: "I am the only man in the world who has ever been so far south!"

All the ships in Drake's fleet but the Golden Hind had either been sunk, broken, or scattered. Now at last he had "leave and life to sail that sea but once"—with one ship alone. The undaunted hero sailed up the western coast of South America to capture treasure from the gold mines of Peru. When he came near Valparaiso, some Spaniards in a ship saw the Golden Hind approach. Never dreaming that an English ship could be in that ocean, they were astonished to see a gun presented through a porthole and to hear an English voice calling on them roughly to surrender. So they stared and cursed under their breath while "the master thief of the western world" took charge of their ship with sixty thousand gold pesos, jewels, merchandise, and a stock of wine.

When the people of Valparaiso heard that the dreadful Drake was in their harbor, they fled from the city. The little English crew entered the town, and stocked up with bread, bacon, and wine, which they enjoyed to the full after many months of famishing. In a day or two the Golden Hind sailed away northward toward Peru.

At another port they waylaid three unguarded barques and captured fifty-seven bricks of silver, each weighing about twenty pounds. When they came to the port of Lima, there were seventeen vessels anchored in the harbor. Not daunted by numbers, Drake sailed right into the harbor, captured them all with his one ship, and made their men prisoners while he plundered the whole Spanish fleet. By this time the alarm had been spread along the coast that Drake was capturing everything in sight, and the{107}
{108}

Queen Elizabeth knighting Drake on board the "Golden Hind"

{108}From the drawing by Sir John Gilbert, R.A.
Queen Elizabeth knighting Drake on board the "Golden Hind"
From the drawing by Sir John Gilbert, R.A.
governor of Peru with two thousand men was waiting for him at Callao.

Drake's good luck seemed now to desert him. In the presence of that waiting army the wind died down and the Golden Hind was becalmed, helpless, and unable to move a yard. The Spanish governor grinned as he went out in boats from the shore with four hundred soldiers, to take back all the precious cargo Drake had lately captured. But before the armed men reached the English ship a gale blew up and Drake sailed away, laughing and waving farewells to his pursuers.

The cargo from the last ship they captured overloaded the Golden Hind with tons of gold, silver and precious gems. It was useless to overhaul any more galleons, for they now had all their ship could carry. Their only thought was to get their treasure home safe and sound. Sailing across the Pacific, they were sixty-eight days without sighting land.

The Golden Hind began to show the strain of her long voyage; so they set up a forge on an island in the South Pacific and spent weeks in making repairs, so that the ship might complete her voyage around the world. After they had sailed more than a month longer, the ship ran on a ledge of rocks. Seeing that they could not get her off, they threw six cannon overboard, then the sugar and spices, then great fortunes in silver. At last they managed to work her off the ledge into deep water. Still it was nearly a year before they reached the harbor of Plymouth, England.

The wildest dreams of the boy Francis Drake were now more than realized. All England buzzed with his astounding exploits. The city bells rang and there was a general{109} holiday, with feasting and dancing. Queen Elizabeth came down from London and dined with the great captain on the Golden Hind. Before she left the deck, the captain knelt before her and she tapped him on the shoulder with his sword, thus knighting him Sir Francis Drake.

After this the greatest of the English knights of the high seas made many voyages, dealing out destruction to Spanish galleons and treasure stores. He attacked cities and burned fleets—reporting to the queen that he had just "singed the Spanish king's beard." Drake was one of the four chiefs in command of the English ships that destroyed the Spanish Armada. No one did more than he to take the sea power away from Spain and give it to England, and thus make it possible for the English to begin the settlement of our country.

SIR WALTER RALEIGH, THE FAVORITE OF GOOD QUEEN BESS

A GAY company was waiting before the old palace at Greenwich, beside the River Thames below the City of London, on a summer afternoon in the days of Elizabeth. They were watching for the queen and her intimates to come down the broad steps in front of the palace.

There had been a shower, and the trees, grass, and bright flowers glistened in the sunshine.

"Here comes Her Majesty!" exclaimed some in the waiting throng as a woman in middle life descended the steps, attended by the Earl of Leicester and other nobles and knights whose names are well-known to history. The{110} queen was slender, with her light auburn hair dressed up from her high, pale brow. Her chief mark of beauty was her small, delicate hands with long, taper fingers, of which she was rather vain. She was richly dressed in a heavy silk brocade, and a collar of costly lace stood up from her shoulders behind her slender neck like an open fan.

The boyhood of Raleigh. As he listens to the sailor's tale of the land beyond the sea, Raleigh resolves to win it for England when he is a man.

From the painting by J. E. Millais
The boyhood of Raleigh. As he listens to the sailor's tale of the land beyond the sea, Raleigh resolves to win it for England when he is a man.
From the painting by J. E. Millais
The court, after receiving her gracious greetings, followed the queen in a grand promenade through the park. Elizabeth soon came to a spot where the recent shower had{111} left a shallow pool of water. A quaint writer describes this scene:

"Her Majesty meeting with a plashy place, made some scruples to go on, when Raleigh (dressed in the gay and genteel habit of those times) presently cast off and spread his new plush cloak on the ground, whereon the Queen trod gently over, rewarding him afterwards with many suits for his so free and seasonable tender of so fair a foot-cloth."

Walter Raleigh was a handsome young man, six feet tall, with curly brown hair and beard. He had been a soldier in France and an officer in Ireland, and had made several voyages of discovery with his gallant half-brother Sir Humphrey Gilbert.

It was the fashion—indeed it seemed necessary then—for men at court to flatter the middle-aged maiden queen, who was foolish enough to believe that she was as lovely as they told her she was. The Earl of Leicester once entertained her at Kenilworth Castle, where he had all the clocks stopped on the moment of her arrival to show that no notice should be taken of the passing of time during her visit there.

So Queen Bess could hardly help feeling flattered when such a gallant and good-looking courtier as Raleigh bowed before her and laid his cloak as a velvet carpet for her to walk upon. Riches, lands, castles, and even happiness go by favor in royal circles. Some time after this, the queen made her favorite a knight, with the title Sir before his name.

One day the queen saw Raleigh taking a diamond ring off his finger and scratching something on a window-pane.

"Fain would I climb, yet fear I to fall."

{112}

Then she took from her own slim hand a diamond and cut in the glass under what he had written, this rhyme:

"If thy heart fail thee, climb not at all."

Of course, each reigning favorite of the queen became an object of envy to the rest of the court. Lord Leicester, who was now slighted by her Majesty for this new knight, did all he could to injure Raleigh. The young Earl of Essex did his utmost, later, to turn the queen against Sir Walter. But for a long time Raleigh remained high in favor.

Raleigh was the first Englishman to attempt to plant a colony in the New World. By way of compliment to the maiden queen, he named the whole region which he was trying to settle, Virginia. Returning from an early voyage, he introduced into Ireland the potato, first found in South America. He also discovered the pineapple (so named because it is shaped like a pine cone) and imported it to England. Another thing Raleigh is said to have introduced into England was tobacco, which the American Indians raised and "drank," as they called smoking, in pipes of copper and clay. Raleigh had a silver pipe made for his own use. One day when he was smoking in his library, a manservant came in with a pot of ale, and, thinking his master was on fire, yelled with fright as he poured the ale over him! It is said that the queen asked Sir Walter to smoke in her presence; but when she tried to learn to use tobacco in that way, she stopped because it made her ill.

Sir Walter Raleigh was in active command of a number of English ships in the fleet which defeated the Invincible Armada, sent against England by King Philip the Second of{113} Spain. For her favorite's part in that great adventure, the queen made him an admiral. Later, he was wounded in a naval battle near Cadiz, Spain. When asked what had been done for him on account of his heroic services there, Admiral Raleigh sadly replied,

"What the generals have got I know least. For my own part, I have got a lame leg and deformed. I have not wanted good words, and exceeding kind and regardful usage; but I have possession of nought but poverty and pain."

Some one must have told the queen of this speech, for she called Raleigh back to the palace and appointed him once more her captain of the guard.

When Queen Elizabeth died, James Stuart, king of Scotland, became king. James's mind had been poisoned against Raleigh, whose enemies told the new king that Raleigh plotted to place James's cousin, Arabella Stuart, upon the throne of England. So Sir Walter was imprisoned in the Tower of London. He was confined there for twelve years, though he proved that the things his enemies had said against him were untrue. One wicked creature who had accused him confessed that his story about Raleigh was made up out of spite.

During the long years of his imprisonment, Sir Walter wrote his "History of the World," and experimented in a rude chemical laboratory which he had fixed up in his prison. He also wrote beautiful poems and many letters to his friends. For some time Lady Raleigh was allowed to visit him with their son, Carew. The older son, Walter, had been killed in an encounter while on a voyage with his father, seeking El Dorado, or the City of Gold, supposed to lie hidden in northern South America.{114}

At last word came from King James that if Raleigh would go and find those fabled gold mines for his benefit, his high treason would be forgiven. So the white-haired knight, lame from a wound he had received in loyal service of England, started out on another voyage of adventure, to fight the Spaniard to the bitter end.

But Sir Walter was only hoping against hope, for there was no such mine there, and the expedition proved an utter failure. Instead of escaping to another country as he might well have done, he went back and bravely told King James that the "El Dorado" story was only a Spanish lie.

So the disappointed king ordered Raleigh back to prison, and a corrupt judge pronounced him guilty of high treason. For that crime, the Raleigh's beautiful home estate might legally become the property of the crown, and Raleigh himself condemned to death.

Raleigh made the best even of this terrible experience. He cheered his wife by telling her he was ready and glad to go where she could come too—where they could be happy together always.

On his way to execution, Raleigh noticed a man with a bald head and no hat. Taking off his own cap he tossed it down to the old man with—

"You need this, my friend, more than I do."

On the scaffold he made a patriotic speech to the assembled crowd. Then he asked to see the axe. He smiled as he tried the edge of it with his thumb, and remarked to the executioner who stood before him, dressed, as was the custom, in black velvet tights, with a black mask over his face,

"This gives me no fear. It is a sharp and fair medicine to cure me of all my troubles."{115}

HENRY HUDSON, THE MAN WHO PUT HIMSELF ON THE MAP

JUST as Magellan set out to discover a way through America from the Atlantic to the Pacific Ocean, so Henry Hudson determined to find a northwest passage from ocean to ocean. The reason for wishing to cross in the north from one ocean to the other was to save going "round the Horn," as sailors call the long voyage around Cape Horn, the southern point of South America. We now know that there is no northwest passage; at least, if there is such a waterway it is so near the North Pole that it is always frozen up. But Henry Hudson, like all sailors in his time, thought that it would be a simple matter to sail through the open polar sea and pass from the Atlantic to the Pacific north of North America.

In 1607 this bold British navigator undertook a voyage in the employ, as he wrote in his journal, of "certain worshipful Merchants of London." The object of this voyage was to explore the coast of Greenland and, as he explained, "for to discover a passage by the North Pole to Japan and China." His crew numbered only twelve persons, including one boy, his own son John. After sailing about for five months, suffering great hardships, Hudson returned to London without discovering that northern passage. The next year he started out again, this time sailing north-east along the coast of Norway, and returned after four months without finding anything but hardships.

Hudson's third voyage was made in the employ of the Dutch East India Company. He sailed from Amsterdam, Holland, with a crew of twenty men and his young son, on the Half Moon. He started out a second time for a north-east{116} passage, but he found so many difficulties that he turned his prow westward again, determined to discover the way past North America. About the 4th of July, 1609, he came to the Grand Banks of Newfoundland, where he saw a fleet of Frenchmen fishing for cod. After catching over a hundred of these fish for themselves, the crew of the Half Moon proceeded to the southwest, as Hudson had heard from his friend, Captain John Smith, that there was an open way to the Pacific south of Virginia.

After wandering down the coast and back, the Half Moon entered a broad bay and anchored beside an island which the natives called Manhattan. Hudson took possession of this region in the name of his Dutch employers and named it New Netherland. Here he traded with the Indians and sailed a little way up the beautiful river which now bears his name. "Here," one of his men wrote in the journal, "the land grew very high and mountainous." Hudson and his crew were afraid of the Indians. They captured two red men and tried to hold them as prisoners. They thought that the other Indians would treat the white men well for fear that Hudson would kill these two prisoners. But they made their escape through a porthole and swam to the shore. As the Half Moon got under way again, the two Indians and their friends stood on the bank, war-whooping, brandishing tomahawks, and calling for vengeance.

The Half Moon sailed on upstream, and towards night came to anchor near what is now Catskill Landing. "There," as it is written in the journal of the voyage, "we found very loving people and very old men, where we were well used. Our boat went to fish and caught great store of very good fish."

The next morning the fishing was not so good, "the{117}

The discovery of the Hudson River

From the painting by Warren Sheppard © 1895, by The Woolfall Co.
The discovery of the Hudson River
From the painting by Warren Sheppard © 1895, by The Woolfall Co.
savages having been there in their canoes all night." In the two days following the ship went only five miles farther up the river. Hudson was kindly received by an old chief who gave him the best cheer he could. The natives came flocking on board the ship, bringing grapes, pumpkins, and{118} beaver and otter skins, which they traded with the sailors for hatchets, knives, beads, and trinkets.

The ship's "log" states that they gave some of the savages brandy to drink. One of these men fell sound asleep, to the astonishment of the others, who feared he had been poisoned. They took to their canoes and paddled for shore. After a long powwow a few of the Indians returned with a quantity of beads. They wanted to pay the white men to lift

48

the spell which they had put upon the sleeping Indian. The next day the intoxicated Indian was walking about, well and happy, after his first taste of "firewater." This made his friends believe in the white men again, and the journal goes on to say:

"So, at three of the clock in the afternoon they came aboard, and brought tobacco and more beads, and gave them to our master; and made an oration, and showed him all the country round about. Then they sent one of their company on land, who presently returned, and brought a great platter full of venison dressed by themselves, and they caused him to eat with them. Then they made him reverence and departed, all save the old men that lay aboard."

Hudson found that it would not be safe to take the ship beyond the site of the present city of Albany; so the Half Moon's prow was turned down stream. On the way back the sailors were met by the two escaped prisoners with quite a company of savages. More than a hundred braves surrounded the ship. One climbed up the rudder and others swarmed over the sides. The crew fired upon them with their muskets, and with the cannon, blew holes in their canoes. The "thunder and lightning" from the guns frightened the Indians so that they fled to the shore and took to the woods.

Hudson himself had had enough. The Half Moon lifted{119} its anchor and sailed away from the river whose name is Henry Hudson's most glorious monument. Stopping in England on his way to Holland, he was engaged by the London Company to make another voyage in their behalf the following year. This time the ship he commanded was the Discovery. The course was past Iceland, around the southern part of Greenland, sighting Desolation Island, which he charted as in the northern part of Davis Strait. Through the strait which now bears his name he entered the sea known for all time as Hudson Bay.

This crew was a bad set of men. One young fellow whom Captain Hudson had picked up and befriended in London proved the worst of the gang. They did not face their hardships and sufferings with real courage. When starvation stared them in the face, every man looked out for himself. They hoarded food, and robbed and fought one another like wild beasts. At last they turned against Hudson, saying that he had brought them there to starve.

The young man to whom Hudson had been kindest of all bound his master. The rest tied up the six men who were most loyal to their chief, and Hudson's son. These eight men were put bound into the ship's boat. Then the crew hoisted the sail of the Discovery. They towed the little boat for a time, as if they were loath to do the dastardly deed that they had planned. But when they reached the open sea they cut the rope, and the little boat containing Henry Hudson and his son was never again seen by white men.

The ungrateful young man met a fate he richly deserved. In a fight with Arctic savages he was killed, and several of the rest were mortally wounded. Still others died of want before the few remaining deserters were picked up, starving,{120} by a passing vessel. Their names are forgotten, and they are only remembered at all because of their wicked treachery. But the map of North America is a fitting monument to the heroic but ill-fated adventurer and discoverer, Henry Hudson.

LA SALLE AND THE MOUTH OF THE MISSISSIPPI

LITTLE is known now of the early life of Robert Cavelier de la Salle, until, at twenty-five or a little less, he came from Rouen, France, to Montreal. But of his life in America, in those days when the land was still a howling wilderness, there is much to tell. He was born a century and a half after Columbus thought he had found the coast of

China; yet this young Frenchman still believed that China was only a little farther west than the land Columbus found, for he had but a narrow idea of the width of America.

The people who were living in Canada, the new country along the River St. Lawrence, were French. They traded with the Indians and trapped and skinned wild animals for their fur. Those were the days of Indian scouts and wigwams, and of war and scalp dances. Many of the French lived like Indians; they played Indian games—running, shooting, snowshoeing, lacrosse—and they learned to hunt and hide, and to travel stealthily through the forests, like real red men.

So the Indians liked the French people better than they liked other white settlers. The French called their scouts wood-runners. These brave, shrewd messengers went out among the Indian tribes and learned their languages and customs. Many of them ran from tribe to tribe, thousands{121} of miles into the wilderness, and came back to the French settlement with skins of the mink, beaver, otter, and other animals. They also had strange stories to tell of meadows, which they called prairies, as level as a floor and hundreds of miles wide, where there were no trees except along the rivers. Down through this thousand-mile prairie region they said there were rivers which flowed together into a wide stream which the Indians called the Mississippi, or Father of Waters, which kept on in a mighty flood to the unknown south country.

These stories fired the fervent soul of Robert La Salle. He believed that mighty river should be used as a water highway to the South Sea—as the Pacific Ocean was still called; and that if they could sail down to its mouth they would find an outlet to China like the outlet which the St. Lawrence gave toward Europe. He was always talking about China and trying in every way he could to raise money for canoes and food and Indian guides to find the way to China through the western wilderness. The French people laughed at his enthusiasm and called some land which he owned beside the rapids above Montreal La Chine—French for China. That suburb of Montreal is still called Lachine, and the rapids are the Lachine Rapids.

Not having wealth enough of his own, La Salle went to France to ask the king to approve his plan, and to provide money for the planting of the lilies of France on the banks of the Mississippi. La Salle's practical way of planting French lilies was to build and maintain forts at different points through all that great western country. Already Fort Frontenac had been built near the outlet of Lake Ontario, and Father Marquette, a heroic French missionary, accompanied by a trader named Joliet had found the Mississippi{122} and explored that great river for hundreds of miles. On his return to a French settlement Joliet wrote to Count Frontenac, governor of Canada, telling of the dangers of his voyage:

"I had escaped every peril of the Indians. I had passed forty-two rapids; and was at the point of debarking, full of joy at the success of so long and difficult an enterprise, when my canoe capsized, after all the danger seemed over. I lost two men and my box of papers within sight of the first French settlements, which I had left almost two years before. Nothing remains to me but life, and the ardent desire to employ it on any service which you may please to direct."

When Robert La Salle had permission from the king and his treasurer, and had borrowed money of his rich relatives in France, he returned to Canada and made up a party of brave French and Indian guides, scouts, and interpreters, who were to fight, if need be, to plant the lilies and forts of France in the great western valley of the Father of Waters.

After they had paddled through Lake Ontario and carried their canoes past Niagara Falls and the rapids above the Falls, they built their sailboat, the Griffin. On this ship they sailed through the lakes to the lower end of Lake Michigan. They paddled their canoes down along the shore of that lake to the St. Joseph River, where they built Fort St. Joseph. Canoeing up this river, which flows into Lake Michigan, they carried their barks across to a little stream which led away from the lake toward the greater rivers of the south country. On their way they saw Indians of the Illinois tribes, and smoked the calumet, or peace pipe, with most of these red men. Some tribes were so savage and unfriendly that the white travelers were afraid to shoot game for food, or even to build a fire lest a band of Indians on the warpath should see it and come to kill and scalp them all. But it seems to have been the fate of most {123}discoverers to find their bitterest foes among those who should be their friends. One of La Salle's own party was caught just in time to keep him from shooting their leader in the back.

Floating down a small stream the travelers came to the Illinois River. On their way, among friendly tribes, they shot plenty of game. Once they captured a huge bison, or buffalo, stuck in a swamp and left behind by the rest of the herd, and feasted on buffalo meat for many days.

At last they came to a place, now called Lake Peoria, where the Illinois is several miles wide. They decided that this would be a good place to build a fort. Seeing smoke, they guessed that it proceeded from the campfire of an Illinois tribe which was said to be hostile to the French. Seeing wigwams in the distance La Salle arranged the canoes in rows, and pulled up to the Indian camp. There was a stir in the Illinois village. The Indian braves came out and received the white men as friends, and there were feasts and games and dances in honor of their French guests.

The Indians said that La Salle and his friends might build a fort there. Built without delay, the fort was named Fort Breakheart, for Robert La Salle had been going through some heartrending experiences. One of these was the loss of the lake boat, the Griffin, with all the supplies and equipments.

When La Salle explained to the Illinois tribe what he was seeking, the chief gave him and his men a solemn warning of perilous falls and precipices, of cannibal tribes and man-eating monsters. He said that if they should get by those awful dangers, the mouth of the river was an awful whirlpool which would engulf them, for no man who had ever gone down into the mouth of the Father of Waters had returned{124} alive. These stories so frightened the men of the party—both red and white—that they deserted their leader. They preferred to endure the ills they had and risk their lives among savages known to be cruel, rather than fly to ills they knew not of.

The ships of France at the mouth of the Mississippi

From the painting in the Versailles Collection
The ships of France at the mouth of the Mississippi
From the painting in the Versailles Collection
So La Salle had to go hundreds of miles back to Canada for more men, funds, and supplies, before he could venture{125} to make the rest of the trip. After many months' delay he started out again from Montreal.

There were now fifty-four in his party—twenty-three Frenchmen, eighteen braves, ten squaws to do the cooking, and three papooses. When they got back to Fort Breakheart, La Salle gave up building a ship, as he had decided to make the voyage down the Mississippi in canoes. There was plenty of game along the river, and in its muddy waters they caught catfish six feet long and weighing about two hundred pounds. They saw wild beans along the banks with stalks "as big as your arm," reminding one of the tale of "Jack and the Beanstalk." They had varied experiences with the different tribes of Indians—Chickasaw, Arkansas, Natchez—along their course, and found that the "man-eating monsters" described by the Illinois chief were only alligators. When at last they reached the mouth of the Father of Waters, there was no whirlpool to swallow them down; but the river calmly divided into three mouths, each leading into a broad expanse of salt water which, they learned, was not the Pacific Ocean but the Gulf of Mexico. On a hill near by, La Salle raised a wooden pillar on which he nailed the coat-of-arms bearing the lilies of France, and buried near it a leaden plate on which letters were engraved to tell future comers that the whole country drained by the Mississippi belonged to France.

At last, the patient worker and traveler had triumphed. He went back to Paris and reported all he had done in the name of his beloved king and country. Robert Cavelier de la Salle had done a greater thing than he realized. One hundred and twenty years later, Napoleon, Emperor of the French, sold to the United States the territory of Louisiana, claimed by La Salle, which is now half of the{126} great republic. This was an achievement which meant more than the discovery of an outlet to China. Although a boat may be sailed through long rivers and short canals from the mouth of the St. Lawrence to the mouth of the Mississippi, this fact is hardly thought worthy of mention in these days. A far greater benefit to America and the whole world was achieved by Robert La Salle, because he enabled the French government to give to the United States her broad empire of the west.

LIVINGSTONE, THE WHITE MAN OF THE DARK CONTINENT

LITTLE Davie Livingstone was a queer, quiet Scotch laddie. His father was a high-minded man, but he was so poor that he had to take Davie out of the village school when he was ten. In those days, the early part of the nineteenth century, children began to work when they were very young. So Mr. Livingstone sent the lad to work, with other boys of his own age, as a piecer in a cotton mill. David worked from six in the morning till eight at night, stopping only for lunch.

With his first week's wages the ten-year-old boy bought a Latin grammar. He was so eager to learn that he went to night school from eight to ten at night. He studied till midnight, and even later, when his mother did not take his books away and send him to bed. His great desire was to be a missionary. So he took up other languages besides Latin, and such studies as would fit him for missionary work. As soon as he was able, he went to London and{127}

{128}

David Livingstone, the brave Scotch missionary

{128}From a photograph taken in 1867
David Livingstone, the brave Scotch missionary
From a photograph taken in 1867
elsewhere to study, working part of the time, to earn enough to pay his way.

On a visit to London Livingstone met Doctor Moffat, a leading missionary in South Africa, and soon decided to work in Africa himself. He had prepared himself to help men's bodies as well as their souls. So he went first as a medical missionary.

Doctor Livingstone's first mission station, or center, was seven hundred miles farther north than Doctor Moffat's, in a region which was dangerous because of savage men, wild beasts, and, worst of all, an unhealthful climate. In this lonely place the new missionary began to tell the ignorant black people about the one true God. He cured them of their illnesses, and showed them how to dig canals and build dams to water their little farms. He also taught them to till these farms in a better way than they had known.

In the region there were many lions. One day, when the missionary was out with a band of natives, he met one of the big beasts. Livingstone and one of his black men shot at the lion, which sprang up with a roar and bounded into the bushes, through the circle the men had made around him. Then two more lions appeared. Before Livingstone could reload his gun, he saw one great brute with bristling mane and angry eyes springing upon him. Its weight bore him to the earth. The lion seized his shoulder with jaws strong enough to carry off an ox. When some one asked him afterward what he thought just then, Doctor Livingstone replied, "I was wondering what part of me he would eat first." In a letter the doctor described this adventure:

"With his terrible roar sounding in my ear, the lion shook me as a dog does a rat; but, strange to say, I felt neither pain nor fear, though fully conscious of all that passed.{129} As I turned to escape the weight of his paw, which was resting on my head, I saw his eyes turn toward Mebalwe [one of the natives], who was about to fire, but his gun missed fire in both barrels. Instantly the lion quitted his hold of me and leaped on Mebalwe, biting him badly in the thigh; then he dashed at another man who was about to attack him with his spear. But at that moment the previous shots the lion had received took effect and he dropped to the ground dead."

Livingstone was bitten in eleven places, his arm was badly mangled, and bones were broken in several places. It was many months before he was well. The broken arm was always weak, and he bore the marks of that big lion's teeth to his dying day.

While recovering from his wounds, Livingstone made the long journey to the home of Doctor Moffat, and married that gentleman's daughter Mary. Miss Moffat was born in South Africa, so that she knew the language and ways of the people. This made her a true helpmeet to her husband in his noble work.

Livingstone called himself "Jack-of-all-trades." "I read in journeying," he wrote, "but little at home. Building, gardening, cobbling, doctoring, tinkering, carpentering, gun-mending, farriering (horse-doctoring and shoeing), wagon-mending, preaching, schooling, lecturing in divinity to a class of three, fill up my time."

When Livingstone reached the country of one of the black tribes, thousands of miles to the north, all the people of the region, numbering six or seven thousand, poured out to see the white man. The missionary was greatly relieved to find that the chief of this region, who was only eighteen years old, was disposed to be friendly. The white man and{130} his party were well cared for and given plenty of good food, of which they were badly in need. They were nearly starved, because unfriendly natives on the way had refused to sell them food. In regions where the Arab slave-traders had robbed, killed, and carried away and sold many of the natives, the people were afraid of Livingstone, for they thought all white men must be robbers and murderers. But in reality the brave Scotch missionary was a great worker against the slave-trade, writing and saying all he could to make people in Europe and England know how wicked it was.

Although Livingstone journeyed about so much, travel was very hard and dangerous. He and his faithful men often had to go up to their necks in swamps where the hot, moist air was filled with poisonous insects, and to cross rivers in great peril from the crocodile and hippopotamus. Not only did Livingstone have numerous hairbreadth escapes from lions, elephants, and other wild beasts, but he was many times stricken with the terrible African fever. Because of his wonderful recoveries the natives thought his life

53

was charmed, and they were afraid he was a wizard who worked cures by magic from the devil. But the good doctor soon won their friendship by his great kindness to them.

Livingstone traveled thousands of miles by water, in clumsy boats. He wrote to a friend, describing the life on one of these river trips:

"We rise a little before five, when it is daylight. While I am dressing, the coffee is made, and after I have filled my little coffeepot, I leave the rest for my companions, who eagerly swallow the refreshing drink. Meanwhile the servants are busy loading the boats, which done, we embark.{131} The next two hours, while the men row swiftly onward, are the pleasantest of the whole day. About eleven we land and eat our luncheon, which consists of what is left from supper the evening before, or of zwieback with honey and water.

"After resting for an hour we enter the boats again, and take our places under an umbrella. The heat is oppressive, and as I am still weak from my recent attack of fever, I cannot go ashore and hunt. The rowers, who are exposed to the sun without cover, drip with sweat and begin to tire by afternoon. We often reach a suitable spot to spend the night two hours before sundown, and as we are all tired, we gladly make a halt.

"As soon as we are ashore the men cut grass for my bed and poles for my tent. The bed is then made, the boxes with our supplies piled on each side of it, and lastly the tent is stretched above. Four or five paces in front of it a huge fire is lighted, beside which each man has his own place, according to the rank he occupies. Two of the Makololos are always at my right and left, both in eating and sleeping, while Machana, my head boatman, lies down before the door of my tent as soon as I go to bed.

"A space beyond the fire is staked out for the cattle, in the shape of a horseshoe. The evening meal consists of coffee and zwieback, or of bread made from maize or Kaffir corn, unless we are lucky enough to shoot something to supply us with a pot of meat. We go to bed soon after, and silence descends upon the camp. On moonlight nights the fire is allowed to go out."

While Livingstone was exploring to the northward, he discovered the great cataracts of the Zambesi, which are even higher and wider than Niagara. He named them{132} Victoria Falls in honor of the queen of England. He also found the lakes from which the Zambesi flows into the eastern sea and the Congo into the western, on opposite sides of the continent of Africa. The two rivers are like two long watersnakes with their tiny tails close together, but their wide-open mouths thousands of miles apart.

Doctor Livingstone had sent his wife to England for the benefit of her health and to educate their children. The people there were greatly pleased with the results of Livingstone's labors in Africa, for all of the country discovered by him would belong to Great Britain. So the British government gave him its support and paid him a small salary for the work he was doing for science and for the world. By this time other missionaries had come to help save the Dark Continent. The wives of two of these were coming out from England with Mrs. Livingstone when she returned. There was great joy on both sides—that of the three husbands in the heart of Africa, and that of the three wives on their way to join them. But Livingstone and both his friends were seized with African fever, and, when their wives came, the two men missionaries had just died. Even Mrs. Livingstone, although she had been brought up in Africa, took the disease and died. The two missionaries' wives soon returned to England, but Doctor Livingstone could not even then be persuaded to leave the needy people to go to England to rest awhile and see his now motherless children.

Besides all these labors, and besides the exact reports he made on the animal life, flowers, trees, rocks, and geography of that new land, he wrote books about his adventures and experiences which had an immense sale. This made him a man of considerable wealth; but, after providing well for{133} his family and for the education of his children, he spent the greater part of his fortune—ten to thirty thousand dollars at a time—for the benefit of his black "children."

When Livingstone did go to England, it was only for a short visit. While absent from Africa he seemed always to hear those millions of poor, ignorant people calling him. Once he purchased the parts of a little steamer and brought it back to Africa. The boat was put together and was run on some of the lakes and rivers he had discovered. The vessel proved to be a poor affair, which ran very slowly and was always breaking down. But the natives were astonished, and would have worshipped it if he had let them. As time went on, larger and better boats were sent out to him. Once he had to discharge his engineer, but he ran the steamboat himself. He found it easier, of course, to make his journeys with the help of steam, though he had to go to many places where the boats could not be taken. A writer has described a trip Livingstone and his friends made in July:

"It was now the African mid winter and the nights were very cold. The tsetse flies were more troublesome than ever. Wild beasts became more numerous every day in this uninhabited region. Herds of elephants, buffaloes, zebras, and many kinds of antelopes were frequently seen, which allowed the head of the caravan to approach within two hundred feet of them. The wild boars, of which many were seen, were very shy; while, on the contrary, troops of monkeys hastily retreated into the jungle at the sight of the travelers, chattering angrily about the coming of the white man. Guinea fowl, doves, ducks, and geese were also plentiful.

"With the darkness a new and even more numerous world of living creatures awoke. Lions and hyenas roared and howled about the camp. Unknown birds sang sweetly or screeched as if in fear, and all sorts of strange insect noises were heard.

"One day Livingstone narrowly escaped losing his life from the attack of a two-horned rhinoceros. This beast was strangely quick,{134} in spite of its great bulk, and very savage, being one of the few animals which will attack a man without being first attacked.

"While making their way through a dense thicket Livingstone had become separated from the others, and was stooping to gather some specimen, when a black rhinoceros made a furious charge at him; but, strange to say, it suddenly stopped short, giving him time to escape. In his flight, his watch and chain became entangled in a branch and, stopping to loosen it, he saw the beast still standing in the same spot, as if held back by an unseen hand. On reaching a safe distance he uttered a shout of warning, thinking some of the party might be near; at this the rhinoceros rushed away, grunting loudly."

While Dr. Livingstone was in England he was welcomed with highest honors. He was invited to visit Queen Victoria and her husband, the Prince Consort. But so strong was the missionary spirit in him that he preferred talking to cotton spinners and the people in the slums of the East End of London. He was quite glad to go back to Africa and escape from the medals, degrees, and other great honors showered upon him.

After his return to the Dark Continent for the last time, he went farther than ever into the interior in an attempt to discover, or at least to prove, where the great river Nile begins. When he had nearly reached the goal, he was driven back by hostile tribes which had recently suffered from attacks of slave traders. At this time the Arabs who carried Livingstone's letters down to the coast to be sent to England destroyed them all, for fear he had written to England about the slave outrages they had committed. For this reason nothing was heard of him for years. It was thought that he had been murdered by savages or had died of African fever.

55

At last the publisher of The New York Herald sent Henry M. Stanley, the newspaper's foreign correspondent, with{135} all the money he needed, to find Dr. Livingstone; or, if he were no longer living, to get any records that could be found. After a long search the American newspaper man heard of a white man hundreds of miles farther in the interior. Trace and trail grew more and more distinct and at last the American company, with the American flag flying, marched up to Livingstone's camp on the shore of one of the great lakes he had discovered. Of this meeting Stanley wrote:

"As I advanced slowly toward him I noticed he looked pale and weary. He had a gray beard, and wore a cap with a faded gold band on it. I could have run to him and embraced him, only I did not know how he would receive me; so instead I walked up to him and said, 'Dr. Livingstone, I presume?'

" 'Yes,' said he with a kind smile. We both grasped hands.

" 'I thank God, Doctor, that I have been permitted to see you!' said I, and he answered, 'I feel thankful that I am here to welcome you.'

"I found myself gazing at the wonderful man at whose side I now sat in the heart of Africa. Every hair of his head, every line of his face, his pallor and the wearied look he wore, all told me what I had longed so much to know."

The two explorers spent months together talking over their discoveries and experiences. Stanley had much to tell of what was going on in the world outside. Nearly all Livingstone's store of supplies had been stolen, but Stanley had prepared for that. He insisted on providing the old missionary with everything he might need. Of Stanley's tenderness Livingstone wrote to his daughter:

"He laid all he had at my service, divided his clothes into two heaps, and pressed one upon me, then his medicine chest, his goods and everything he had, with true American generosity. To coax my appetite he often cooked dainty dishes for me with his own hands. The tears often started to my eyes at some fresh proof of his kindness."

{136}

As Dr. Livingstone was again recovering from a very severe attack of fever Stanley begged him to go home to England with him for a year of rest, but the aged missionary shook his head sadly. Stanley returned to the outside world.

About a year after this, David Livingstone was found kneeling beside his bed in a hut built of bamboo poles and coarse grass. He had died while praying. Millions of natives in the heart of the Dark Continent were heartbroken when they heard of the medical missionary's death. They spent months in wailing and mourning, for they had lost their "White Father."

Two devoted black men carried the body of their beloved master hundreds of miles through the swamps and jungles of Africa, and placed it on shipboard, to be taken back to England. That ship was met at the English seaport by a special train heavily draped in mourning, which carried the honored remains up to London. Great Britain had strong reasons for honoring David Livingstone. He had added a million square miles to the known world, and put great lakes, rivers, mountains, and countries on the map of Africa.

There was a magnificent funeral in Westminster Abbey, where the great missionary and explorer was buried beside the sacred ashes of kings, queens, princes, and statesmen. Thus he received the highest honors England can bestow upon her most illustrious dead. On the black marble slab which marks David Livingstone's final resting place are the last words he is known to have written. They are about the cruel slave trade:

"All I can say in my solitude is, may Heaven's rich blessing come down on every one—American, English, Turk—who will help to heal this open sore of the world."

{137}

FOR hundreds of years after Columbus, explorers sought the Northwest Passage through the frozen seas of North America. It was not until 1853 that such a channel was actually traced. Even then it was so filled with ice that no sailor, however brave and skilful, could make his way through. Long ago the search for the Northwest Passage gave place to the great desire and purpose to reach the North Pole.

Of course, there is no pole standing out of the northern half of the world. The axis, or axle, of the earth is only an unseen line which scientists have thought of as if it ran straight through the center of the earth. The place in the middle of the top of the globe where this line, if there were one, would come out, is named the North Pole, and the same place at the opposite end is called the South Pole.

It is easy to see how many boys could have a great longing to run away to sea and seek their fortunes in foreign lands; but it is hard to understand why any young man should wish to undertake the awful hardships of bitter cold and blizzards, with the risk of falling down ice-cracks hundreds of feet deep, and of starving or freezing to death, in trying to get to the Pole, especially when there is nothing but snow and ice to see there if he ever could find the place.

Yet, in his youth, Robert E. Peary had a strange desire to visit the Inland Ice region of Greenland. Robert was a Pennsylvania lad whose father had died when he was three. He grew up to care for his widowed mother. He went to an eastern college and was graduated second in a class of fifty-one. Then he passed the rigid tests for Engineer in the United States Navy. Like young Robert E. Lee,{138} Robert E. Peary was first assigned to engineering duty on the eastern coast, in Florida. Then he was sent as one of a number of experts in science to survey a route through Nicaragua, as many people believed that a ship canal should run through Nicaragua rather than across the narrow isthmus where the Panama Canal was dug afterward.

Peary in Arctic dress with his Eskimo dogs

©1909, Doubleday, Page & Co.
Peary in Arctic dress with his Eskimo dogs
©1909, Doubleday, Page & Co.

So it was not until he was thirty years old that Robert E. Peary was able to realize the dream of his boyhood and explore the bleak and frozen plains even beyond "Greenland's icy mountains." Five years later he started out to go farther north than any white man had even been. His first attempt to reach the Pole was in 1891, when he took{139} with him his young wife. This was the first time a white woman ever had made the journey into the unknown regions of the "Great White North." With the Pearys in this dangerous undertaking went Dr. Frederick A. Cook, a surgeon, and Matthew Henson, the Pearys' colored helper. On board the Kite—the special ship for this journey—the leader's leg was broken by the sudden slipping of the rudder. This accident kept them from advancing farther north that fall. Through the constant care of his wife, the faithful Matthew, and Dr. Cook, Lieutenant Peary was restored to health and strength by the following spring.

Peary knew how to make the best of everything. The half year he was laid up by this accident was that of the Arctic night. For six months in the year—spring and summer—the sun in the Arctic regions can be seen moving in a complete circle up in the sky. In other parts of the world, what is called the sunset is just the turning away of one side of the earth from the sun; and sunrise is the whirling round of that side into the sunlight again. What is called night is the time when the sun is shining on the other side of the earth. But the sun moves north in spring and summer; so that during those seasons in the Arctic region it never sets, and there is daylight all the time. In the fall and winter the sun moves south, and then in the Arctic region it never rises. So there is night for six months.

While nursing his broken leg during this Arctic night, Lieutenant Peary was by no means idle. He sent the Kite thousands of miles back to the United States. He made friends with the Eskimos, his little fat, red-faced northern neighbors who lived in igloos, as they called their small dome-shaped houses built of blocks of ice. He learned all he could of their language and their ways. He found out{140} how to hunt the reindeer, the musk-ox, and other big game of the north, and studied and trained the Eskimo dogs, which would draw his sledges the thousands of miles he must yet go to reach the Pole. At last, when his leg was entirely well, it was early spring, when the sun could be seen rising, shining a little while in the middle of the day, and setting just above the frozen plains and icebergs to the south of them.

In May, when the sun was circling a little higher in the sky for several hours every day, Peary and a small party harnessed sixteen dogs to four sledges and started off on a camping trip towards the Farthest North. With one companion who was used to the life in cold northern countries, he climbed a mountain of ice nearly a mile high. These two heroes kept on alone, across bleak regions broken up by ice-cracks, called crevasses, hundreds of feet deep, over slippery hummocks or ice-mounds, through deep snowdrifts and fogs, in constant danger of precipices and pitfalls. On the Fourth of July, they reached a body of water which they named for the day, Independence Bay. Here they climbed an icy height which they called Navy Cliff. From here they beheld a splendid expanse of clear country stretching still farther away toward the north.

It was now the Arctic midsummer. They were surprised to find flowers blooming in sheltered nooks and to hear the hum of bees and flies. There were birds also—snow-bunting and sandpiper—flitting and flying about. On the little patches of bright green that showed through the snows of ages, musk-oxen—which look like both sheep and buffalo—were grazing. Peary shot five of these to supply meat for men and dogs on the return journey of five hundred miles or more.{141}

The way back was beset with even greater dangers than before. While they were on their way north they had known that the shifting and breaking up of fields of ice might cut them off forever from their friends and supplies. So every few hundred miles they had "cached," or buried, tools and provisions, and marked the places so that they could find them again when a little food might save them from starving. In spite of such precautions, many exploring parties found only hardship, starvation, and death in the cruel ice. But Peary and his party succeeded in making their return to the Inland Ice fields, the region of young Peary's boyish dreams, through violent wind-storms, drifting snows, and freezing fogs. Even the hardy little Arctic dogs were half famished and worn out. Finding the Kite, with other explorers, waiting for them there, the Peary party sailed down to the United States, meeting mountain-like icebergs, and shooting walruses and polar bears by the way.

Lieutenant Peary at once went to work preparing for a second attempt at the discovery of the North Pole. Mrs. Peary again accompanied her husband into the Arctic regions, and the twelfth of September, 1893, the first white baby ever seen in that far northern country was born. This was the Pearys' little blue-eyed daughter, "bundled deep in soft, warm Arctic furs, and wrapped in the Stars and Stripes." During the first half year of her life, Marie Snowbaby Peary—as they named her—never saw the sunlight.

Before the sun began to show above the southern horizon again, Papa Peary started off on another twelve-hundred mile ice journey. This time he took with him eight men, twelve sledges, and ninety-two Eskimo dogs. But some{142} of the dogs were strangers to the rest, and those from different places fought one another. As it is hard enough to separate only two fighting dogs, it was impossible to stop the wholesale dog-fight that went on constantly and kept the party from going forward. The cold became even more intense; the temperature went down to sixty degrees below zero. Conditions were so much worse than on the previous trip that Peary decided to cache all the provisions and other things they did not need to preserve life, and returned to the place where he had left his wife and baby. The feet of the men, even of the Eskimos of the party, were badly frozen, and when they returned to their base of supplies, out of the ninety-two dogs, there were only twenty-six left.

But the heroic explorer would not give up. He and his little family stayed north of the Arctic Circle while he made discoveries and proved the truth of the statements of those who had been there before him. Little Snowbaby also made her observations. She saw Eskimo children living in their small round hives of ice, and heard them teasing their mothers for whale blubber and other kinds of grease, just as the children at home plead for candy or ice-cream. An Eskimo child likes a tallow candle much better than a stick of candy, and will chew the cotton candle-wick until there is no more grease left in it.

Lieutenant Peary made eight trips to the Arctic regions. Sometimes he would advance farther north than any explorer before him; then, when he was almost within reach of the Pole, everything would fail and he would have to retreat and go back thousands of miles to the United States and begin to raise a fortune for the next attempt. At one time his ship, on the way to the north, would be{143} caught in the ice and crushed like an egg-shell. On another occasion the boat would be frozen up in miles and miles of ice, so that he and his men would have to wait for spring to come and thaw it out of the clutches of the terrible white giant, Jack Frost.

It needed the patience of Job to endure and overcome the trials which came thick and fast upon him. One summer the wealthy friend died who had promised him all the money he needed to reach the Pole; but a newspaper owner in London, England, offered his yacht, the Windward, for the next polar trip. This time the great Arctic explorer froze both his feet and had to have eight toes cut off. The cold was awful—from fifty-one to sixty-three degrees below zero. After many weeks of acute suffering, he was removed to a less severe climate.

In 1902, for the seventh time, Peary came within a few degrees of the Pole, and finding that he could not go farther, was forced to return to the United States. In the first gloom of this defeat he wrote:

"The game is off. My dream of sixteen years is ended. I have made the best fight I knew. I believe it has been a good one. But I cannot do the impossible."

But this hopeless state of mind did not last long. Peary spent six more years in preparing for one last desperate attempt. On the sixth of July, 1908, he left New York City for his eighth voyage to the Arctic, on his latest ship, the Roosevelt—determined to reach the Pole or die in the attempt. This time, when he came within a few degrees of his goal, he decided to leave all behind but the faithful Matthew and one Eskimo, while he made the last dash. When he came within a few miles of the spot he had sought for nearly twenty years, he was prostrated by overwork{144} and excitement. After a short rest he went on and stood, on the sixth of April, 1909, in the place called the North Pole. There was nothing to see—not a living thing but themselves and their dogs. But he was now on the top of the world. There was no North, no East, no West—only South. The only

59

North he could see was up in the cold, gray sky. Directly overhead was the North Star, toward which the Pole points.

Peary stayed in that desolate neighborhood thirty hours, taking observations and "planting" five United States flags to show to future comers that America had been first to discover and take possession of the North Pole. One flag he mounted on a pole which he set in the top of a hummock of ice, as if the North Pole were a flag pole standing up out of the surface of the earth. This was called "nailing the American flag to the North Pole." Then he wrote this postal card to mail to his wife:

"90 North Latitude, April 7th, 1909.

"My Dear Jo:—I have won out at last. Have been here a day. I start for home and you in an hour. Love to the kidsies.

"Bert."

{145}

COLONISTS AND PIONEERS

JOHN SMITH, THE CAPTAIN OF MANY ADVENTURES

STORIES of the strange adventures of Columbus, John Cabot, and other explorers made a restless lad of little motherless John Smith, of Willoughby, England. When he was fourteen he had made ready to run away from home; but then his father died and left him the owner of an estate, in the charge of guardians. Those mean men cared more for the property than for the boy who was to have it when he was old enough. So they gave him only a little pocket-money and hired him out by law as apprentice to a tradesman, who treated the well-to-do lad as if he were a slave.

Captain John Smith

Captain John Smith

In less than a year young John Smith ran away in good earnest, leaving master, guardians, and property behind. He had attended two free schools and had gained what would be equal to a common-school education in these days. He went right to Paris, because France and Spain were at war just then; but peace was declared almost as soon as he was able to enlist.

After several hard experiences, young Smith engaged in the service of the duke of a little kingdom which was fighting the Turks. In one of his books, John Smith describes his adventures in these desperate battles. He tells of killing three Turks single-handed in mortal combat, and{146} of how his princely master designed for him a coat-of-arms having in it three Turks' heads.

But ill fortune soon befell young Captain John Smith. In a battle with the Turks he was wounded and left for dead, and became the property of a Turkish chief, who, as Smith goes on to tell, "sent him forthwith to Constantinople to his fair mistress for a slave. By twenty and twenty, chained by the necks, they marched in file to this great city where they were delivered to their several masters."

The princess, to whom Captain John Smith was sent, was too young to own any kind of property. Afraid her mother would sell her white slave before she was of age, she sent him to her brother, a distant chief, asking him to be kind to her prize. But the brother treated his sister's slave so brutally that Smith killed him and escaped in his master's clothes to Russia. Here he found people who were unfriendly enough to the Turks to file off the iron collar which he still wore. On his way back to England, Smith found himself on the ship of a friendly French pirate, where he had to fight for his life against two Spanish men-of-war. The French ship succeeded in escaping from the Spaniards into a port on the northern coast of Africa. From here Smith took ship for London and entered the service of the Virginia Company, whose business it was to carry on the settling of America, begun by Sir Walter Raleigh.

The Virginia Company secured a charter from King James and in December, 1606, sent more than a hundred men to America. It was a strange company for such an enterprise. There were four carpenters, one blacksmith, one bricklayer, one mason, one tailor, one sailor, one drummer, two surgeons, two "boys," or men-servants, and only {147} twelve laborers. But there were forty-eight "gentlemen," of whom some were ne'er-do-wells and others downright criminals, who could not work because they did not know how to do anything useful. Even before they reached Virginia, quarrels broke out among members of the party and Captain John Smith was falsely accused of conspiracy and condemned to be hanged. He escaped, however, and afterward forgave the conspirators.

The king had sent out the colony with sealed orders, which were not to be opened until they reached Virginia. When the orders were opened, John Smith was found to be among the seven men appointed as council for the colony. But the men highest in control were unfit to command such an enterprise. They spent seventeen days searching for a good site for a settlement. The place which they finally chose was a long distance from the coast, was hard for a sailing vessel to reach, and lay in an unhealthy place between the shallow river and a bad swamp. The river was named the James and the settlement Jamestown, both in honor of the king.

As for Captain John Smith, the others of the party were jealous of him. They thought he knew too much, because he saw how little they knew. Most of the party expected to get rich quick, and they did not care how they did it, so long as it was at the expense of some one else. So, instead of fishing for oysters, planting gardens, and clearing farms, they went hunting for gold and making trouble with the Indians. They did discover something they thought was gold, but Know-it-all Smith told them the yellow stuff was only "fool's gold," which is the common name for iron pyrites. Instead of following Smith's advice and working all together to prepare for the future, they became so {148} spiteful that they would have imprisoned him if he had not been too shrewd for them.

The Indians grew more and more hostile. The condition of the settlers was fast becoming hopeless. Smith himself wrote of their condition:

"What toil we had, with so small a power (twelve laborers out of more than one hundred men) to guard our workmen a-days, watch all night, resist our enemies, and effect our business—to re-lade the ships, cut down trees and prepare the ground to plant our corn."

The settlers' provisions were disappearing faster than they expected. One of them wrote at this time of the sad state of affairs: "Our drink was water; our lodgings, castles in the air." The foolish president of the council was soon displaced. The man elected in his stead was said to be "of weak judgment in dangers, and less industry in peace"; but he had the sense to leave the management of affairs to John Smith.

That capable captain now took hold with a firm hand. He fought the Indians till they gained a wholesome respect for him and the English. Then he played on their curiosity and superstition so as to get them to bring Indian corn, venison, and wild turkeys to feed the white men. He set the idlers to work at chopping down trees and the like.

61

When he had things going right in Jamestown, the tireless captain went out exploring the wilderness. Captured by a hostile tribe of Indians, he showed them his compass and told them a story which made them afraid to kill him. So they took him, as a great prize, to the Powhatan, or head chief of all the tribes of that part of the country.

The Powhatan and his chiefs knew too well that this was the mighty chief who had thus far kept the white men out of their clutches. They held a solemn powwow and{149}

The marriage of Pocahontas
The marriage of Pocahontas
{150}
condemned the troublesome captain to death. They laid his head on a stone and a chief was lifting his war-club to dash out the prisoner's brains, when Pocahontas, the Powhatan's beautiful daughter, rushed out and threw herself between the death-club and Smith's head. She pleaded so earnestly, threatening to kill herself if Smith was harmed, that her father gave orders to stop the execution, and to keep the white man prisoner. With the help of the Indian girl, he soon made his escape.

Pocahontas proved a true friend to the English. More than once she warned Captain Smith of the deep-laid plans of the Virginia tribes to murder all the white settlers at a stroke. She became a convert to Christianity, was christened Rebecca, and was confirmed in the Church of England. Then a young settler, John Rolfe, married her and took her to England, where she was received in the homes of lords and ladies, and entertained by the queen as Lady Rebecca and the Princess Pocahontas. Some of the "First Families of Virginia" proudly prove that this beautiful and devoted Indian girl was one of their ancestors.

Not long after his escape from the Indians, John Smith was seriously injured by the explosion of some gunpowder, and was compelled to return to England for treatment. His work in Virginia was done. But the restless soul of the old Captain could not let him be content to remain at ease in England. He made other voyages of exploration along the coast to the north of the Dutch island of Manhattan. From his careful observations he drew a good map of that northern country and gave it the name New England. So besides starting the greatest southern colony of North America, he prepared the way for the Pilgrims to settle at Plymouth.{151}

CHAMPLAIN, THE FATHER OF NEW FRANCE

IN Samuel de Champlain's earlier life he was both a soldier and a sailor of France. He was a great adventurer, who came to visit the new country in America claimed for France by Jacques Cartier about seventy-five years before. He was a personal friend of Henry of Navarre, who became Henry the Fourth, king of France.

Champlain was a great lover of king and country. He said to the high officials at court: "Spain has her 'New Spain,' and England her 'New England'; why should not we have our 'New France' in America?" The king and the rich nobles thought it was a good idea, and one leading man at the French court sent Champlain to carry out his own project. The brave explorer started a settlement on the coast near the wide mouth of the St. Lawrence, but on account of the wars France was engaged in, this wealthy Frenchman found that he could no longer spare money to carry on the enterprise, and Champlain had to give up the settlement he had so nicely started and go back to France.

But Samuel de Champlain was a plucky soul whom nothing could frighten or discourage. He had a romantic nature, to which the wild life in America appealed. It was

62

not long before he was back in the New World, sailing up the St. Lawrence. There he saw a high, steep cliff at a narrow point in the wide river, and decided that it would be a good place to build a fort and make a settlement.

He started both at once—placing the fort on the head of the cliff and building several houses at its foot. Champlain, who was quite an artist, made a drawing of this small group of houses and named the little settlement Quebec. On account of its high cliff above a narrow place in the{152} river, Quebec is called "the Gibraltar of America." Gibraltar is the name of a high rock on the coast of Spain guarding the entrance to the Mediterranean.

In this narrow settlement Champlain planted a garden with as many roses and other flowers as he could. He had a kind heart and a pleasant face, and soon became as great a friend to the Indians as William Penn in Philadelphia. Champlain encouraged his French friends to treat the men of the forest as their brothers. As he was a devout Catholic, he did everything he could to make the savages Christians, sending good men to live among them and teach the natives how to live right. He not only tried to help pious men to convert the Indians, but he went himself to trade and hunt with the neighboring tribes and make them his friends. More than this, he sent young Frenchmen to live among the different tribes and learn the language and the ways of the Indians. These hardy young heroes were called "wood runners," and became the first white guides and scouts in the wilds of America.

It was necessary for Champlain to make several voyages home to Old France. On one of these visits "the Father of New France," now forty years of age, married Hélène, the young daughter of a wealthy citizen of Paris. But, instead of taking her to share his rough life in the wilds of the St. Lawrence, he sent her back to school to fit herself better to aid him in teaching the Indians when she was old enough to come with him to the New World.

When he went back to Quebec he went farther up the St. Lawrence to an island which Cartier had called Mount Royal, and started another little settlement, which he named Montreal. Here he made everything as beautiful as he could, planting roses and other flowers, as he had{153} done at Quebec. The island in the river opposite this new settlement he named Sainte Hélène, for the child wife he had left behind in Old France. This island, now known by the English name, St. Helen's, is a park and pleasure ground for the people of Montreal.

"The White Governor" found before long that the Indians around Quebec were not satisfied with a friendship which showed itself in teaching them to be Christians and in trading beads for the furs the savages had gathered by shooting and trapping in the forests. It seems strange that tall, stern red men should be so childish as to care much for beads, but it must be remembered that the Indians used beads of special colors in weaving bands and strings of wampum which they used for money. Their own beads were very hard to make from shells; so they were as eager for glass beads of certain colors as white men are for the smallest grains of gold.

The Indians were less trouble to Champlain and his friends than the English—and other Frenchmen, too—who tried to turn the Indians against him and his settlers. Other ships than those of Champlain's company landed every now and then at points along the St. Lawrence to trade with the Indians. These white men would try to make the savages unfriendly to Champlain, so that they would trade only with the newcomers, somewhat as a business house to-day tries to take customers away from other dealers.

The simple men of the forest could not understand these tricks of trade of the wily white men. Champlain, in one of the stories of his adventures, relates that the Indians came to tell him about some fur traders from other parts of France.{154}

"They tell us that they would come and fight for us against our enemies if we liked. What do you think of it? Are they telling the truth?"

"No, they are not," said Governor Champlain earnestly. "I know well enough what they want. They tell you this only to get your trade."

"The white governor is right!" shouted the Indians. "Those men are women; they only want to make war on our beavers!"

By this they meant that the other Frenchmen were willing to promise anything in order to get all the beaver and other fur skins the Indians might have to sell. As the Indian squaws were not allowed to go into battle, the savages showed their contempt for white men by calling them "women"!

Champlain knew that the Indians would not accept him as a real friend unless he would fight for them against their enemies—the cruel and powerful Iroquois, who lived south of the St. Lawrence. The tribes of the Iroquois were the most daring and warlike of the red men and were feared by all their neighbors.

The Indians looked upon "the White Governor" and his men as workers of miracles with their "fire-sticks," as they called the rude guns which the French called arquebuses. In one of his accounts Champlain describes the first of a number of battles he helped the Indians to fight against the Iroquois. After describing how his red friends met the enemy at night and agreed to fight next morning, he continued:

"Meanwhile the whole night was spent in dancing and singing on both sides, with many insults and other taunts, such as how little courage we had, how great their power against our arms, and when day broke we would find this out to our ruin. Our Indians did not fail in talking back, telling them they would witness the effect of arms they had never seen before.{155}

"After each side had sung and danced and threatened enough, day broke. My [white] companions and I were always concealed for fear the enemy would see us preparing our arms the best we could, being separated, each in one of the canoes belonging to the St. Lawrence savages.

"After being equipped with light armor, we took each an arquebus and went ashore. I saw the enemy leave their barricade. They were about two hundred men, of strong and robust appearance, who were coming slowly toward us with a gravity and assurance which greatly pleased me, led on by three chiefs. Ours were marching in similar order, and told me that those who wore three tall feathers were the chiefs, and that I must do all I could to kill them.

"The moment we landed, our Indians began calling me with a loud voice, and making way, placed me marching at their head—about twenty paces in advance—until I was within thirty paces of the enemy. The moment they [the Iroquois] saw me, they halted, gazing at me and I at them. When I saw them preparing to shoot at us I raised my arquebus, and aiming directly at one of the three chiefs, two of them fell to the ground by this shot, and one of their companions received a wound of which he died afterwards. I had put four balls in my arquebus. Our Indians, on witnessing a shot so favorable for them, set up such tremendous shouts that thunder could not have been heard, and yet there was no lack of arrows on either side.

"The Iroquois were greatly astonished, seeing two men killed at once, though they were protected by arrow-proof armor, woven of cotton thread and wood, this frightened them very much. While I was reloading one of my [white] men in the bush fired a shot which so astonished them anew that they lost courage, took to flight, and abandoned the field and their fort, hiding in the depths of the forest where I followed them and killed some others. Our savages also killed several of them, and took ten or twelve prisoners. The rest carried off the wounded. Fifteen or sixteen of ours were wounded by arrows; they were promptly cured.

"After gaining the victory, they amused themselves plundering Indian corn and meal from the enemy, also the arms which the Iroquois had thrown away in order to run faster. After feasting, dancing and singing, we returned three hours later with the prisoners.

"I named the place where this battle was fought Lake Champlain."

{156}

"The White Governor" went on to tell about the devilish delight his friends, the St. Lawrence Indians, took in torturing their Iroquois prisoners. The braves, and even the squaws, would try to think of something to do that would make the dying Indians' sufferings still more terrible. If the victim cried out or uttered the least sound, the torturing Indians would laugh and dance about for joy. Champlain begged his friends to stop this fiendish sport, but they could not understand why. The Iroquois would have tortured them just as wickedly if they had won. So "the White Governor" shot several of the suffering victims to put them out of their agonies. After that, when the St. Lawrence Indians gained a victory, Champlain would demand as many prisoners as he could for his share. These he would not allow to be tortured, and, in time, would contrive to let them escape.

By being friends with the neighboring tribes in war, Champlain made bitter enemies of the Iroquois who lived in New York, so that in the later wars between France and England those powerful tribes fought with the English against the French, and in the end helped to place New France in the hands of the British.

Champlain's sympathetic and romantic nature made him a welcome visitor, whether in the wigwams of the savages or in the palaces of the kings and noblemen of France. He did all he could to help the people of Old France and New to understand one another. He sent a young Frenchman up into the country some distance north of Montreal to live among the savages. After this youth had spent the winter in the north, he came back to the St. Lawrence with glowing stories about the finding of a "salt sea" much farther north. He was taken to France and became the{157} lion of the day there, for explorers from all lands were still looking for a northwest passage across America to "the South Sea" and China. Just about this time Henry Hudson had discovered the Hudson River and was lost in Hudson Bay in his search for this passage; but this was not yet known in Europe.

So Champlain, with his strong desire to explore and to prove a great benefit to mankind, arranged to command an expedition into the far northern wilds and make his young friend's boasted discovery of actual use to Old and New France. With the young explorer and an Indian guide, the Governor and a company of men reached the lake and island belonging to the tribe with which the young Frenchman had stayed. In talking with those Indians about the great discovery, Champlain spoke with pride of his young friend's energy and success. They laughed and told him he had been fooled, for that young man had never gone farther north than the island on which they were standing!

This was a bitter experience for the good "White Governor."

The Indians, who had told him before that there was no salt sea anywhere near that region, taunted Champlain with,

"Now who were your friends? Don't you see that he wanted to cause your death? Give him to us and we promise you he shall never lie again."

Champlain knew too well that with the savages' hatred of a liar and their cruel modes of punishment they would have tortured that young Frenchman to death. Of course, the kind-hearted governor could not permit this. But he did make the fellow stand before all the Frenchmen at Montreal and confess that he had been guilty of lying and committing{158}

When brave and courteous Champlain surrendered Quebec, the English obtained their first foothold in Canada.

When brave and courteous Champlain surrendered Quebec, the English obtained their first foothold in Canada.

{159}

a great fraud. After that, as Champlain himself expressed it, "We left him to the mercy of God."

At last, Sieur de Champlain brought his young wife to Canada. Her brother, who had been a settler on the St. Lawrence for years, exclaimed when he met her, "You are a brave girl to come here!" The Indians, always glad to welcome the great white chief, were now doubly glad to see his young "squaw"! They greatly admired "the little white witch," as they called her, and would have worshiped her if she had let them. She wore a small mirror—the fashion in Paris then—as a sort of charm. When she allowed the Indians to see their painted faces in this, they said, "She carries each one of us in her heart!" She used her good influence over her dusky admirers to persuade them to be baptized. Of a very devout spirit, Madame de Champlain returned to France after a short stay in the western wilds, and entered a convent in Paris.

Once more England and France were at war, and King Charles the First looked with jealous eyes upon the fair islands and settlements of the St. Lawrence. English warships appeared before Quebec, claimed possession, and threatened to take that place. "The White Governor" wrote back, with French courtesy, to the impudent enemy:

"We will await you from hour to hour and shall endeavor if possible to dispute the claim which you have made over these places. Upon which I remain, Sir, your affectionate servant,"

The English commander did not dare dispute the claim then, but he came again with a powerful force and "the White Governor" was forced to yield and go back to France. But at the end of the war, England returned Canada to{160} France, and the Father of New France came again to Quebec, his capital, amid the rejoicings of all the people, both French and Indians, and even of "our friends our enemies," the English. Here he lived like another French knight, "without fear and without reproach," until he received the call of the King of kings in the Far Country, on Christmas Day, 1635.

MYLES STANDISH, THE BRAVE LITTLE CAPTAIN OF PLYMOUTH

LITTLE is known of the life of Myles Standish before he sailed from Holland among the hundred and two passengers of the Mayflower on its way across the stormy ocean to the wilderness of America. The brave men and women who had been driven out of England, on account of their religion, by foolish King James, had made their escape to Holland. Although the Dutch who lived in that country were very kind to them, the English people decided to go to America where they could live and worship as they wished and teach their children their own language and ways of living; for, though their king was silly and mean, they still loved dear Old England.

The Mayflower was a poor, clumsy, leaky craft about the size of a coastwise schooner, which would not be allowed to risk a voyage across the ocean to-day. The Pilgrims, as the Mayflower passengers were called, did not know just where to land. The part of America to which they had chosen to go was called Virginia, but that was the name of the country all along the eastern coast, from the South nearly to New{161} York harbor, which had been claimed by the Dutch only a few years before. The Pilgrims had a vague idea of landing about halfway between New York and Jamestown, which had been settled some years before by John Smith and a company of men from England. But storm after storm drove the Mayflower farther and farther northward, till the Pilgrims found themselves just within the long, protecting arm of land called Cape Cod.

They were very tired of being huddled together and pitched about in the little ship. Many of them were ill from the close quarters, as well as from terrible seasickness. During the long voyage they had had nothing but mouldy bread and salt pork to eat, for there were no canned meats, vegetables, and fruits in the fall of 1620, when the Pilgrims made their long voyage across the sea.

The first thing they did was to go ashore near the end of Cape Cod, where the Pilgrim Mothers did their much-needed washing. The Cape was a long, low, sandy arm of land extending far out to sea. The ship's carpenter worked to finish the shallop, or small sailboat, which he had started to build during the voyage. It was intended for the purpose of sailing in shallow water to find a good place to live, where there were trees for shelter and springs of water and, if possible, a good, safe harbor in which the Mayflower and all coming ships might stay at anchor.

The Pilgrims held a meeting in the cabin of the Mayflower and signed a paper which they called "The Compact," by which they agreed to live and be governed. They elected John Carver, the oldest man in the company, governor. Although they are called "The Pilgrim Fathers," they were nearly all young or middle-aged men. Elder Brewster, the minister, was about forty years old, and Myles Standish{162} was thirty-six. William Bradford, who wrote the story of the settlement in his diary, and John Alden, the cooper, were still younger.

The Pilgrims chose twenty of their number to go along the shore of Cape Cod toward the mainland to find a place to build their cabins and spend the winter, for it was late in November and very cold. While waiting for the shallop to be finished, this Pilgrim "Lookout Committee," led by Myles Standish, started out afoot on their great search, not knowing what might happen to them. Captain John Smith had explored that part of the country after he lived two years at Jamestown, Virginia; he had made a map of all that region which he named New England. The men went ashore from the Mayflower and had walked along the Cape a mile or more when they saw a party of Indians with a dog coming toward them. When the red men saw the white strangers they hid in the bushes and whistled to their dog, which followed them out of sight. Myles Standish and his men tried to catch up with the Indians and speak with them, but they were afraid of the strangers who wore helmets and armor over their bodies and thighs, and carried "fire-sticks," as the Indians called the guns.

The Pilgrims followed the natives about ten miles without seeing them again. Then they built a hasty camp of logs and brush in which eighteen men slept while three stood on guard outside. Nothing happened that night to disturb them.

Next day they saw wild ducks and deer and discovered a kettle and some fresh mounds of earth, "which," William Bradford wrote in his diary, "we digged up, and found a fine, great, new basket, full of very fair corn of this year, with some six and thirty goodly ears of corn, some yellow,{163} and some red, and other mixed with blue. The basket

67

was round and narrow at the top. It held about three or four bushels, which was as much as two of us could lift up from the ground, and was very handsomely and cunningly made. But, whilst we were busy about all these things, we were in suspense what to do with it, and at length, after much talk, we concluded to take as much corn as we could carry away with us; and when our shallop came, if we could find any of the people, we would satisfy [pay] them for their corn. The rest we buried again; for we were so laden with armor that we could carry no more."

The march of Myles Standish.

From the painting by G. H. Boughton
The march of Myles Standish.
From the painting by G. H. Boughton
As they walked slowly on, noting all the strange things they met, they found a deer trap. One of their number wrote down afterward just what happened at this point: "As we wandered we came to a tree where a young sapling was bowed [bent] down over a bow and some acorns strewed{164} underneath. Stephen Hopkins said it had been to catch some deer. So as we were looking at it, William Bradford, being in the rear, when he came and went about, it gave a sudden jerk up and he was caught by the leg. It [the deer trap] was a pretty device, made with a rope of their own making and having a noose as well made as any ropemaker in England can make." Even those solemn Pilgrims had to laugh to see Brother Bradford with one foot up in the air and his head on the ground!

The men returned to the ship and reported what they had seen. When the shallop was completed they sailed away in that, and went farther on little voyages of discovery; but Cape Cod is a long peninsula, and they went back and forth several times between the land and their ship, which remained at anchor near the end of the Cape.

One time they came back from their site-hunting and found that another Pilgrim had been born in the Mayflower. This baby (William White was its father) was the first white child born in this part of America. They named the baby Peregrinus, the Latin word for Pilgrim; so he was called Peregrine White.

There was a mischievous small boy in the Mayflower—"that Billington boy," the Pilgrims called him—who found some gunpowder and proceeded to make trails of it on the deck, then touched a live coal to it and made it flash up. So young Francis Billington made the first fireworks in New England. He also shot off a musket. There were two kinds of musket; one called the matchlock, lighted by punk or "slow match" (there were no friction matches for two hundred years after that); and the other kind called the snaphance, or flintlock. While playing with fire, "that Billington boy" flashed a line of powder which ran back to{165} the kegs of gunpowder and came very near blowing up the Mayflower and all on board!

Another time the home hunters had had a hard day, and, being tired and hungry, made their camp and went to rest after placing men on guard. Bradford wrote in his journal:

"About midnight we heard a great and hideous cry; and our sentinels called, 'Arm, arm!' So we bestirred ourselves, and shot off a couple of muskets, and the noise ceased. We concluded that it was a company of wolves or other wild beasts, for one told us he had heard such a noise in Newfoundland.

"About five in the morning we began to be stirring; and two or three [men who] doubted whether their pieces would go off or no, made trial of them, and shot them off, but thought nothing at all. After prayer we prepared ourselves for breakfast, and for a journey; and, it being now twilight in the morning, it was thought meet [best] to carry the things down to the shallop.

"Anon, all of a sudden, we heard a great and strange cry, which we knew to be the same voices, though they varied their notes. One of the company came running in and cried, 'They are men! Indians! Indians!' and withal their arrows came flying amongst us.

"Our men ran with all speed to recover their arms, as by the good Providence of God they did. In the meantime, Captain Myles Standish, having a snaphance ready, made a shot; and after him another. After they two had shot, other two of us were ready, but he wished us not to shoot till we could take aim, for we knew not what need we should have; and there were four only of us which had their arms there ready.

"Our care was no less for the shallop; but we hoped all the rest would defend it. We called unto them to know how it was with them; and they answered, 'Well, well!' everyone; and, 'Be of good courage!' We heard three of their pieces go off; and the rest called for a firebrand to light their [punk] matches [for their matchlock muskets]. One took a log of the fire on his shoulder, and went and carried it unto them. The cry of our enemies was dreadful, especially when our men ran out to recover their arms. Their note was after this manner, 'Woach! woach! ha ha hach woach!' "

This "hideous and great cry" was the first Indian warwhoop the Pilgrims ever heard. It must have curdled the{166} blood of those quaint old Puritans who had never heard a modern college yell! The white men's matchlocks and snaphances seem to have scared the Indians even more than their warwhoop and arrows—tipped with brass, buckhorn, and eagles' claws—frightened the white men. So the red men ran away and lived to fight another day.

The Indians who first fought with the Pilgrims proved to be the Nausets, an unfriendly tribe living on Cape Cod. The white men named this place, "The First Encounter." The Lookout Committee went on after this until they reached the main land and soon found the site they had been searching for so long. Bradford's diary contains the record:

"On the Sabbath day we rested; and on Monday we sounded the harbor, and found it a very good harbor for shipping. We marched also into the land and found divers cornfields and little running brooks—a place very good for situation. So we returned to our ship [Mayflower] again with good news to the rest of our people, which did much comfort their hearts."

Though Bradford did not then think it worth mentioning, there was a big boulder in the edge of the harbor upon which these men sprang out of the shallop. This happened on the 21st of December, 1620, and is known as the Landing of the Pilgrims on Plymouth Rock. December 21st is celebrated now, more than three hundred years after that event, as Forefathers' Day. This place was marked Plymouth on Captain John Smith's map of New England, and the Pilgrims, who had sailed from Plymouth, England, were glad to give their new-found settlement that name.

Four days after this landing, the Mayflower sailed from the end of Cape Cod and came to anchor in Plymouth harbor. The first thing the Pilgrims did was to build a common house of logs to be used later as a sort of town hall.{167} Then they erected a square cabin on top of the hill for both church and fort. On its flat roof they mounted three brass cannon. Christmas Day came while they were building their first cabin, but they worked all that day, for they were too strict even to celebrate Christmas. While they were building their village of log cabins with thatched roofs, some of them stayed in their quarters on the Mayflower.

It seemed a long time before they saw Indians again. But one day while the grave and reverend Pilgrims were holding a council in their common house, a tall red man came stalking up to their door, saying: "Welcome, Yankees! Welcome, Yankees!" "Yankees" was the nearest the Indian could pronounce "Englishmen"! From this, the people of New England are still called Yankees.

This Indian's name was Samoset. He had learned a little English from some fishermen farther north on the New England coast. He came again to Plymouth bringing another red man named Squanto, who, years before, had been carried away with other savages by an English captain and sold into slavery. Squanto had been taken to London and learned to speak English. He was glad to stay with the Pilgrims and talk for them to the tribes around Plymouth, for while he was away a slave in foreign lands, his own people had been taken with a dreadful disease called a plague, and when he came back they had all died, and poor Squanto was left alone in the world.

The Pilgrims elected Myles Standish, who was the only soldier in the company, their captain. But about the first work Captain Standish had to do was to take care of the sick, and he did so, according to the poet Longfellow, "With a hand as gentle as woman's."{168}

In the spring there were only fifty-one of the Pilgrims—just one-half the number that had landed on Plymouth Rock. Among the first to die was Rose Standish, the Captain's beautiful wife. Although they were not attacked that winter, they knew the Indians were lurking about, so the Pilgrims did not make mounds of the graves in their poor little burial ground on the hill for fear the savages would see how few white men were left, and attack them while they were all so ill. At one time only two men were well enough to nurse all the rest and bury them as fast as they died.

In April the men were well enough to plant corn and do other work. It was so hot that Governor Carver, the oldest of all the Pilgrims, was prostrated by the heat and died. William Bradford was elected Governor in his place.

When the Pilgrims had erected cabins enough to house all who were left of them, they built a stockade, or wall of upright logs, around the settlement. In April, 1621, the Mayflower started back to England. Much as they had suffered through the long, dreary winter, none of the Pilgrims wished to return home on their little ship. That plucky band of men and women had come to America to stay.

They marched to their church-fort on the hill every Sunday, led by their governor, minister, and captain. The men carried their muskets to be ready to defend themselves if the Indians tried to surprise them while at their worship. The Pilgrims believed in watching and fighting as well as praying.

After a long time, Massasoit, the great Indian chief, came with a company of his braves to see the Pilgrims, and the white men and the red made a treaty of peace and{169} friendship. Afterwards the chief of a more distant tribe sent an Indian runner to Plymouth with a bundle of arrows tied together with a rattlesnake skin. Captain Standish promptly filled the snake skin with powder and bullets and sent it back. This frightened the Indians, for they thought the white "medicine man" had the power to send a plague among them which would make them all sicken and die.

After a time the people of Plymouth were comfortable and at peace with their Indian neighbors. Then a lad known as "that Billington boy" disobeyed the rules by going outside the limits and was lost. The settlers were alarmed, and Captain Standish took a small company of men and made a search for the lad. They found him with the unfriendly Nausets, the Indians they had fought with at "The First Encounter."

The Indians around Plymouth laughed at the little red-headed white captain because he was so small. He was so quick-tempered that they named him "Little-Pot-That-Soon-Boils-Over." Once when a tall, wiry Indian north of Plymouth insulted him, the fiery little captain had all he could do to control himself. Standish and three other white men had gone up to that place for the purpose of punishing the Indians who were threatening the whole colony with death. Watching his chance, the white captain sprang upon the big Indian chief who had sneered at him, snatched the savage's own knife, and killed him with a single stab. The other white men dispatched their Indians. The account of this brave deed of the Captain of Plymouth was reported among the Indians far and near, and the Pilgrims had long years of peace because the red men had gained a wholesome respect for Myles Standish, whose name they now changed to Sword-of-the-White-Man.{170}

JOHN WINTHROP, A PURITAN MAKER OF MASSACHUSETTS

John Winthrop can not be called a boy's hero; yet he was a hero, and his life was strange and interesting. He was a son of a good Puritan family in England. When a young man he met Oliver Cromwell, who became Lord Protector of England. He was acquainted with John Milton, the blind Puritan poet who wrote "Paradise Lost," one of the greatest poems in the English language. John Winthrop had also to transact certain business with Cromwell's cousin, John Hampden, the great English patriot who opposed King Charles when he sought to impose taxation upon the people without their consent.

Governor John Winthrop.
Governor John Winthrop.
Young Winthrop was married the first time when he was seventeen, and his son Henry was born when the young father was eighteen. In 1629, the father decided to go to America where he could worship God as he thought best.{171} He and four hundred men and women set sail from England in a fleet of small ships, intending to join the settlement at Salem, started a year before. One of these ships was the Mayflower, in which the Pilgrims of Plymouth had sailed nine years before.

On their second morning out from England they spied eight ships coming behind them. The captain of the Arabella, the ship on which Winthrop sailed (as he wrote in the logbook or journal of the voyage),

"caused the gun-room and gun-deck to be cleared. After noon we still saw those eight ships to stand towards us. Having more wind than we, they came up apace. We all prepared to fight with them, and took down some cabins which were in the way of our ordnance [cannon] and out of every ship were thrown such bed matters as were subject to take fire. We drew forth our men and armed them with muskets and other weapons and instruments for fireworks. To try it our captain shot a ball of wildfire fastened to an arrow, out of a crossbow, which burnt in the water a good time.

"The women and children were removed into the lower deck that they might be out of danger. All things being thus fitted, we went to prayer upon the upper deck. It was good to see how cheerful all the company appeared; not a woman or child showed fear.

"It was now about one of the clock, and the fleet seemed to be within a league of us; therefore our captain, because he would show he was not afraid of them, and that he might see what was to be done before night should overtake us, tacked about and stood to meet them. And when they came near, we perceived them to be our friends.

"So every ship (as they met) saluted each other and the musketeers discharged their small shot; and so, God be praised, our fear and danger was turned into mirth and

71

friendly entertainment. Our danger being thus over, we espied two boats fishing in the Channel. So every one of our four ships manned out a skiff, and we bought of them great store of excellent fresh fish of divers sorts."

The voyagers were seventy-six days—nearly eleven weeks—crossing the Atlantic. They had passed through {172} storms, but when, early in June, they sighted America, Winthrop wrote in his journal:

"We had now fair sunshine weather, and so pleasant a sweet air as did much refresh us; and there came a smell off shore like the smell of a garden. There came a wild pigeon into our ship, and another small land bird."

In four days the Arabella was anchored in Salem Harbor. The poor little settlement welcomed some of the newcomers with "a good supper of venison pasty. In the meantime most of our people went on shore upon the land of Cape Ann, which lay very near us, and gathered store of fine strawberries."

"Salem, where we landed, pleased us not," wrote one of the men on board to a countess in England. Winthrop, who had been elected governor of the colony they were to found, looked about for a better place to settle, and decided on a site they called Charlestown, on the Charles River. Although they had left England because of their obstinate and foolish king, Charles the First, they named rivers and towns for him, and one of their earliest churches was called King's Chapel. When no one was allowed to think for himself, or even to wear such clothes as he saw fit, it would have been regarded as almost a crime to speak a word against the king, no matter how much he deserved a bad name.

When Governor Winthrop came back from Charlestown to Salem, he wrote in his journal: "We went to Massachusetts to find out a place for our sitting down." By "Massachusetts" he meant only that part of the country along Boston Harbor, about fifteen miles south of Salem. Just after his return, his eldest son Henry, who had come over on another ship, arrived at Salem. That very day the young man started with several of the ship's officers to {173} visit some Indian wigwams. In his journal the father describes what happened:

"They saw, on the other side of the river, a small canoe. He would have had one of the company swim over and fetch it, rather than walk several miles on foot, it being very hot weather, but none of the party could swim but himself; and so he plunged in, and, as he was swimming over, was taken with a cramp a few rods from shore, and drowned."

"My son Henry! My son Henry!" wrote the bereaved governor to his wife in England. "Ah, poor child. Yet it grieves me much more for my dear daughter. Yet for all these things (I praise my God) I am not discouraged."

Henry, the son of John Winthrop's first wife, had been married in England. He had come without his bride to the western wilds to build a little home before sending for her.

Heartsore but not dismayed, Governor Winthrop took his followers and tried to make the settlement at Charlestown, now part of the great city of Boston. But their sufferings were not over. As at Jamestown, on the James River in Virginia about twenty-five years before this, the settlers were ill with malaria and some of them died.

Then a strange old hermit, who had lived about twenty years alone on a tree-topped hill on the other side of the river, came to see the new governor, and invited him to come over the river and build his town on the hill which had been named Three-mount, Tri-mountain, or Tremont. So Winthrop and his people moved once more and named the new place for the city of Boston in England. The old hermit proved to be William Blackstone, a minister from old England. On the Three Mounts he tilled a small farm which extended down into the now historic Boston Common. He had brought from

72

England his library, and spent his {174} time reading, farming, and raising apples. He had left England because he would not worship according to the legal forms there. But he did not like the way the Puritans wished him to worship, either. So he moved away from Boston as soon as he could dispose of his house and other real estate.

Blackstone also had been kind to the Indians. His influence did much toward keeping the red tribes friendly with the white settlers of Boston. On the highest of the three mounts was placed a sort of lighthouse or beacon which sailors could see far down the harbor. This gave the name of Beacon Hill to that part of Boston. On this hill the State House has since been erected. This building has a great dome covered with gold-leaf which glistens in the sun and can be seen for many miles around. "All roads lead" to the dome of the State House in Boston, as the spokes of a wheel come together in the hub. Because of this fact, a humorous writer gave Boston the title of "The Hub of the Universe."

Though the Indians gave the early settlers very little trouble, the wolves which howled around the settlement were alarming, and sometimes dangerous to the little children. Sometimes a bear would come ambling into "Boston Town." The people's cows were pastured on the Common. This made some people who wished to make fun of Boston claim that the narrow, crooked streets of that city were laid out by the cows, as they wandered down from the Common to drink at a certain spring.

Sometimes the town suffered from disease and famine. One day, when Governor Winthrop had divided his last cupful of cornmeal with a starving beggar, he appointed a day of fasting and prayer to God for food. On the very {175} day set for this fast, a ship arrived from England with provisions, and the people had a feast instead. Another time when the people did not have enough to eat, an Indian chief named Chickataubot came and presented the governor with a great quantity of corn. As with the Indians, so with the white settlers at first, it was either feast or famine.

The people of Boston were kinder to the Indians than to the white men who failed to agree with them in religion. They banished the Baptists and hanged the Quakers. Besides Roger Williams, they drove out a good woman named Anne Hutchinson, because she argued too well against some of their beliefs. This gifted woman and her family were murdered and scalped by Indians in the log cabin in which they lived after they were banished from Boston.

Governor Winthrop finally sent for his wife and his other children. One of his sons became governor of Connecticut. John Winthrop was twelve times elected governor of Massachusetts. More than once he was chosen deputy governor. He was good to the poor and unfortunate. In this he was far in advance of his time. It was said that he kept his private purse open for the public. Once, when he found that a man was stealing wood from his pile, he laughed and said he would stop that. He did so by inviting the man to come in the daytime and help himself to all the wood he needed. But the man never came again.

Cotton Mather, one of the greatest of Boston preachers, said of Governor Winthrop that he was—

"The terror of the wicked, and delight of the sober, the envy of the many, but the hope of those who had any hopeful design in hand for the common good of the nation." {176}

ROGER WILLIAMS, A MINISTER WHO LIVED THE GOLDEN RULE

WHEN the Pilgrim Fathers left Europe in the clumsy little ship, the Mayflower, they came to America to have freedom to think and act as they believed right in matters of religion. Many men in England who wished to have their own religious beliefs were called Puritans because they wished to purify the Church of England from things which they thought were wrong. King James of England had announced that they must all worship in the ways of the Church of England or he would "harry them out of the land."

Puritans and other people who would not conform to the service of the Church of England were called Nonconformists. The group of Nonconformists who went away from their own country in 1620, to come as strangers to America, were called the Pilgrims. They came to America in the Mayflower, and landed on a big boulder in the edge of the harbor at a place they named Plymouth. Companies of Puritans sailed from England a few years later and landed on the shores of Massachusetts Bay, some at Salem, and some at a place they named Boston, for another town in England. John Winthrop was the leader of this last company, and was made governor of Massachusetts Bay Colony.

The Puritans soon found that there were some of their number who did not believe just as they did. It seems strange now that those who had come from England just to find a place where they could worship God in the way they saw fit could not let others do the same. They came to do what their consciences told them was right, but they would not let others think that any other way was right.{177}

So when members of the Society of Friends, called Quakers, came, dressing differently and thinking it wrong to fight and treat the Indians cruelly, the Puritans sent them away. If the Quakers came back to Boston after being sent away, they were hanged on the Common. A man who did not think what his neighbors believed was likely to have a hard time of it. For any one to dress differently from others was considered a great offense. It was the same all over the world, especially in England. The first man who tried to wear a silk hat in London was chased through the streets. The mob battered his hat and tore his clothes, and he barely escaped with his life.

Therefore, when Roger Williams, a bright young minister from England, came to preach in the first church of Boston, the people soon found that he believed in a different form of baptism from theirs, and some were angry enough to wish to kill him for being a Baptist. So he left Boston and went to live at Plymouth. The preaching of those days was not so much about doing good and living by the Golden Rule as about certain fixed beliefs. This often led to angry arguments, and some good people became very violent. On this account Roger Williams soon had to leave Plymouth. Then he went to Salem and built a little church there which is still standing, about three hundred years old. Here the young minister kept on preaching what the leaders thought were strange and wicked teachings. It was decided that such a reckless preacher should be arrested and sent in chains to England to be tried, and imprisoned or put to death. But Roger Williams heard of this decision and did not wait to be arrested. When the captain and his men from Boston came to the Salem minister's house, they found that he had left there three days before.{178}

When the people of Boston, Salem, and Plymouth next heard of Roger Williams, he was settled on Narragansett Bay. The Indians there received him gladly, for he had been one of the few white men who treated them kindly, as William Penn, fifty years afterwards, dealt with the Indians along the Delaware River.

Williams and his friends built a group of log houses and named their settlement Providence, because they believed that, in the providence, or care, of God, they had found a safe retreat among the savages from the severity of the pious Puritans of Massachusetts. Quakers and other religious people, who were driven from the Puritan colonies, came and settled near Roger Williams. Even here the people of different beliefs quarreled over religious matters, and good Pastor Williams had all he could do to keep them from fighting and injuring one another.

Soon the savage Pequot Indians tried to persuade all the Indian tribes to join together and kill at a stroke all the white men who had come over the Great Water and taken from the natives certain parts of their country. When the white men of Boston and Plymouth heard of this they sent and begged Roger Williams to use his good influence with his neighbors the Narragansetts, a large and powerful tribe, to prevent them from joining in the plot to murder all the white men—as the Indians could have done if all the tribes had joined together and attacked all at once.

Here was a chance for Roger Williams to get even with those who had wished to kill or imprison him and who had driven him from place to place. But the minister of Providence returned good for evil. Taking his life in his hands, he went to the Indian village. The Pequot braves were there in the wigwam of Canonicus, the Narragansett chief,{179}
{180}

The Landing of Roger Williams.

{180}From the painting by Alonzo Chappel
The Landing of Roger Williams.
From the painting by Alonzo Chappel
trying to persuade him and his tribe to take part in a war against the "palefaces." Roger Williams was a hero. He stayed with those Indians, sleeping with them at night without showing the least sign of fear, though he very well knew that a savage Pequot might stab him in his sleep.

The Providence minister was successful. Canonicus refused to join with the Pequots. Because the Narragansetts stayed out of the war, other tribes also kept out of it. The Pequots went ahead, but the white men defeated and destroyed them. By his conduct at this time of need, Roger Williams set both red men and white a noble example. He taught them all by his life that a true Christian loves his enemies and does good to those who treat him badly. The man who founded the town of Providence and the state of Rhode Island was the friend both of white men and red because he lived the Golden Rule.

LORD BALTIMORE, CALVERT AND CLAIBORNE, THE THREE FATHERS OF MARYLAND

GEORGE CALVERT, of Kipling, England, was such a fine man that he was beloved by king and people alike. King James gave him the title of "Sir" George Calvert, and made him Secretary of State. As the king and the church in England were Protestant, Sir George felt it his duty to give up his royal honors when he became a Catholic. But King James' son, Charles the First, instead of taking Calvert's rank away from him, made him "Baron" Baltimore. A baron is higher in position than a knight, who is called "Sir."{181}

A few years after the Pilgrims came to America and settled at Plymouth in order to worship God as they thought right, Lord Baltimore asked permission to make a settlement for himself and the Catholics of England who were persecuted because of their religion. The first place chosen by him for a Catholic settlement was in Newfoundland. But though the climate was lovely and cool there in spring and summer, the settlers found it so cold in winter that they had to go back to England. King Charles then granted Lord Baltimore another great tract of land much farther south, between the English settlement at Jamestown and that of the Puritans at Plymouth in New England. Lord Baltimore named this region "Mary Land," in honor of King Charles' wife, the queen of England.

George Calvert, Lord Baltimore
George Calvert, Lord Baltimore
As all the other English settlements in America were Protestant, the party had great trouble in securing supplies and getting started for the New World. Before they were{182} quite ready, the first Lord Baltimore died, and his eldest son, Cecil Calvert, who then became Lord Baltimore, inherited Maryland as part of his father's estate. But some of the land granted to Lord Baltimore had been settled years before and was claimed by the colonists of Virginia. On account of this, young Lord Baltimore had to stay in London to look out for his rights in America. Therefore his younger brother, Leonard Calvert, was sent to act for him as governor of Maryland.

At last the voyagers sailed away in two ships, the Ark and the Dove. There were one hundred and twenty-eight passengers, not counting servants and children. There were others on board who, not having money, bound themselves by law to work for a certain time in America to pay their passage across the sea.

The two ships were caught in a terrific storm on the way and the Dove was not to be seen anywhere. After many days of hoping against hope, those on the Ark gave up for lost the Dove and all their friends on it. Then the Ark sailed on alone, stopping, after many weeks, at one of the islands of the West Indies. While they were anchored there their sorrow was turned to joy, for the Dove caught up with them. It had been driven out of sight by the fierceness of the gale and had found refuge in a harbor near by.

The two sister ships now sailed northward and entered the mouth of the Potomac. Of this river Father White, one of the company, wrote:

"Never have I beheld a larger or more beautiful river. The Thames seems a mere rivulet in comparison with it; it is not disfigured by any swamps, but has firm land on each side. Fine groves of trees appear, not choked with bushes and undergrowth, but growing at intervals as if planted by hand, so that you might easily drive a four-horse carriage through the midst of the trees."

{183}

Governor Leonard Calvert had heard so many stories of the fierceness and cunning of the Indians that he did not land at once. After the two ships had cruised about the rivers and the bay awhile, he decided to settle at the mouth of a small river, which they named St. Mary's, and built a group of cabins, calling this place St. Mary's also.

They were quite surprised to find their Indian neighbors friendly, bringing corn and provisions, and showing them all they could about planting and trapping and hunting. The settlers soon learned that the Indians were friendly because they wanted the white men to help them when they went to war with their savage enemies. The red men thought the strangers' "firesticks" (guns) worked magic, like lightning and thunder from above. The children of young Maryland saw much to entertain and sometimes to frighten them. When the Indians painted themselves with red, black, and yellow stripes, they looked even uglier than before. The white people had heard of the savages' war dances and scalp dances, but they now found the natives had also their corn dances, something like a harvest or Thanksgiving festival.

The Maryland colonists were kind to the tribes and gained their friendship, as Champlain had done and as William Penn and the Quakers of Philadelphia were to do about fifty years later. The Indians in and around Maryland learned to believe in the goodness of the people of the Baltimore colony.

Most of the trouble Governor Calvert had in settling Maryland was with a white leader named Claiborne, who had settled on the largest island in the bay. He claimed that this land, which was named Kent Island, was part of Virginia.{184}

Governor Calvert visited Jamestown, and the governor of that colony said that the island was part of Lord Baltimore's land. Then Claiborne announced that Kent Island was not only separate from either colony, but that it belonged to him. He had made friends among the Indians, far and near, and began to boast that he was going to drive all the other white people out of that country.

The Marylanders went to work like so many beavers, building a fort and other defenses to be ready for an attack. When they heard that the people on Kent Island had fitted out a large sailboat as a man-of-war, Governor Calvert fitted up two pinnaces, or small boats, and mounted a cannon in each. Then the men of Maryland sailed for Kent Island and captured it, after a battle in which several persons were killed. After this there was no more trouble with Claiborne, and since that time Kent Island has belonged to Maryland. Lord Baltimore held the rights over Maryland by a grant from the king, somewhat as William Penn afterward came to own Pennsylvania. Although Cecil, Baron Baltimore, was never able to visit his property in the New World, his name was given to Baltimore, the greatest city of Maryland, and Anne Arundel County was named for his wife.

The purpose of the colony was not all religious. Trading and business were also the objects of those brave settlers, and some of the most successful merchant princes have sprung from that old Maryland stock—"the best out of Old England." The women of Maryland have been far-famed for their beauty. There is good reason for naming the loveliest of climbing roses, "Baltimore Belles."

The best thing grown in old Maryland was its patriotism. When the Fathers were signing the Declaration of Independence,{185} the chief man from Maryland was Charles Carroll. As there was another Charles Carroll, the hero in Independence Hall signed his name "Charles Carroll of Carrollton." The patriotic spirit of the colony still lives in that song, popular in all the states: "Maryland, my Maryland!"

WILLIAM PENN, THE FOUNDER OF PENNSYLVANIA

WHEN William Penn was born, his father, Admiral Sir William Penn, was sailing out to sea on an English battleship. Little William's mother was a lovely woman from Holland, and as good as she was beautiful. While in college at Oxford, young Penn attended Quaker meetings, which had been started by followers of George Fox, the founder of a religious sect, the Society of Friends, or Quakers, as they were commonly called.

William Penn.

In State Capitol of Pennsylvania
William Penn.
In State Capitol of Pennsylvania

The professors in charge of Oxford University did not believe in such meetings, so they turned out of the college those who attended them. When William Penn went home, sent away from Oxford, his father was so angry that he gave his Quaker son a beating and drove him from home.{186} Young Penn would have had to starve or beg in the streets but for his good mother, who sent and helped him secretly. Even after that William was found at a Quaker meeting in London and put in prison for eight months.

William Penn's father was a great man, a friend of King Charles the First. When that king was put to death, Admiral Penn became the friend of Cromwell, who had fought against the king. After Cromwell died, the Admiral attached himself to King Charles the Second, and to the king's brother, the Duke of York, who afterward became James the Second. Although these four rulers were different—even bitter enemies to one another—shrewd Admiral Penn managed to keep the favor of them all. He was ambitious also to have his eldest son become the favorite of kings. He allowed William to come home after he was free from prison, in order to send him away to Paris, as he hoped the youth would forget his queer belief in the gay life there. The father asked the son's friends, who were sons of English noblemen, to influence William while in Paris to do everything that was against the Quaker belief. One day a stranger met young Penn in the street and picked a quarrel with him, drawing his sword and challenging the peace-loving young man to a duel with swords. Penn was forced, much against his will, to fight. He had always been an active youth and fond of sports. While at college he had been very good at fencing. By skilful play he disarmed the quarrelsome fellow and ended the duel without hurting the stranger, as if it were all done in sport. This pleased all who saw the sword-play and it did credit to the heart as well as to the skill of the young Quaker.

When William returned home he was so handsome and had gained so much in courtly manners that his father was{187} thoroughly pleased. But the Great Plague broke out in London then, carrying off nearly seventy thousand people in that city alone. This frightened even the most worldly into leading religious lives, and made William Penn's conscience trouble him. Repenting of his gay life, he finally joined the Friends for good and all, and became one of their most earnest members and preachers. His father ordered him out of the house and threatened to cast him off utterly.

William was now imprisoned in the London Tower because of something he had written against the Church of England. While in prison he wrote "No Cross, No Crown," and other works in defense of the Quakers. His father, whose heart was touched by his son's courage and unselfishness, appealed to the Duke of York, King Charles' brother, and got William out of the Tower.

Admiral Penn died soon after this, leaving William a rich man. The royal treasury owed him immense sums of money loaned to King Charles and his brother James. But young Penn was again arrested because he was a Friend, and imprisoned in Newgate, where the worst criminals were kept. When he was again set free he began to seek some good place outside of England where he and his Quaker followers could serve God and their fellow-men without being treated like criminals. Learning of a certain region in America, he went to King Charles and asked for it in payment of the large amount of money Charles owed him.

As the king was still unable to pay the great debt in money, he was glad to grant Penn a charter for the vast tract of land. When Penn came before the king and the council to have the state paper signed and sealed, he did not remove his hat, as Quakers think it wrong to show such{188} reverence to any one but God. King Charles allowed Penn to keep his hat on, but removed his own, to the astonishment of all, and said with a smile, "It is the custom at court for only one person to remain covered."

Penn suggested calling the tract of country they were ceding to him, Sylvania, which meant "forest land"; but the king insisted on naming it Pennsylvania, or Penn-forest. This name was written in the charter, so William Penn had to abide by it, though he thought it vain to have the land named for himself. The religious leader was now happy in having a country where he and his people could live and love God and one another in their own simple way. Sailing across the ocean in his good ship, Welcome, Penn bought the country from its rightful owners, the Indians. He made a solemn treaty with them which was "never sworn to, and never broken."

No Quaker ever hurt or wronged an Indian, and no Indian ever injured a Friend, though the red savages murdered settlers belonging to other religious faiths. William Penn laid out a town which soon became the largest city in America. For this place he made up a name, Philadelphia, composed of two Greek words meaning "Brother" and "love."

Grand as it was to own such a great country as Pennsylvania, and to found a large and flourishing city like Philadelphia, it was even grander to teach people to live by the Golden Rule, and to help along religious liberty. It was most fitting that the Declaration of Independence should be adopted and signed in the State House of Pennsylvania, in Philadelphia, the city of William Penn.{189}

William Penn's treaty with the Indians.
William Penn's treaty with the Indians.
{190}
PATRIOTS OF THE REVOLUTION

PATRICK HENRY, THE "FIREBRAND OF THE REVOLUTION"

"PAT HENRY'S a good-for-nothing fellow. Just lounges about his father-in-law's tavern telling stories and fiddling."

This was the verdict of the people of Hanover Court House, Virginia, when Patrick Henry was a young man. When he was but a youth he had married the tavern-keeper's daughter. He had tried farming and failed, people said, because he was "too lazy to do anything but go a-fishing." But he was a great reader and had studied law in a random, listless way.

The door of opportunity opened one day before this young man of whom the neighbors had so little good to say. There was a case in court called "the Parsons' Cause." This famous lawsuit arose in the following way: An old law required each church in Virginia to pay its minister sixteen thousand pounds of tobacco as his yearly salary. Later the legislature of Virginia passed another law which permitted each parish to pay its minister a smaller salary in money. The King of England set this law aside and then the "parsons," as the clergy were called, brought a lawsuit to collect the unpaid parts of their salaries. Young Patrick Henry's sympathies were with the men who were sued and he offered his services in their defense.

When the people of Hanover Court House heard of this, they laughed as if it were a huge joke.{191}

Patrick Henry delivering his celebrated speech, May, 1765.
Patrick Henry delivering his celebrated speech, May, 1765.

79

"The good-for-nothing! What can he do, with his low, tavern talk?" they asked in scorn. "His stories may do for a bar-room, but for such a fellow to speak in such an important case will be an insult to the court."

The courtroom was well filled on the day of the trial. The opposing lawyers had promised to make short work of Patrick Henry, and teach him a lesson he would not soon forget. There was a strange stillness when the young man rose to speak. At first he seemed unable to control his voice, and some of those present nudged each other and whispered: "He's going to break down! I told you so. He ought to have known better than attempt a big case like this."

Then young Henry's will seemed to come to his rescue. He straightened up. His face flushed eagerly. His eyes blazed with indignation. His words soon came in a torrent of eloquence. He declared that the people of Virginia had the right to make their own laws and that if the King interfered he was no longer the father of his people, but a tyrant whom they need not obey. The jury, carried away by the young lawyer's fiery appeal, decided that the parsons should have only one penny more money.

The people who had come to sneer now began to cheer. They carried the young lawyer out of the courthouse on their shoulders.

That success showed that the "ne'er-do-well" was really a great lawyer. After that Patrick Henry spent his time in his law office instead of going fishing or loafing about the hotel. He studied to improve his mind, and practiced in correcting his errors of speech, while learning to make good use of his new-found gift of speaking in public.

Honors were showered, thick and fast, on the fiery lawyer. {193} Other cases were brought to him and he won them right and left. Soon he was sent to the House of Burgesses, or the legislature of Virginia.

When other leaders hesitated to take the steps necessary to obtain their rights, Patrick Henry did not falter. He seemed to see farther than other men into the future. He made the halls of the lawmakers ring for liberty, beginning his great liberty speeches ten years before the colonies were prepared to meet and declare their independence.

When Virginians were sent to the first Congress of the United Colonies in Philadelphia, Patrick Henry was one of those chosen to go with George Washington and Richard Henry Lee. Here, in a fiery speech, Patrick Henry exclaimed: "I am not a Virginian—I am an American!" He had to leave Congress before signing the Declaration of Independence; but soon after he became the first governor of Virginia, which was now no longer a British colony but a new state. He was four times elected governor of the state.

Patrick Henry was "the firebrand of the Revolution"; that is, his burning words spread like a prairie fire from south to north, and inspired the people with a burning zeal for liberty which could not be quenched till all thirteen colonies had gained their independence and had become the United States of America.

It has been said that Patrick Henry "rocked the world with his voice." The best known of his speeches was made just a few weeks before the battle of Lexington, which was the first skirmish of the Revolution. Here are the closing words of that great speech:

"Gentlemen may cry, 'Peace! Peace!'—but there is no peace. The war is actually begun. The next gale that sweeps from the north will bring to our ears the clash of resounding arms! Our {194} brethren are already in the field. Why stand we here idle? What is it the gentlemen wish? What would they have? Is life so dear, or peace so sweet as to be purchased at the price of chains and slavery? Forbid it, Almighty God! I know not what course others may take; but, as for me, give me Liberty or give me Death!"

NATHAN HALE was a country boy, the sixth of ten children. When he was twelve his mother died. It had been her wish that Nathan should study to be a minister. So the lad entered Yale College when he was only fourteen. Young as he was, Nathan became president of the debating society. He was a big, strong, handsome fellow, full of fun and fond of sports. He was best at what was known as the broad jump. For many years "the Hale jump" made the record for the college. He was a strong swimmer and excelled in shooting at the mark. In going about the college grounds, Hale was often seen placing one hand on top of a six-foot fence and vaulting over it with ease. One of his chums has told how Nathan would stand in one hogshead, with his hands on his hips, and jump up out of that into the second hogshead; then, in the same manner, leap into the third hogshead and from there out on the ground—"all without touching." His athletic feats were so wonderful that the boys used to boast of the things "Young Hale" did for "Old Yale."

When he was seventeen, the young athlete also showed himself such a ready and eloquent speaker that he was chosen for the highest honors of the debating society. One address of his is still kept in the records of Yale University. {195} One of the questions he proposed and took part in debating was: "Is it right to enslave the Africans?"

Right after his graduation, at the age of eighteen, young Hale began to teach school and do tutoring besides, to pay his way while studying to be a minister. But early in 1775, when he had been teaching less than two years, the news of the first battles in the War for Independence fired the fervent soul of the young patriot, and he joined the army.

Nathan Hale was appointed lieutenant in a company sent by Connecticut, his native state, to become part of General Washington's army which was trying to take the city of Boston, then in the hands of the British. The army then was without uniforms, proper arms, or training. During the summer Lieutenant Hale "turned" twenty-one and was promoted to the rank of captain.

When the time for which the Connecticut men had enlisted was nearly up, the young captain was shocked and hurt to find that some of the men in his own company were not willing to serve a little longer. Here is a short, signed entry he made in his camp-book in November:

"28. Tuesday. Promised the men if they would tarry another month they should have my wages for that time. Nathan Hale."

The youthful Connecticut officer and some of his men were among the few who stayed till the British were driven out of Boston by sea. After this the commander-in-chief, foreseeing that New York must be the next point of attack for the British, sent all his soldiers on ahead to that city. In the first brigade to go was Captain Nathan Hale, with as many of his little company as he could command.

While officers like Hale were recruiting new soldiers and drilling the raw recruits, Washington went to consult with {196} the Congress then in session at Philadelphia. During this visit he designed the first American flag and ordered it made. It was the summer of the Declaration of Independence.

Washington and his untrained troops, less than fourteen thousand in number, had to defend and hold New York City, Brooklyn, and the surrounding country against an army nearly three times as large. The British troops under General Howe were well fitted out and trained, and were aided by a fleet of warships commanded by the general's brother, Admiral Lord Howe. The Howes and their regular soldiers thought it would be an easy matter for their army, numbering three to one of their enemies, to capture the

American army and carry Washington and the other ring-leaders of the rebellion back to England to be hanged for treason.

When, late in August, Washington learned that Howe was landing his army on Long Island from Staten Island, he sent General Putnam to meet and hold the British back. As the British outnumbered Putnam's company five to one, this was impossible, and the Americans retreated to their defenses. This engagement was called the battle of Long Island. At nightfall the British encamped around the cornered Americans, and the commander told his staff that they would take that "nest of rebels" in the morning.

A dense fog came in from the sea, and Washington, under cover of it, got as many boats together as his sailor soldiers could manage, and they rowed away from Long Island in the silent watches of the night. Next morning, when Howe came to capture the nest, the birds had flown.

Washington was now forced to fly with his army from place to place, and the danger of being captured was greater than before. So he needed to learn, if possible, what{197} General Howe's plans were. Captain Nathan Hale was selected for this dangerous service.

There were some people in the colonies who believed that Washington was a traitor and that his men were rebels. These people called themselves Loyalists, but others called them Tories. Because of Nathan Hale's frank face and sincere manner it was thought that he could make friends with these Tories and find out what was desired through them and their friends, the British officers. Also, he was an educated gentleman. He could take a position as tutor in the family of a rich Tory. British officers visited these Loyalists and often discussed plans with them.

Captain Hull, a college friend of Captain Hale's, was now an army comrade also. When he heard that Hale was chosen, he called to beg him not to go as a spy. He argued:

"Your nature is too frank and open for deceit and disguise. General Washington— nor any commander—has a right to ask you to assume the garb of friendship for the betrayal of others."

Hale hesitated a moment at this, but when he spoke his voice was clear and firm:

"I think I owe it to my country to do the thing which seems so important to General Washington, and I know of no other way of getting the desired information than by assuming a disguise and passing into the enemy's camp."

"But," urged his friend almost in despair, "think of the disgrace of it! If you were caught, you would be hanged as a criminal! Dear Nathan, I beg of you, don't go."

Nathan Hale could not help being deeply moved. He said gently: "He took upon himself the disguise of the men He came to live among, for the good of many and the cause of the right. He was arrested and hanged—on a{198} cross! Who am I that I should set up my judgment against His example and General Washington's will?"

Still, Captain Hull could not give up. He has left on record his last attempt to persuade the young man whose love of country had become a religion: "I urged him for the love of country, for the love of kindred, to abandon an enterprise which would only end in the sacrifice of the dearest interests of both. He paused—then, affectionately taking my hand, he said, 'I will reflect, and do nothing but what duty demands.' He was absent from the army and I feared he had gone to the British lines to execute his fatal purpose."

Naturally very little is known of the spy in the few weeks that followed. Sergeant Hempstead has told of going with him to the point chosen for crossing on a waiting sloop to Long Island, many miles from the British camp. Hempstead says Hale was then "dressed in a brown suit of citizen's clothes, with a round, broad-brimmed hat." When the captain and the sergeant wrung each other's hands in farewell, Nathan Hale gave into

82

Hempstead's care his private papers and letters and his shoe-buckles. The letters were to Hale's aged father and to the girl whom he expected to marry.

At the end of several weeks Nathan Hale had succeeded in carrying out General Washington's instructions, even to making a number of sketches. So far as he knew, he had not been suspected. This, he thought, was rather surprising, for there were Tories everywhere.

It was late in September, "in the dark of the moon," when Hale slipped away from the British on Long Island and strolled down to the water's edge where he was to meet the sloop and sail back to his own army. He waited some{199} time for the ship, but it did not come. After some delay a sailboat came in sight and made up to the shore. He was greatly relieved, for it did not occur to him that there was anything wrong. As the boat drew near he hailed it with a happy shout. When it was too late, Hale saw that some of the men in the boat were in British uniform. In a moment more, he was their prisoner. He had been betrayed—it was never known by whom. He had a Tory cousin who was blamed at first, but his innocence was proven in time.

The last words of Captain Nathan Hale, the hero-martyr of
the American Revolution

From the painting by F. O. C. Darley
The last words of Captain Nathan Hale, the hero-martyr of the American
Revolution
From the painting by F. O. C. Darley
He was taken to General Howe's headquarters. The telltale sketches and data were found in his shoes. He did{200} not attempt to deny that he was a spy. It was not necessary to try him after he confessed. He was turned over to the provost marshal to be hanged next day.

Of course, no one knows what Nathan Hale thought that last night, but it may well be believed that he did not waste his last hours in despairing regrets. If he was permitted to write farewell letters that night, they were never delivered. In the morning Hale asked if he might speak with a minister, but that was curtly denied him. "Will you lend me a Bible a moment, then?" was his dying request. "No!" snapped the marshal.

A kind-hearted British officer, who noticed the pure, honest face of the young American spy, offered him shelter from the sun in his tent during a brief delay. The heart of this enemy captain was touched, and it was he who preserved Nathan Hale's noble words for future ages. If the young spy could have known that his death would strengthen the hearts of patriots to fight for liberty, and that what he was about to say would go resounding down the ages, it would have added to his joy that hot September day. A poet has described the moment when they came and led him out:

"To drum-beat and heart-beat
A soldier marches by;
There is color in his cheek,
There is courage in his eye;
Yet to drum-beat and heart-beat,
In a moment he must die."

They led him to an apple tree near at hand. While they were fastening his arms behind him and tying a rope around his ankles, he gazed up into the tree. On his handsome face rested the resigned expression which is shown in the{201} bronze and

83

marble statues of Nathan Hale in the Yale yard where he used to play, and in the park before City Hall, in New York.

"Well, have you any confession to make?" asked the marshal. This called Nathan Hale's mind back. He smiled at the needless question, for he had confessed the night before and had thus made a trial unnecessary. Hesitating only a moment, he answered the officer with simple courtesy, in the bravest words ever uttered by mortal man:

"I only regret that I have but one life to lose for my country."

LAFAYETTE, THE BOY HERO OF TWO WORLDS

IN a great stone building among the tree-covered hills in the south of France there lived a little boy who at birth received fourteen names and titles. He belonged to the noble French family of the Lafayettes, who had been knights for at least seven hundred years. The boy never saw his father, for shortly before the child was born, his brave young soldier father was killed in a battle with the English. The home in which this fatherless boy lived was a castle, but it looked like a great prison or a modern storage warehouse with a huge, round tower at each end. Across its few small windows were iron bars.

Out of all the Lafayette boy's names, the family called him Gilbert. When he was eleven years old Gilbert was sent to a school in Paris where sons from French gentlemen's families were taught the things it was thought proper for young nobles to know. First of all, they studied heraldry, which explained the coats-of-arms of their royal and noble relations and was really a sort of family history of France.{202} The boys also learned to ride and to fence and to talk politely—even wittily, if they happened to be bright enough. Besides their own French language they learned Latin so that they could write and even speak it. Then the youths who had a taste for history were instructed in that study, not the history of the whole French people, but the records of the royal and great families, and the battles and schemes of the kings and princes.

In this boys' college the rooms were very small, dark, and narrow, like prison cells, and the pupils were locked in at night. Gilbert was never allowed a holiday. If his mother came to see him she was permitted to talk with him in the presence of a tutor, almost as if he were a prisoner. The masters feared that a good, motherly chat with her son would distract the boy's mind from his studies.

Madame de Lafayette wished to do all she could to help her son in his future life. So she moved to Paris and was presented at court; that is, she was introduced to the king and queen and the highest nobles of France. When Gilbert was thirteen his mother died, leaving her son almost alone in the world. He had a rich uncle who might have been his guardian, but he also died, leaving young Lafayette another fortune and making him a very wealthy marquis.

Boys and girls in French noble families were often betrothed in infancy and brought up expecting to marry each other when old enough. Marriage seemed to be rather a question of the family fortunes than of the young people's real love for each other. When young Marquis de Lafayette was left without parents to plan a proper marriage for him, a rich duke who was a great favorite with King Louis decided to arrange for the orphan boy to marry his own daughter Adrienne. In order to bring this about, Adrienne{203}'s parents invited Gilbert de Lafayette to come and live in their palace, where they all could care for him as a son until it was proper for him to marry their daughter. There was a wonderful wedding when Lafayette was sixteen and Adrienne fourteen years old.

From that time, besides all the wealth of the Lafayettes, the riches of his father-in-law, the duke, gave the young marquis a splendid position at the court of France. If the boy bridegroom only had enjoyed that sort of high life he might have been very happy.

But the things which interested the young nobleman were of quite a different sort. While he was at a dinner, in honor of a younger brother of George the Third, king of England, he heard that the American people had started their fight for independence. Lafayette's sympathies for the unhappy people across the sea were so aroused that he began at once to plan to leave his palace home, his lovely young wife, and his baby daughter, in order to help the American people in their struggle. To find out how best to do this, he went to see Dr. Franklin and Silas Deane, the agents for the United States in France. Knowing how much the American people needed Lafayette's money and influence, these statesmen encouraged him in every way.

The young marquis fitted out a ship and made ready to start, taking with him several Frenchmen of high rank who also expected to be made officers in the American Army. But Lafayette's father-in-law did not relish the youth's idea of fighting for the common people against kings and nobles, so he persuaded the king to order the marquis not to leave the country. In spite of King Louis's command, Lafayette walked on board his own ship, under the detectives' noses, disguised as the bodyservant of a stranger{204} from another country who also was going to fight for American liberty.

The Marquis de Lafayette reached the American army, near Philadelphia, after many dangers and hardships. General Washington could not help smiling at the earnestness of "Major-General" Lafayette, aged nineteen, who could command only as much of the English language as he had learned while crossing the Atlantic. Though "the Marquis," as everyone learned to call him, volunteered to serve anywhere without pay, Washington offered him a place on his staff. Once when the commander-in-chief asked Lafayette how to improve the discipline of the American troops, the noble youth replied, "I am here, General, to learn, not to teach."

General Lafayette wounded at the Battle of Brandywine.
General Lafayette wounded at the Battle of Brandywine.
{205}
General Lafayette received his first wound in the Battle of Brandywine, where he fought hard to keep the British back from Philadelphia. While riding his horse at the head of his men he was shot in the leg. He recovered from this wound in time to come to Valley Forge and suffer with Washington the hardships of the long, bitter winter there.

While at Valley Forge the young general was sent to keep the British from coming out from Philadelphia and attacking the American camp. Lafayette took his station at Barren Hill near the Schuylkill River. When the British commander had word of this he sent out three companies to surround the boy general from three directions, and make him their prisoner. So sure were they of making this capture that they planned a dinner in honor of their noble French prisoner, and invited their friends in Philadelphia to be present and meet the Marquis de Lafayette.

But the boy general was too shrewd for them all. Quick as a flash he saw a way out of the trap they had set for him. Ordering the heads of his columns to stand in the edge of a grove where they could be seen as if in battle array, he ordered a retreat by a secret path. When the three British lines marched up the hill, even the Americans in the edge of the woods had disappeared, and the companies only met one another and looked sheepish as they marched down again. Their game had gotten away, and they had to eat that dinner without their prisoner-guest.

Howe and his men soon heard that the French were sending ships and men to help their American friends, so they went away from Philadelphia as quickly as possible.{206}

On the way to New York, Washington met them and gave battle at Monmouth, New Jersey. He appointed General Lafayette second in command; but General Charles Lee was offended because "that French boy" was placed above him. To relieve his chief, Lafayette gave up the command. This was the battle in which Lee disobeyed Washington's command and prevented the American army from winning a real victory. It was Lafayette who saw that something was going wrong and helped to save the day for the Americans.

Hearing of his wife's illness and his little daughter's death, Lafayette asked leave of absence to go home to France. He returned to America as soon as he could, after persuading the French government to send more money, more men, and more ships to help bring the long war with England to an end. Soon after his return, "the Marquis" was sent with his regiment to meet Cornwallis and defend Virginia.

Cornwallis laughed when he saw that "the Boy" had been sent against him. But "the Boy" was more than a match for the British commander in the south. He kept retreating and advancing up and down the James River. One day Cornwallis would think he was trapping Lafayette, but the next day he found himself only moving farther from his base of supplies. "The Boy" did this just to gain time, for he had learned that the expected fleet was in American waters with a French army on board, and that Washington was on his way down from near New York to meet the French ships and men and surround Cornwallis. It was now the British general's turn to retreat. He retired to Yorktown, where he was surrounded by the Americans and French and was soon forced to surrender.{207}

As soon as the fighting was ended, General Washington gave a dinner to the French officers and their English prisoner, Lord Cornwallis. The defeated general was so well treated by Washington and his men that the two commanders became good friends.

When the Americans had gained their independence, General Lafayette returned to France, where he was received as a hero, even by the king whose command he had disobeyed by running away to help America. The people were so fond of the brave young marquis, that King Louis appointed him a marshal of France, though he was only twenty-four.

The French Revolution soon broke out, but it was very different from the American Revolution, because the people of France had the wrong idea of liberty. They killed the king, the queen, and many of the nobles in a savage and cruel way. They even imprisoned and put to death some of their early leaders, who loved liberty, but who were not willing to do such savage deeds to obtain it. Lafayette was one of the lovers of liberty who suffered much from the French people during the Revolution, because he did not believe in going to extremes.

Washington and Lafayette did not forget each other. They wrote devoted letters to each other as if they were father and son. The French nobleman named his son for Washington, who, during the troublous years in France, received and cared for the boy as if he were a grandson.

Nearly fifty years after Lafayette's first coming to America, he made his fourth voyage to our country, bringing with him his son, George Washington de Lafayette. He came, at the invitation of President Monroe and Congress, as the guest of the United States. Because of the{208} enthusiasm with which he was welcomed all over the country, his visit was remembered as one of the brightest times in the history of the United States.

One hundred and forty years after the Marquis de Lafayette's first coming to help America, four millions of American young men were enrolled to rescue republican France from her brutal enemy. A million soldiers had crossed the ocean, and another million were on their way when a company of Americans visited the last resting-place of

Lafayette. As they laid a wreath upon the tomb of the "Friend of America," General Pershing, the commander of the American forces, exclaimed, "Lafayette, we are here!"
THE IMMORTAL REPLY OF JOHN PAUL JONES

OF the millions of boys who have had "sea fever," perhaps none suffered with it more than John Paul, a bright, sandy-haired Scotch lad. His father was a gardener on the estate of a noble lord. John went to school but little, yet he studied hard while he was there. He had learned to sail a boat quite well when he had a chance, at twelve years old, to go to America as a cabin boy. When the owner of the ship soon after failed in business, John Paul entered the Royal Navy as a midshipman. He learned all he could in the short time he was a "middy," but, as his father was poor, he saw no chance to get ahead there.

He left the navy and found work on a merchant ship running between Scotland and the West Indies. Coming back from a voyage to Jamaica, the ship's captain and mate both died, and John Paul, though still a mere boy, sailed{209} the ship home. So he became a captain before he was twenty. In those days, shipmasters treated their men roughly, and once young Captain Paul had to flog the ship's carpenter. The man died some time afterward of fever, and, to spite the young shipmaster, he claimed that he had been fatally injured by John Paul's cruelty. After that, on another voyage, the sailors mutinied or turned against their captain, and tried to kill him. In self-defense the young master knocked the leader down stairs and he died of the fall.

The next time John Paul was heard from, he was living in America with a wealthy man named Jones. It was just at the beginning of the War for Independence, and the young Scotchman was so in love with liberty and the new country that he decided to become an American. In doing this he took the name of his new-found friend Jones. Instead of John Paul, the British subject, he now called himself Paul Jones, American. He went to the Congress in Independence Hall, Philadelphia, in May, 1775, to offer his services. He was promptly given command of several ships to defend the colonies against Great Britain. The next year the Declaration of Independence was signed. On the 14th of June, 1777, the Congress appointed him to the command of the American ship-of-war, Ranger. On the same day the Congress adopted a flag and made this record:

"Resolved, That the flag of the thirteen United States be thirteen stripes, alternate red and white, and that the union be thirteen stars, white in a blue field, representing a new constellation."

Captain Paul Jones had a silk flag made at once and raised it on the Ranger, on the first birthday of the United States, July 4th, 1777. The first voyage of this ship was to France, and the young United States captain announced to{210} the French admiral, in the harbor he was about to enter, that he would expect the French fleet to salute the new American flag. After some delay, the French officer consented and the Ranger sailed into port between two rows of French ships-of-war, which had French flags flying, and French sailors and soldiers manning the yardarms, and cannon booming all along the line, in honor of the Stars and Stripes. That was a great day for the United States, for this was the first time a foreign kingdom recognized the new republic of America.

France not only treated the United States as an equal, but she went to war with England and helped the Americans win their independence. Captain Jones was a little, peppery man, and had been an American only two years, but he was trying to make up for lost time. He believed so much in the people's right to be free, that he considered being an American citizen the highest honor in the world. He begged the high French officials and Doctor Franklin, who represented the United States in France, to let him take the Ranger out and fight England all by himself. The British had taken American prisoners and treated them as spies and traitors, instead of as prisoners of war. Captain Jones wished to capture some British prisoners and teach the enemy how prisoners of war should be treated.

When the Americans in Paris and the French tried to convince the brave little captain that it would be dangerous for him to go out with but one ship, he replied that he liked nothing better than "going into harm's way," and he finally went. He waited outside an English port till the warship Drake came out. The British commander stared at the new flag, for he had never seen it before. "What ship is that?" he asked. "It is the American ship Ranger." {211} Some one on the Drake made fun of the new flag, saying it looked like a patchwork quilt. "Very well," retorted Captain Jones, "we will cover your Union Jack with it, then."

The battle between the Ranger and the Drake lasted just one hour and four minutes. When it was over, the Drake had lost her captain and first lieutenant and thirty-eight men, killed and wounded, while the loss on the Ranger was only two killed and six wounded.

When Captain Jones returned to the shores of France he brought with him the Drake as a prize, with a goodly crew of British prisoners to exchange for Americans. As he had promised, the Stars and Stripes were at the Drake's masthead over the British flag. There was no trouble then about saluting the American flag. All France and America went wild over this victory. In fact, nearly every nation under heaven—excepting Great Britain—was greatly pleased with the escapade of brave little Captain Jones.

Of course, Captain Jones had just had enough to make him long to be "going into harm's way" on a larger scale. But France now had her own troubles with England. She needed all the ships and men she could raise to make a navy able to beat the big fleet Great Britain was getting ready for a great naval battle. Still, Captain Jones would not be put off. With Doctor Franklin's help the French found him a poor old ship which they told him to arm and man and go ahead with. Jones did his best, but the foundry did not fill his order for cannon, and he was obliged to take some old guns which were too heavy for the positions he had to give them. It was bad enough to be forced to fight the whole British navy with a poor, slow, rotten old hulk with out-of-date guns, but the men he had to take {212} to do the fighting were worse. Among them were Portuguese and Malays who could not understand orders in either French or English; but, worst of all, there were a hundred or more English prisoners, who would watch their chance to stab or shoot the few Americans in command, and surrender the ship to their own countrymen.

Dr. Benjamin Franklin's "Poor Richard" almanac had been published as a French book, under the title of "Bonhomme Richard," or "Goodman Richard." So Jones, in compliment to his genial friend and helper, named his newly-made-over ship, Bonhomme Richard. Before he got this craft ready, several French commanders and crews wished to join him. These men were not capable commanders, but they had better ships and crews than Captain Jones, the one man best able to use them to advantage.

When Jones started out with the Richard, he was followed by a sort of private fleet, among which were the Alliance and the Pallas. The commanders of the other ships refused to obey orders unless they happened to feel so disposed. Most of the other ships got lost or started off, like pirates, after prizes for themselves, so that when Jones met the leading ships of the British, there were only the Richard, the Alliance, and the Pallas left.

When the three ships came round a high point called Flamborough Head and saw there the British men-of-war, Serapis and Countess of Scarborough, Commander Jones ordered the Pallas to engage the Countess while he, with the Richard, tackled the Serapis.

The commander had one lieutenant, Richard Dale, an American who had escaped in the most mysterious way from an English prison. Without the heroic aid of this officer

Jones might have lost the day—or the night, for the{213} battle did not begin until dark. There were hundreds of people on the shore watching the fight. At the very beginning they saw—and heard—the old cannon on the Richard bursting and killing nearly all the gunners and powder-boys serving them.

Meanwhile the Serapis, which was a brand-new ship with twice the number and weight of guns that Jones had, was raking the Richard fore and aft, and shooting great, ragged holes in her sides. The sea came pouring into the ship and the British prisoners came running up, yelling frantically, "We are sinking!" By sheer force of will and fear of eye, Paul Jones and Richard Dale drove those excited Englishmen back into the hold to work the pumps, as though they would pump the North Sea dry.

Jones sailed his ship close to the Serapis, intending to catch hold of its side with hooks called grappling-irons. This made it possible for the men on both ships to fight hand to hand. The Richard came alongside with such force that a spar which stuck out at the side (called the jib-boom) was driven into the ropes which held the mast nearest the stern of the Serapis (called the mizzenmast). The grip which Captain Jones now had on the Serapis was like that of a Boston bulldog who has an English mastiff by the throat. If one ship went down, the other would have to go too.

"Well done, my brave lads. We have got her now!" shouted Jones; and he ordered the sailing master to haul the Richard's cable over and tie the jib-boom of the Serapis to his own mizzenmast. When the cable caught and became tangled the master uttered an oath.

"Don't swear," said Jones calmly. "In another moment we may be in eternity; but let us do our duty."{214}

The ropes and spars of the two ships were now so tangled that the men in the top of the Richard scrambled across into the rigging of the enemy, like monkeys in two treetops. In spite of all the captain's efforts, the Richard was now on fire in a dozen places. The people on shore cheered, for it looked as if the English were burning the "pirate" ship. The master-at-arms, hearing a report that the captain and Dale had both been killed, started with two others to surrender to the commander of the Serapis, all three shouting, "Quarter!" The commander of the Serapis, hearing the cry, asked Jones if he was ready to give up.

"No," shouted the American commander, "I have not yet begun to fight!"

By this time even the masts of the Richard were burning; but an American sailor saw a chance to do great harm to the enemy. Seizing a hand grenade, or bomb, he crept across the yardarms of both ships and threw it down upon the deck of the Serapis. The bomb fell and burst on a train of gunpowder scattered by broken cartridges. The flame blazed along past several of the big guns, ending in a terrific explosion.

This turned the tide of the battle. The Americans swarmed on board the Serapis and took possession of it. The English commander surrendered by pulling down the flag of his ship. In giving up his sword to Jones he said, with a sneer,

"It is painful to me that I must resign to a man with a halter around his neck."

The American captain seemed not to notice the intended insult. Every American boy and girl has a right to be proud of Paul Jones for his noble reply:

"Sir, you have fought like a hero."{215}

John Paul Jones commanding the "Bon Homme Richard" in the battle with the "Serapis."

89

John Paul Jones commanding the "Bon Homme Richard" in the battle with the "Serapis."

{216}

The Pallas had captured the Countess of Scarborough after an hour's fighting. The Bonhomme Richard, when cut loose from the Serapis, sank to the bottom of the sea. Before the rest of the enemy's fleet could stop them, Jones and the commander of the Pallas sailed away with the Serapis and the Countess to a safe neutral port in Holland. The British now offered a reward of more than fifty thousand dollars for Captain Paul Jones, dead or alive. The people of Holland begged him not to fly the American flag, as there were two British fleets waiting outside that Dutch harbor to capture him. But Paul Jones insisted on flying the Stars and Stripes, not only in that port, but when he came out and ran the gauntlet of more than forty British men-of-war. He passed them all with colors flying, and reached a French port in safety.

Captain Paul Jones was one of the heroes of the world. The French made him a knight and King Louis presented him with a magnificent gold-handled sword. The United States Congress voted him a gold medal in honor of his greatest victory and passed a resolution commending "his zeal, prudence and intrepidity," assigned him to the command of a new ship of the line then being built, and proposed to create for him the rank of real admiral, until then unknown in the American navy. General Washington wrote him a letter of congratulation in which he said: "You have won the admiration of the world."

Thus the son of a poor gardener became our greatest naval hero in the War of the Revolution. But above all the honors he received at home and abroad, this was Paul Jones's proudest boast: "I have ever looked out for the honor of the American flag." {217}

GENERAL MARION, THE CAROLINA "SWAMP FOX"

A HUNDRED years ago, when boys had but few books of any kind, "The Life of General Marion" was their favorite book of adventure, because of its short stories of rare bravery and hairbreadth escapes. General Francis Marion, of whom the book tells, was a southern man, born the same year as General Washington, and a commander of some of the American troops in the War for Independence.

During that war, when the British found that they could accomplish little in the northern states, they decided to carry the war into the south. Lord Cornwallis was the British commander; under him Colonel Tarleton was a cavalry officer notorious for bullying and cruelty who became a terror to the whole region. Another commander of British troops in the south was a former American general, Benedict Arnold, the traitor, who joined the British after he had failed to deliver West Point into the hands of the enemy.

General Horatio Gates was sent by the Congress to defend the south against the British. But General Gates was not a great or brave commander. He was defeated by Cornwallis at Camden, South Carolina. He lost two thousand men, and the rest of his soldiers were scattered. Because of this terrible defeat—the worst in the whole War for Independence—the southern people were deeply discouraged.

What was to be done? In the south there were many Tories, as the people were called who believed that those who fought against England for liberty were rebels. Besides fighting in the British campaigns, the southern Tories went about in bands, shooting and injuring all the "rebels" they {218}

90

General Marion, the Carolina "swamp fox."
General Marion, the Carolina "swamp fox."
{219}
could. So the southern patriots gathered together in small companies to defend their families from the British and the Tories, and to prevent the British from capturing the whole southern country before Washington could send down a better general and another army.

During the months after the defeat at Camden, the fight was carried on in what was called guerrilla warfare—guerrilla being Spanish for "little war." Small bands of Americans hid in the woods and swamps, and when they caught the British off guard, suddenly pounced upon them, taking or rescuing prisoners. The greatest leader of this kind of warfare on the American side was General Marion.

These southern soldiers had very poor weapons. Most of their guns were the kind used in shooting birds, and were loaded with shot instead of bullets. For swords they had wooden-handled saws with the teeth ground down to a smooth edge. They had but little to eat—often only potatoes, which they could bake in the ashes of their campfires.

Their horses, however, were the finest and fastest in all that country. Although these men had to deny themselves food and clothing, their horses were well fed and groomed, for often the masters' lives depended on the fleetness of their steeds. And the horses sometimes acted as if they understood and enjoyed the terrible game of life and death their masters were playing.

Some of the bravest men in the south, seeing no other way to save or to serve their country, came and offered themselves to General Marion, to fight under the greatest hardships and risks in the most dangerous adventures. Among these was the famous Sergeant Jasper, who was one of the first to risk his life for the flag. Nine British ships-of-war{220} attacked a fort in Charleston Harbor. They shot away the staff on which the American flag was flying; but Jasper jumped out, caught the banner before it touched the ground, and climbed up and nailed it in place, while the guns were aimed at him as well as at the starry ensign.

While Sergeant Jasper was under General Marion he was often sent out on scout and spy duty. He had a natural talent for disguising himself. He went once to visit a sergeant in a British regiment. While he was there a number of American prisoners were brought in. Taking it for granted that a guard of ten British soldiers, with these prisoners, would pass a certain spring, Jasper left the British camp to obtain help. He found only one American who could go with him. The two hid themselves near the spring, surprised the ten redcoats, disarmed them, and, with the former prisoners, marched gaily back to Marion's headquarters with the ten captured British soldiers.

Once when General Marion came to a river ferry, he heard that a company of ninety British regulars were taking more than two hundred captured Americans to the prison-ship at Charleston. The prisoners already in the hold of the ship were starved and neglected. Besides, smallpox had broken out among them, and many of the best men among the patriots were dying of that loathsome disease. So General Marion ordered his men to ride through the darkness to the ford where the British and their prisoners had crossed the river a few hours before. Here they learned that the redcoats and their charges were going to stay that night at a country tavern called the Blue House. The Americans approached this place with great caution. When they came to a wooden bridge, they took horse-blankets{221} and laid them down on the bridge to deaden the sound of the horses' hoofs.

Before deciding how to make an attack, General Marion sent several scouts to find out the lay of the land. With tread as sure and silent as that of moccasined Indians, the scouts returned and whispered this report:

"The officers are carousing in the house. Some of the men are outside. Many of them must be asleep, as we could not get a glimpse of them. A few sentinels are lounging about, without a thought of being attacked."

Marion told his men to lie down under the trees for a little rest. Very early in the morning, when all the British, including the sentinels, seemed to be asleep, he roused the men and ordered the attack.

The odds were over three to one against them, but Marion's men were used to that. They were taking a great risk, but there was much to be gained—guns, equipment and British prisoners who could be exchanged so as to release Americans from the prison-ship. Best of all, each man of the thirty might be the means of setting ten other Americans free.

When the men were well awake, General Marion sent a lieutenant ahead, directing him as follows:

"Take a few men with you, make a wide circle, and come in behind the house. Get as close to them as you can, and wait till I give the signal. Then close in on them and see that no one gets away. We must make quick work of this. See that your guns are all right."

To the men waiting with him he said: "Are you ready?"

"Ready, sir," they whispered back.

"Come on, then," he commanded. "Follow me. Don{222}'t make any noise. Don't speak. Watch me. Don't fire till I say the word."

They crept around the Blue House like Indians, testing every twig lest it snap, and feeling their way in the darkness. Suddenly a shot rang out in the early morning air. A sentinel on the other side of the house must have seen the lieutenant's men. The British soldiers, roused from a sound sleep, jumped about, peering this way and that in the darkness. No one knew what had happened, or what would happen next.

The officers came tumbling out, swearing and yelling. As the Americans came rushing in from all sides, shouting and shooting, the British thought they were attacked by an army instead of by thirty guerrillas. Marion's men grabbed the rifles of the British soldiers, shooting some and knocking others down. Some of the British shouted, "Quarter!" and General Marion ordered his men to stop firing.

There was a wholesale surrender, and the hundreds of American prisoners were set free. Many of them joined Marion's men. When the British saw how they and their prisoners had been taken in, ten to one, they looked sheepish.

But the British leader, the bullying Colonel Tarleton, had made his escape. His motto seemed to be—

"He who fights and runs away
Will live to fight another day."

He ran away, at least, though he did not do any fighting first.

Five months after the battle of Camden, there was another battle at Cowpens. The British army, commanded by Tarleton, was only a little larger than the American.{223} The redcoats were so badly beaten that they lost over nine hundred men, while the American loss was only seventy-two.

One day, not long after, Tarleton was bullying a southern woman in her home, where he and some of his officers were quartered. There was, on the American side, a Colonel Washington, a distant relative of the commander-in-chief. In his insulting way, Tarleton asked, when the lady said this officer was a relative of hers:

"What does Colonel Washington look like? I have never had the pleasure of meeting him."

"You might have seen him," said the lady, sweetly, "if you had looked behind you at the Battle of Cowpens!"

This polite way of calling him a coward made Tarleton very angry, but he was no match in wit for a brave and brilliant southern woman.

Though many of the wealthiest people of the south were Tories, some of them were true patriots. A widow named Motte had just built a beautiful home on a hilltop, and had furnished it elegantly, when the British decided that it would make a fine fort, and promptly took possession of it. General Marion and his guerrilla band surrounded the mansion and told Mrs. Motte, who was then staying in a neighbor's house, that if he could set her house afire he could "smoke out" the British and capture them. That woman patriot was glad to sacrifice her lovely home for the good of her country; so Marion burned down the mansion and made the redcoats his prisoners.{224}

WINNERS OF THE WEST

WOLFE AND MONTCALM, THE RIVAL HEROES OF QUEBEC

MORE than one hundred years after Champlain returned from France to his beloved Quebec, France and Great Britain were at war. In America this struggle was called the French and Indian War, because the English colonists had to fight against the French and their Indian allies, who came down from Canada to keep the English out of the country along the Ohio River. In Europe this strife, in which several other nations took part, was known as the Seven Years' War.

During this war young George Washington was first heard of. He was sent into the western wilderness in the dead of winter to carry a message from the English governor of Virginia to the French commander at a fort in western Pennsylvania. A few years later, General Braddock came over with an army of British regulars to fight the French and their allies in the region where the young messenger had been. Major George Washington was on the English general's staff, and saved many of the British regulars after Braddock fell, defeated, near Fort Duquesne, where Pittsburgh now stands.

The British attacked the French also at Louisburg, in Nova Scotia, and at Ticonderoga, near the southern end of Lake Champlain; but the most important point to attack was Quebec, "the Gibraltar of America," which Champlain{225} had built nearly one hundred and fifty years before. The general then in military command at Quebec was the Marquis de Montcalm, a true Frenchman, devoted to his king, and to his mother, wife, and children, from all of whom he was separated because of his warm love of country.

The Marquis de Montcalm, the brave defender of Quebec.

The Marquis de Montcalm, the brave defender of Quebec.

In his frequent letters to his mother and his wife, Montcalm told all his troubles with the governor of Canada and the Canadian volunteers. He had brought from France to Quebec an army of regular soldiers. They looked with scorn upon the French Canadian raw recruits, who seemed about as rude as their Indian neighbors. The Canadian governor, on his side, saw with jealous eyes the French marquis who had come from Old France to command the Canadian companies along with his own French troops. It needed rare tact and true love of country for Montcalm to keep friendly with the

Canadian governor, who pretended to be {226} the friend of the marquis while secretly turning everybody he could against him.

When the general won a great victory at Oswego, hundreds of miles away, the governor, who was not there, wrote to his friends and the men over him in France about "my" victory and what "I" planned and "I" did with such great success. But though Montcalm wrote about his trials and troubles to his wife and mother, he managed to keep on good terms with the governor and to prevent an outbreak between the French regulars and the Canadian soldiers and Indian warriors.

General Montcalm knew that the British would attack the French stronghold of Quebec. To keep this fortress at the narrow point in the St. Lawrence River might mean the saving not only of all Canada, but also of the French forts and territory along the Wabash and Mississippi rivers, more than a thousand miles away to the southwest.

The fortress at Quebec seemed impossible to take, for it was on top of a high, steep cliff looking over the St. Lawrence. The lower part of the town lay along the level of the river far below, but the town would be of no use whatever to an enemy that could not take the fort, frowning directly overhead. It seemed that the only way the fort might be reached by an enemy was by way of the St. Charles River, just below the town. Troops might be taken up this river, and reach Quebec by going a long distance around back of the city. Montcalm had logs chained together, making a "boom," and threw that across the St. Charles where it flows into the St. Lawrence. Then no ship or large boat could enter there and land soldiers behind the fort.

Not only was the St. Lawrence River narrow at Quebec, but there were many rocks in the swift channel below, so {227} that no ship without a skilled pilot could pass up to the town. Montcalm, however, wishing to make Quebec doubly safe, posted most of his army below the town, to prevent the approach of the enemy.

Meanwhile William Pitt, the British prime minister, decided, as Montcalm had foreseen, that Quebec must be taken. Pitt made up his mind also that a young British officer named Wolfe was the right man to place in command of the British army, to capture the Canadian fortress. Wolfe's father had been a general, and from the age of sixteen the son had been a soldier. As a colonel under General Amherst at Louisburg, James Wolfe had shown himself so fearless as to be even rash, and so devoted to his duty that he seemed not to care for his own life. He was so daring and reckless that some one tried to warn the king of England by saying, "That young Wolfe is mad."

"Mad, is he?" snapped King George. "Then I only hope he will bite some others of my generals!"

Colonel Wolfe was as keen and wise as he was brave; so the king appointed him general and commanded him to capture Quebec.

James Wolfe was as devoted to his mother as Montcalm was to his—even more so, for Wolfe had neither wife nor child to divide his affection. He wrote home often about his army life, his hopes, and his aims. With all his successes and honors, General Wolfe was a very modest young man.

He sailed up the St. Lawrence with a small army—only nine thousand men. Of these he wrote to William Pitt:

"Our troops are good, and if valor can make amends for the want of numbers, we shall probably succeed."

To the astonishment of Montcalm and the French army and people, the British ships sailed up to the Isle of Orleans {228} opposite Quebec as if there were no dangerous rocks in the rapid river there. Wolfe had taken some Canadian pilots on board farther down the St. Lawrence, and had threatened to hang them if one of the ships ran upon a rock.

Still, Montcalm told the people that there could be no danger. The hated English had only run into a trap. They could go neither upstream nor down, and when winter came their ships would be frozen in the ice and become an easy prey. So the French general refused to risk an attack. He decided to play a waiting game and let time and nature fight for France. On the day when Wolfe's fleet arrived, a violent storm came up, and several British ships and floats were dashed on the rocks and badly damaged. After that, Montcalm sent out burning ships to set fire to the English fleet and destroy it. But Wolfe's men bravely towed the French fire-ships out of the way, and the only men lost were the Canadian captain in charge of the fire-ships and six of his sailors, who were burned to death.

Next Wolfe tried to enter the country on the Quebec side of the river, near the Falls of Montmorency, where the water falls two hundred and fifty feet over high cliffs. These falls are so beautiful that some of the English risked being shot by the Canadians in order to see them. The region between the Falls of Montmorency and Quebec was so well guarded by French and Canadians that Montcalm was sure the English could never get behind Quebec. He sent word to the British general: "You will, no doubt, demolish the town, but you shall never get inside of it." Wolfe answered back: "I will have Quebec if I stay here till the end of November." But every English attack failed, and even the brave young commander became discouraged.{229} He had never known good health, and he was now quite ill.

When he was urged to attack the English general and capture or drive him back, Montcalm said with a smile, "Let him amuse himself where he is. If we drive him off he may go to some place where he can do us harm."

But the French made another attempt to set fire to the British fleet with seventy rafts, small boats, and schooners. Again they failed, and the French themselves explained that this was due only to the courage of the English sailors, who swarmed out in little boats to fight the fire before it could do any harm to their fleet.

In August General Wolfe was ill in bed, and it was reported in the British army that he was not likely to live long. But even while he was so ill, the young commander's one thought was the capture of Quebec. On the last day of August he said to his physician that he now had a plan to carry out if he could only live to lead his army in person. "I know too well that you cannot cure me," he continued, "but pray make me so that I may be without pain for a few days, and able to do my duty. That is all I want."

In his letter to his mother that day he wrote:

"The enemy puts nothing to risk, and I can't in conscience put the whole army to risk. He has wisely shut himself up so that I can't get at him without spilling a torrent of blood, and that perhaps to little or no purpose. The Marquis de Montcalm is at the head of a great number of bad soldiers, and I am at the head of a small number of good ones that wish for nothing so much as to fight him, but the wary old fellow avoids an action."

Early in September Wolfe seemed himself again, though he realized that he had only a few days to live. The French saw the British fleet pass their fort on the way up the river{230} at night, although the cannon of the fort belched lightnings and bellowed thunder at them. Montcalm wondered what the English were going to try to do, after all. "They mean to land somewhere," he said.

Wolfe did "mean to land somewhere," and that somewhere was the very place Montcalm did not dream of, a steep cliff back of the town. When any one spoke of the danger of the capture of Quebec, the French general would shrug and smile and say, "But the English cannot fly!"

One night when it was very dark, sixteen hundred British soldiers came floating down the river in their ships' boats till they came opposite the town. Wolfe was with them in person, as he had hoped and prayed to be. As they were slowly floating, the young commander repeated the familiar lines by Gray,

"The boast of heraldry, the pomp of power,
And all that beauty, all that wealth e'er gave,
Await alike the inevitable hour—
The paths of glory lead but to the grave."

"I would rather have written those lines," he said with deep feeling, "than take Quebec to-morrow!"

As their boats stole in to the shore, a sentinel called out in French, "Who goes there?"

"France," answered a voice in French.

"What regiment?"

"The Queen's," again in good French, by a Scotchman who had seen service in France.

A little later another sentryman challenged them.

"What is that?"

The Scotchman whispered, "Provision boats. Sh! the English will hear us!"

In this way they reached a point at the foot of the steep{231} cliff. Twenty-four men started to climb up where it seemed impossible. As they kept on, others started up after them. Then came others, General Wolfe among the number. In a short time quite a large company, in red coats and Scotch kilts, had reached the top and dragged several small cannon after them. The French felt so safe from attack that the small guard on the Plains of Abraham, as the level top was called, was taken by surprise and easily overcome.

The death of General Wolfe on the Plains of Abraham.

From the painting by Alonzo Chappel
The death of General Wolfe on the Plains of Abraham.
From the painting by Alonzo Chappel

An alarm spread. A Frenchman on horseback came dashing over to Montcalm's headquarters, gasping: "The English—on the Plains of Abraham!"

There was a great fight on top of that cliff. Wolfe was{232} seen here—there—everywhere! But before the British drove the French back, the young general had fallen—shot three times.

"Shall I go for a surgeon?" asked an Englishman.

"There's no need," Wolfe whispered. "It's all over with me."

A little later a man shouted, "See how they run!"

"Who run?" repeated Wolfe, opening his eyes.

"The enemy, sir. They are giving way everywhere!"

Wolfe roused up long enough to send a brief order to the next in command, telling him just how to go ahead and capture the fort. Then he lay down wearily, smiling as he closed his eyes. "Now God be praised, I shall die in peace," he said.

The French hero of Quebec also was shot through the body in that last short fight. "How long have I to live?" he asked.

"Not more than twelve hours," said the surgeon in charge.

"So much the better," said the dying Montcalm. "I am happy that I shall not live to see the surrender of Quebec."

DANIEL BOONE, THE GREAT INDIAN FIGHTER OF KENTUCKY

OF all the great American hunters, trappers, and Indian fighters, Daniel Boone was the leader. He was born in Pennsylvania, but while still a boy he moved with his parents to North Carolina. Besides learning to do farm work and help his father at the loom and the forge, the{233}

{234}

Daniel Boone, the great Indian fighter of Kentucky.

{234}From the painting by Chappel

Daniel Boone, the great Indian fighter of Kentucky.

From the painting by Chappel

Boone boy found time for trapping, hunting, and learning the arts of a woodsman. Father Boone, though of Quaker descent, encouraged this son to go hunting and to learn the woodcraft of the Indians. When the lad was twelve his heart was delighted by the gift of a light rifle from his sensible father.

Of course, Daniel did not have much chance to go to school, but he acquired mathematics enough to fit him for the business of backwoods life and to make him a fair land surveyor. But he never had the gift of spelling. For many years a giant beech-tree was pointed out where he had had a bear-fight; it was a kind of monument to Daniel's poor spelling. In the bark, high on its trunk, he had cut these crooked letters: "D. Boon cilled a bar on this tree in the year 1760." Yet, although he did not spell even his own name correctly, Daniel Boone was the best educated of all the pioneers, for he had just the kind of knowledge that his country needed most at that time.

When Daniel was twenty-one a call came to North Carolina for men to help the soldiers of General Braddock, who had been sent by the king of England to fight the French and Indians. The English wished to keep control of the country north and south of the Ohio River. Young Boone volunteered and was in the battle of Fort Duquesne, when Braddock was defeated and killed, and when young Major George Washington led the colonial troops, who fought Indian fashion and saved a small part of Braddock's army from being killed and scalped. This fight proved a turning point in the life of the North Carolina soldier, for he met in the ranks a scout named John Finley, who had been on a hunting trip in the wild country south of the Ohio. Finley drew a picture of this wild region that warmed{235} the heart of Daniel Boone. One of the chief beauties there for the born hunter was that the Indians did not inhabit the country. They only went back and forth across it, so that they did not kill or scare away the game.

Daniel went home to North Carolina and married a beautiful girl of seventeen, and they kept house in a cabin the young husband had built with his own hands. He lived there several years with his wife and little boy, near his father's family. But he was restless, going on hunting trips farther and farther from home, until he had followed the game over the mountains into the region of the Tennessee River.

The friend of the French and Indian War, John Finley, came to visit the Boones one fall, and they made him stay all that winter. "The call of the wild" was too strong to let Boone stay at home long after that. In the spring he and Finley, with four other men, on

97

six horses, with bedding and a small cooking outfit on six packhorses, started off, early one bright morning, on their wonderful shooting and trapping trip. They were armed with hunting-knives, tomahawks and their trusty rifles.

When they had crossed the mountains they hunted the bear, buffalo, elk, and deer, and trapped little fur animals with such success that they soon had quite a fortune in furs. As they prepared to start east with these, a band of Indians appeared on the scene, broke up their little camp, and captured everything they had. The savages spared the white men's lives; but they made signs that they would kill them all if they found them there again, and they took Boone and another man prisoners. The rest of the party, badly frightened, took up their weary march for home, empty-handed. Boone, and his companion, when they{236} escaped, only went far enough to make the Indians think they also were afraid; then they came back and hunted alone in all that wild region.

After long, lonely months, Boone's brother came and brought gunpowder and supplies, and the Boones hunted and trapped there two years longer. They started home with a rich store of furs, but some Indians came along and robbed them again. The red men afterward killed the brother, but Daniel, after hairbreadth escapes, reached North Carolina, safe and sound, but poorer than when he went away.

Still, Daniel Boone was rich in wood lore and Indian craft. He gave such attractive accounts of the beautiful country and the chances to get rich quickly that quite a number of heroic people were persuaded to go back with him and settle in the land. He started over the mountains again with ten in his own family, besides neighbors and friends. No one could have followed the way but a cunning scout like Daniel Boone, to whom every leaf, every sound, every mark in the earth had its own secret message. During the journey the party were attacked by Indians, and Boone's eldest son, a lad of seventeen, was killed.

This experience discouraged the others and they tried to induce their leader to go back with them. He sturdily refused, saying, "There are nearly a hundred of us. We can beat the Indians yet." Nevertheless, it seemed wiser to wait awhile before pushing on across the mountains; so they went back a little way and settled for a year or two on a little mountain river.

By this time many people in the Carolinas and Virginia had heard about the Promised Land of Daniel Boone. He was engaged to mark the way or "blaze the trail"{237} through to Kentucky. This trail was afterwards traveled so much that it was called the Wilderness Road. Taking thirty men with him, Boone once more set out on the way to settle Kentucky. They came to a halt in the heart of that country, and built a stockade on the Kentucky River. This enclosure, a little longer than a square, with a fort at each of the four corners and eight smaller cabins in the space inside, was surrounded by a high fence of sharpened logs standing upright. To this strong stockade the rest of the party gave the name of Boonesboro, in honor of the Kentucky pioneer. Later, Boone returned for his family and brought them to their new home.

Many and exciting were the adventures of the settlers. One afternoon two girls went out canoeing on the river with the daughter of Daniel Boone. When the three girls had passed a bend in the river and were too far away for their shrieks to be heard at the fort, a fierce-looking Indian sprang out from the bushes on the farther bank and pulled in their canoe. Other savages stifled the girls' cries and plunged with them into the darkening forest.

Before long the absent ones were missed and the alarm was given. The empty canoe was found, and a search party was formed, led by the fathers of the missing girls. The hunt lasted two days and two nights. On the morning of the third day the anxious fathers saw smoke rising from an Indian camp. As the camp was over fifty miles from

Boonesboro, the savages had become careless. Boone and two other men crept up near the camp and shot the two Indians guarding their three white captives. The other red men jumped and ran for the woods. The happy fathers and their friends returned to their anxious families at Boonesboro with the daughters unhurt. {238}

While Washington and his little armies were waging the War for Independence along the eastern coast, Daniel Boone and his pioneers were fighting just as bravely for their country. Though they did not realize it then, the Backwoods Territory formed by far the greater part of the future United States. Boone was the leader who remained on guard while others did the things which are oftener described in the history of the country. He helped the pioneers with his advice, and defended the families of the men who went out and fought in the historic battles.

One reason why the Indians feared and revered this "White Chief" was that Daniel Boone, as if by magic, had often escaped death at their hands. But once his good fortune seemed to fail him. Near Boonesboro was a salt "lick," or a spring of salt water, where salt was left spread around the spring like frost or a white powder on the ground. Deer, buffalo, and other animals often came there to lick up the salt, and pioneers often hid near by and shot them. Boone and thirty men had come from the fort to gather a supply of salt to have on hand in case they should be attacked by Indians. Boone and his men were surrounded and captured; and, as this was during the War for Independence, they were taken to Detroit to be dealt with by the British Governor Hamilton. On the way through deep snows and zero weather they were all in danger of starving. At a solemn council some of the Indians proposed to get rid of their prisoners by torturing and burning them to death. There were one hundred and twenty of the savages, and the vote stood fifty-nine for the killing to sixty-one against. There was no doubt that the Indians' regard for Daniel Boone saved the lives of all those white men. Though this seemed to have been done{239} by a single vote, it was a strange thing that sixty-one hostile savages were willing to keep alive and feed their prisoners at the risk of starving themselves.

At Detroit, Hamilton offered the Indians five hundred dollars if they would let Daniel Boone go free, as he wanted to use him as a British scout. The savages refused and took him to their chief village in the Ohio country. Boone knew their language, but he pretended not to understand a word they said among themselves. He seemed to be very fond of their mode of life and acted pleased when they told him they were going to make him a chief. He won their good will by not wincing when they tortured him to see if he could prove himself worthy of that great honor.

The white chief was the best marksman in all the tribe. When they let him go off hunting by himself they counted the bullets and measured the gunpowder they gave him. But he cut the bullets in two and used very small charges of powder, thus saving nearly half to use when he should find a chance to escape. Hearing the others talking of an attack they were going to make on Boonesboro, he slipped away one morning while out hunting, when he would not be missed till night. Not daring to shoot game for food, nor wishing to waste time to dress and cook it, he was nearly starved when he reached the Kentucky fort, after going one hundred and sixty miles through a region full of hostile tribes.

The Indians must have wasted many days searching for him, as it was six weeks before his adopted tribe and other savages arrived at Boonesboro. Daniel Boone held the fort for ten days, with fifty white men and boys and twenty-five women and children, against four hundred and fifty red men. Several times the Indians set fire to the fort,{240} but the brave white men put out the fire at great risk to their lives. The Indians tried to tunnel under the log fence, but the cunning white chief met and beat them back at every point. At last the savages gave up the fight and slunk away.

Now that so many settlers had moved to Kentucky, the old hero found that country too crowded to suit him, so he and his family moved to a wilder region on the Missouri River, "to find elbow room," he said. After hundreds of thrilling adventures and narrow escapes, the Indian hunter died in bed, with his wife and three of his children around him. A friend who was near him in his latter days said of Daniel Boone: "Never was old age more green nor gray hairs more graceful."

GEORGE ROGERS CLARK, THE YOUNG HERO WITH A GREAT IDEA

SOON after the beginning of the War for Independence, George Rogers Clark, a tall, broad-shouldered, red-haired, blue-eyed young man of twenty-four, left his home in Virginia and went over the mountains to join the settlers in Kentucky. He had already had some adventures in the wilderness along the Ohio River, hunting wild game and fighting wilder Indians. Not long after Clark's arrival, the pioneers joined together and sent him and another man back to Virginia to see if they could have Kentucky adopted as a county of that state. Virginia had just been declared one of the thirteen United States. Clark and his companion were also to try to get the legislature to grant them money{241} enough to buy gunpowder, which was now the greatest need of the Kentucky settlers in fighting the Indians.

When the two young delegates, in coonskin caps and leather leggings, arrived at the Virginia capital they found to their dismay that the legislators of the new state had just adjourned and gone home. Patrick Henry, the fiery orator who had shouted in that very capitol building, "Give me liberty or give me death!" was now governor of Virginia. The young men from Kentucky went and told him they must not go back without that powder; so Governor Henry got them five hundred pounds, and arranged to make it all right when the State legislature should meet again. Clark succeeded also in having Kentucky made a county of Virginia.

Colonel George Rogers Clark.
Colonel George Rogers Clark.
While the battles of the Revolution were being fought along the Atlantic coast, there was a terrible state of affairs in the great valley of the Ohio. Henry Hamilton, the{242} British governor at Detroit, then in charge of the forts and trading posts on the Wabash and Mississippi rivers, was doing one thing that made the settlers' blood boil wherever they heard of it. He had hired all the Indians he could to fight on the British side by furnishing them with scalping-knives and paying them a bounty, or money prize, on every scalp they brought in to prove that they had killed an American man, woman, or child. The savages went everywhere on the warpath, murdering as many people as they could to earn as much bounty money as possible.

In the midst of this horrible warfare a bright idea came to George Rogers Clark, but he kept it to himself. He sent two men across the Ohio and up the Mississippi and Wabash rivers to see what was going on at the British trading-posts there. The word they brought back made the young man start at once for Virginia—this time alone. He called again on Governor Patrick Henry and on his old neighbor, Thomas Jefferson. Both of those great patriots approved his plan and charged him on no account to let it leak out before he was ready to act, for fear some wily Indian or dishonest Frenchman might give warning and spoil it all.

When George Rogers Clark started again from Virginia he wore the badge of a colonel in the Continental army; and he had the promised support of the state. He went west by way of the Ohio River as far as what is now Louisville. The settlement he started there owes its name to the news which Clark heard from some men who joined him there; that the king and the people of France had pledged money, men, and ships to help the United States in the War for Independence. The new town was named in honor of the French king.{243}

The first thing the young commander had to do was to raise a company of about two hundred men for his secret purpose. All he told his recruits was that they were to go on a mission to put a stop to the terrible outrages of the "British" Indians upon the settlers. It was not until they were again floating down the Ohio River toward the Mississippi that he told them that they were out to capture three towns on the Mississippi and the Wabash, which, as his two friends had found out for him, were not well guarded by the British. Most of the people in these towns were French settlers, but were under British rule. When they had nearly reached the place where the Ohio flows into the Mississippi, they left their boats and marched through tangled forests and across the plains toward Kaskaskia, the nearest of the three towns. They arrived on the Fourth of July, 1778, the second anniversary of American independence. They hid for a whole day in a clump of trees and bushes on the shore of the Mississippi. After nightfall Clark detailed half his men to surround the village, and led the rest to the fort, where he found the French commander of the fort giving a dance by the flaring light of several torches. Some of the women of the settlement and several Indians were present. The young Virginian went right in and stood there smiling—it was so different from what he had expected!—when an Indian spied him and gave an ear-splitting warwhoop.

The dancers stopped as if shot. All stared at the tall young officer with the keen but kindly eyes. After a moment the newcomer raised his voice and said, "Go on with the dancing, but I wish to announce that you are no longer subjects of King George. This fort and this place now belong to the State of Virginia." As he spoke, his {244} men burst in and took the French officers prisoner. Clark added, to the village people,

"You can go to your homes, but you must stay there. All who leave their houses to-night will do so under pain of death. The town is guarded by my men."

The French settlers spent the night in fear, for Clark disarmed the village at once. Some of their chief men came to him next day to beg him to spare their lives. The young commander shook hands with them and told them that they need not be afraid of any one but the British. "King Louis of France," he explained, "is the friend of America. He is going to help us in our fight for liberty."

The French were all glad to hear the good news and lost no time in swearing to be true to the United States government.

In his record, Clark went on:

"The scene was changed from almost dejection to that of joy in the extreme—the bells ringing, the church crowded, returning thanks—in short, every appearance of extravagant joy that could fill a place with almost confusion."

To Colonel George Rogers Clark and his sturdy pioneers this easy campaign so far seemed like a pleasure excursion. They were well received also at Fort Cahokia, on the Mississippi across from St. Louis. Then a French volunteer took a few men to Fort Sackville at Vincennes and placed them on guard there. Thus the three scattered strongholds of the British in the Northwest Territory came to belong to the new State of Virginia.

When Governor Hamilton got word, by Indian runner, of all that had happened, he came down from Detroit to Vincennes on the Wabash with five hundred English and Indians in canoes. He easily retook Fort Sackville, for{245} Clark had not been able to spare more than half a dozen men to hold it.

By that time winter had come on, and the Wabash began to rise and flood its banks. The river overflowed this part of the country so regularly that the region was called "the drowned lands." The flood, of course, made it impossible for Hamilton to march his men to the Mississippi. He announced that he would wait until spring before retaking the other forts. So he sent away his Indian allies and ordered part of his troops back to winter quarters at Detroit.

When the young Kentucky colonel heard of this he saw a chance to spring another surprise. He started out with one hundred and seventy men to travel two hundred and fifty miles through, rather than over, trails almost impossible to pass because of snow, ice, and overflowing streams. The worst part of all the journey was at the last, near Vincennes, where the whole country looked like a large lake. Clark himself led the way, feeling out the path with his feet. He placed the tall, stalwart men among those who were smaller and weaker. Sometimes they had to wade in the icy waters up to their necks. Only the hardiest of the pioneers could endure long hours in such cold water. Some of the men became numb and unconscious. Their robust companions carried them in their arms or held them on floating logs until they came to a dry knoll like an oasis in the desert. There the active men would rub and warm the chilled bodies of the rest. Meantime a meal would be prepared of duck, venison, or other game, which Clark and his more able-bodied men had been able to shoot, dress, and cook in the ways best approved by hungry pioneers. After they had eaten and dried their clothes, they would make up lost sleep. Clark himself was a wonder of endurance,{246} cheerfulness, and tact. He started his men singing the favorite songs of the frontier, like, "Keep Your Powder Dry," and encouraged and animated them by every means in his power.

It took five days to wade the last nine miles. Washington's crossing the Delaware in boats was a short and easy passage compared with this feat of George Rogers Clark. But the humor of the American pioneer, who made a joke of his hardest experiences, saved the day. Clark wrote of the "antic little drummer-boy" who floated across a river on his drum; but he did not tell how a tall soldier took that drummer on his shoulder and led the way through deep waters, while the boy beat a merry march for that shivering, laughing company.

Near Vincennes they met a man out shooting ducks. From him they learned that Hamilton and his garrison did not dream of being attacked. By this man Clark sent in to the people of the settlement this warning:

"To the Inhabitants of Post Vincennes:

"Gentlemen: Being now within two miles of your village with my army, determined to take your fort this night, and not willing to surprise you, I take this method to request such of you as are true citizens and willing to enjoy the liberty I bring you, to remain in your houses; and those, if any there be, that are friends to the king, will instantly repair to the fort, and join the hair-buyer general and fight like men! Those who are true friends of liberty may depend on being well treated; and I once more request them to keep out of the streets, for every one I find in arms on my arrival I shall treat as an enemy.

(Signed) G. R. Clark."

As a result of this notice, the Indians took to the woods and the French villagers shut themselves in their homes. Clark and his men soon rushed into the town and surrounded Fort Sackville. The next day a party of "British" Indians{247} came into town on their ponies, grinning and shaking the scalps they had taken from a number of Kentucky settlers. These Indians on the warpath did not know of the presence of the little American army until some wrathful Kentuckians fell upon and killed every one of them in plain view of Hamilton and his soldiers. The besieged garrison fought desperately for days, but the pioneer sharpshooters with their deadly aim forced them to surrender.

The British never attempted to take the little river fortresses again. And when the treaty of peace was signed between the young United States and old England, that vast Northwest Territory was safe in the hands of the new nation. But for the great thought so heroically carried out by George Rogers Clark and his men, that western empire—now occupied by the states of Michigan, Ohio, Indiana, Illinois, and Wisconsin—would at the end of the war have belonged to England. As Clark said to Governor Patrick Henry when he outlined his plan of capturing the three river forts and holding all that territory for the United States of America: "A country which is not worth defending is not worth claiming."

LEWIS AND CLARK, TWO ADVENTURERS IN THE FAR WEST

WILLIAM LEWIS, a nephew of General Washington's sister Betty, lived near Thomas Jefferson's beautiful estate in Albemarle County, Virginia. Two years before Jefferson wrote the Declaration of Independence, a boy was born into the Lewis family. This baby was given his mother's maiden name, Meriwether.{248}

Twenty-five years after writing the Declaration Jefferson became President of the United States and went to live in the still unfurnished White House in the new city of Washington. Then he chose for his secretary Meriwether Lewis, whom he had seen grow up from boyhood. He was such a remarkable young man that later ex-President Jefferson wrote, in a story of the life of his former secretary:

"When only eight years of age, he often went out in the dead of night alone with his dogs into the forest, to hunt the raccoon and opossum (which, seeking their food in the night, can then only be taken), plunging through the winter's snows and frozen streams in pursuit of his object.

"His talent for seeing things led him to a true knowledge of plants and animals of his own country. At the age of twenty, yielding to the ardor of youth and a passion for more dazzling pursuits, he engaged as a volunteer in a body of militia called out by President Washington. At twenty-three he was promoted to a captaincy and appointed paymaster of his regiment."

In 1803, President Jefferson, acting for the United States, bought of France, through Napoleon, all the country west of the Mississippi, which LaSalle had claimed and named Louisiana. That vast region was sold for fifteen million dollars, which amounted to only two and a half cents an acre. This act is known as the Louisiana Purchase. The new country, called Louisiana Territory, was an unknown region thousands of miles in extent. Traders had gone up the Missouri River a few hundred miles, and voyagers along the Pacific coast had traded with the Indians at the mouth of the Columbia River; but no one knew much about the wide expanse of territory lying between, or of the rise and course of either of those great rivers. So it was decided that some one should undertake the long and dangerous journey among savage tribes and wild beasts,{249}

Lewis and Clark on their expedition into the Far West.

From an old painting

103

Lewis and Clark on their expedition into the Far West.
From an old painting
and find out all about the region. Young Lewis had wished years before to explore
that country and had been kept from going, so now he begged the President to let him
take charge of the great hunt for facts. The President had good reasons for consenting.
He knew that Captain Lewis was brave, firm, and persevering, and that nothing
could{250} turn him from his purpose. He was well acquainted with the character and
customs of the Indians, and was used to the hunting life. He had carefully studied the
plants and animals of his own country. Above all, he was honest, fair-minded, and
truthful, so that whatever he might report would be sure to be true. For these reasons the
President felt no hesitation in trusting Captain Lewis to do so important a task.

With fatherly pride ex-President Jefferson afterward wrote that young Lewis was not
certain that he could do this great work right; so he attended a scientific school to learn
more about plants, animals, minerals, physical geography and astronomy. He wanted all
he should see to be of the highest value to his own country and to the other nations
which claimed the great tracts next to the vast territory he had been appointed to explore.
Besides, he went to a factory where firearms were made, so as to gain the working
knowledge he might need some time to save the lives of his party.

He started down the Ohio by boat from Pittsburgh. At Louisville he picked up his
former neighbor, William Clark, brother of George Rogers Clark. He had been a mighty
hunter and Indian fighter, and had served his country under General Anthony Wayne.
Captain Lewis thought it best that there should be two leaders, in case of any accident to
himself. The two captains were real comrades and generous commanders, keeping the
respect and friendship of their men through the many hardships of their wanderings in
the wilderness.

They started out from St. Louis in May, 1804, with thirty-two experienced hunters,
scouts, and woodsmen, on their great adventure. They had only a barge with sails{251}
and two smaller boats to go up the "Big Muddy," as the Indians called the Missouri River.
With the aid, later, of a few Indian canoes they were to find their way to the far-distant
purple mountains and into the hazy regions of mystery beyond. The President had
charged his two young neighbors: "Keep in peace and good-will with the savages," so the
wise partners and their picked men joined in councils and powwows with the various
Indian tribes all the way up the long river. They had brought with them bright medals
which the chiefs admired. Though the red men could not read the words printed on them,
"Peace and Friendship," they could understand the two clasped hands, one red and the
other white, under the lettering, for that was the way they expressed the same thought in
the Indian sign language. And the big chiefs hung the shining medals around their sturdy
necks, and grasped the white captains' hands in token of their lasting good-will.

The Indians were experts in signs. When a red scout came to invite the white
travelers to join in a council with the chief men of his tribe, he would hold a folded
blanket above his head, and, with a slow flourish, unfold it. Then he bent forward and
spread it on the ground like a carpet, sat on it himself and motioned to the white "chiefs"
to do the same. Then he would tell them, with signs, that his chief had invited them to
come and join in a solemn "peace-smoke talk" at the Indian lodge. The city which stands
on the place of one of these friendly powwows is called Council Bluffs.

Captains Lewis and Clark made careful records of the adventures they had and the
strange things they saw and heard as they journeyed and camped across half the
continent. Their diaries fill three thrilling volumes. During the{252} first summer,
Captain Clark jotted down in his journal: "The mosquitoes were so numerous that I could

not keep them off my gun long enough to take sight, and by that means missed." One morning Captain Lewis, who was away exploring by himself, awoke to find that he had a huge rattlesnake for a bedfellow. Another time they all lay down to sleep on a soft, dry sandbar, in the middle of the river. In the night the men on watch woke them. The strangest thing was happening. Whether they were lying on a quicksand or over an ancient volcano, their sandbar was sinking. It was so uncanny to feel the earth giving way under them that they trembled as they got into the boats—just in time to save their lives!

Of all the dwellers in those western wilds the grizzly bears seemed most to object to the white strangers who prowled about their country. Unlike the Indians, the grizzlies attacked the explorers. The great, angry brutes rushed up and stood on their hind legs, threatening the strangers with wicked eyes and red, wide-open jaws, and striking with their great clumsy paws. Some of the party brought back big bearskins as trophies of their hairbreadth escapes. The buffalo were almost as eager to look at their white visitors as the strangers were curious about them. A few of the awkward beasts would follow the travelers about as if fascinated. One night a blundering buffalo bull came into the camp, sniffing right and left, between the rows of sleepers. The travelers waked up and tried to teach that big bison better manners than to call on strange gentlemen at such unseemly hours.

The captains made several copies of the records of the trip and placed them in charge of different members of the party. One of these was carefully written on a kind of{253} birch-bark paper which they believed would stand the hardest tests of time, dampness, and rough usage. They explored for a little distance up every river flowing into the Missouri and put down on their maps what they found out. They shot deer, antelope, and buffalo, and noted down what they could about all the small animals, and the birds, trees, fruits, flowers, soil, and minerals they found.

It took the explorers nearly six months to examine sixteen hundred miles of the Missouri Valley. They went into winter quarters among the Mandan tribe of Indians, building a stockade like a high picket-fence of logs, with cabins inside, near where Bismarck, North Dakota, now stands, and naming it Fort Mandan.

If they had not had so much to do in exploring and making friends with the redskins, the party might have moaned, like the Indian in "Hiawatha," "O the long and dreary winter!" But Lewis and Clark found plenty for one and all to do. They met the chiefs of the neighboring tribes around their council fires. They told all about the "Great Father" in Washington who loved the red men as his own children, and showed them a portrait of kindly, gray-haired President Jefferson. At these love-feasts the savages rubbed cheeks with the white men. Of course, the greasy red paint rubbed off, and the explorers must have laughed at one another in secret, for they did look funny with their faces all smeared and mottled. But the Indians were so in earnest that they would have been deeply offended if a white man had dared to smile. After a love-feast they had another kind of feast, on buffalo meat, venison, and wild duck. Then they exchanged presents. The white men gave the Indians beads—blue and white were the colors the red men liked best—with knives, guns, pewter mirrors,{254} and trinkets. And the Indians made return presents of ponies, and of Indian corn and other food-stuffs. Then the travelers showed the Indians how white people danced, and the red braves gravely performed their war, peace, scalp, and snake dances for their guests. Big Indians solemnly played a game in which one side passed around a piece of bone while the rest tried to guess where it was, as in the children's game of "Button, button, who's got the button?"

The Mandan tribe told the strangers about the fierce Sioux, the Shoshones, the Blackfeet, and other tribes farther west. As the great river grew shallower and was

105

obstructed by falls and rapids, Lewis and Clark tried to buy Indian ponies for the trip over the mountains. At Fort Mandan they found a French scout whom they engaged as their guide and interpreter for the rest of the way. He had a young Indian wife, Sacajawea, or Bird Woman, who insisted on going with him. She had a funny little papoose, only two months old, that could not be left behind, of course. Absurd as it seemed to take a weak woman with a little baby on such a hard and dangerous journey, the party soon found that they could not have gone much farther without her. She was most useful as an interpreter. In some places, for example, Captain Clark would say in English what he wished to tell a certain chief. One of the other men would repeat this in French. The Indian woman's French husband would translate that into an Indian dialect she spoke. She would then repeat it in another language which an Indian in the strange chief's party understood; and he, in turn, would translate into the dialect of the chief to whom Captain Clark had addressed his original remark. Roundabout as this method was, it was far better than {255} not to be able to talk at all and make friends of the red strangers.

The Bird Woman's greatest service was yet to come. They had finally discovered the source of the Missouri—a cool, clear, crystal brook, very different from the "Big Muddy" a thousand miles below. An Irishman in the party stood astride this narrow streamlet and called out, "Sure, an' I never thought to see the day I could stand a-straddle of the big Missouri River!"

Captain Clark and other men of the party started out in different directions to "forage for facts," and try to find the small beginning of the other river which the Indians said would take them down to the great western sea. One day Lewis met a party of Shoshones and tried to persuade them to go with him and act as guides. He needed help moving the baggage over the mountains which are called "the Great Divide" because they separate the rivers which flow east into the Mississippi River from those which run west to the Pacific Ocean. Though he offered the Shoshones presents and other favors, they still refused to go. Then he appealed to the Indians' curiosity by telling them that if they would come with him he would show them a black man with curly hair, for Captain Clark's negro servant was one of the party; also that there was an Indian woman of their own tribe in the white men's camp. This was more than the chief and several of his braves could resist, so they returned with Lewis. To the surprise and joy of all, the Shoshone chieftain discovered that the Bird Woman was his long-lost sister, who had been carried away by a hostile tribe, many years before. The Bird Woman helped her own tribe to a better understanding of the white men, and persuaded them to furnish horses, canoes, guides, and {256} helpers over the Divide to the headwaters of the Snake River, which empties into the Columbia.

When they were in their canoes, floating down this beautiful stream, they laughed to think how much easier it is to go down than to pull up against the current. But their speed greatly increased the danger. They rushed into rapids and nearly plunged over falls. One canoe ran upon a rock and they had a hard time rescuing from the boiling waters several men who, strange to say, could not swim. Once Lewis and one of the men, while climbing cliffs, slipped over the brink of a lofty precipice and narrowly escaped being dashed to pieces on the rocks far below.

When they were floating down the Columbia they saw their first live salmon, and the Indians cooked some for them. At one place a great rock jutted far out into the channel, leaving it very narrow and swift, so that the water swirled about in dangerous rapids and whirlpools. The cliffs on each side were so high and slippery that the two captains decided to risk "shooting" or steering a canoe through these rapids, though several passing Indians had warned them not to attempt it. Landing the rest of their party

106

and their precious records, Lewis and Clark made the trial trip and shot through without an accident. After this they steered the other boats and men through in perfect safety.

Before long they noticed that the water was a little salt, showing them that tidewater from the Pacific came up there. Farther down they saw three European ships at anchor near the mouth of the river. On the 7th of November, 1805, they reached a point from which they could see the surf heaving and rolling in the west. The happy young captain wrote of this first view:{257}

"The fog cleared off, and we enjoyed the prospect of the ocean—that ocean, the object of all our labors. This cheering view exhilarated the spirits of all the party, who were still more delighted on hearing the distant roar of the breakers and went on with great cheerfulness."

They built seven wooden huts on the shore of the Pacific, calling this winter camp Fort Clatsop. They made friends with the Indians of the Columbia River region, and gathered data for the government and supplies for their return trip. As instructed by President Jefferson, they sent two of their number back around the world on a ship by way of China and the Cape of Good Hope, with copies of records and information they had thus far collected. In March, 1806, Lewis and Clark started back on their journey of more than four thousand miles, reaching St. Louis in six months, after many more thrilling adventures and hairbreadth escapes. They had been gone from St. Louis two years and four months, and during that time had traveled altogether a distance of almost eight thousand five hundred miles. Often the party suffered terrible hardships and were in almost constant danger from wild animals, the winter cold and the lack of supplies and comforts. For fourteen months they were shut off from all communication with the world and their friends were very anxious about their safety.

Lewis and Clark had accomplished great things by their expedition. They had made friends of the natives and learned many things about the wonderful regions they explored. Their work helped to keep Russia and England out of the valley of the Columbia River and to give that rich country to the United States. The task of opening up the west, begun so long before by brave French explorers, was now completed by those American patriot partners, Meriwether Lewis and William Clark.{258}

DAVY CROCKETT, THE HERO OF THE ALAMO

MOST of the great men in the new West a hundred years ago were born poor; but few were ever as poor as little Davy Crockett. His father seemed to be unable to get along well and was always in debt. When Davy was still a lad he was hired out for twenty-five cents a day, but he did not receive the pay himself; it was given to his father.

Once a drover to whom Davy's father owed money hired Davy to help drive cattle from the Crocketts' log cabin in East Tennessee over the mountains to a place in Virginia, four hundred miles away. Though Davy had had a poor place to live, it made him homesick to stay away from there long. He knew what that lonely man meant when he wrote, while a stranger in a foreign land,

"Be it ever so humble, there's no place like home."

The drover wanted Davy to stay and work for him in another part of the country, but he did not treat the boy very well, thinking that a twelve-year-old lad four hundred miles from home could not help himself. But that hard-hearted man did not know Davy Crockett. The boy found a man who was going in a wagon to a place within a hundred miles of his home in Tennessee. Davy planned to meet this man very early one morning, about seven miles from where he worked.

The lad did not sleep much that night, and at four o'clock next morning he was on his way to keep his word, though he had to wade seven miles through the deep snow in a blinding blizzard. He met the man with the wagon and was soon happy in being headed for home. The roads {259} were rough and the heavy cart jolted over logs and stumps. The boy could not stand it, not because it was rough, but because they went so slowly. He soon got off to walk the two or three hundred miles that remained. But after he had hurried on foot a hundred miles or so, he saw, to his great joy, a drover whom he recognized, for the man had stopped at his father's log tavern in Tennessee. The drover took him about a hundred miles on his way, but turned off before reaching the place where Davy lived. The boy had to walk on quite a distance farther, swimming rivers and wading swamps. He did not mind that, for his heart was light—he was going home! He had a happy time telling the family—Davy had seven brothers and sisters—all about his strange journey over the mountains and back.

David Crockett, hero of the Alamo.

From the painting by A. L. de Rose
David Crockett, hero of the Alamo.
From the painting by A. L. de Rose
The boy was soon hired to pay another of his father's debts. When Davy expected to be paid in money, the man gave him a note instead. But Davy was glad to be able to help in this way. Another time he went and hired out on purpose to pay a bill his father owed. As his wages were small, it took a long time to pay a few dollars. {260}

When Davy was thirteen he could not read nor write. At that time he was working for a good Quaker neighbor. The boy asked permission to work two days a week, just to pay his board, and spend the other days in school. Young Crockett learned "the three R's—Readin', 'Ritin', 'Rithmetic"—well enough to do the simple business of pioneer life.

Davy's highest ambition was to own a horse and a gun. When he had a rifle and a pony he thought he was old enough to marry a girl of seventeen. He seems not to have thought much about having a home of his own. The boy bridegroom took possession of a deserted log cabin. The bride's father gave them a cow, and the good Quaker lent the young couple fifteen dollars to start housekeeping. Davy Crockett wrote, after they had bought many fine things with that fifteen dollars, "We were then fixed up pretty grand, so we thought."

After three years the young Crocketts owned, besides the horse and gun, two cows, two calves, two colts and two children. But now that he had a home of his own, the young hunter was too restless to stay in it. When that region became so thickly settled that neighbors lived within a mile or two of one another, the nervous young pioneer moved hundreds of miles, to a newer country where he could find "elbow room." His devoted wife took their little children and went with him to the rougher region among Indians, bears, and other wild animals.

Davy Crockett found friends wherever he went. He was happy-hearted and full of funny stories. He had a humorous way of saying things that pleased those rough-and-ready western people. His homely yarns had a meaning deeper than the surface, like those told twenty years {261} later by a young man named Abe Lincoln. Crockett's backwoods stories and western slang were quoted all over the country. He told of "treeing a coon" once, and of how, as he was about to shoot, the raccoon exclaimed, "Don't shoot, I'll

108

come right down. I know I'm a gone coon!" "I'll come right down" and "I'm a gone coon" became popular expressions everywhere.

Crockett became a great hunter. He killed all the bears in the country around him and had exciting times hunting big game wherever he lived. He was wise and sensible in helping and advising his neighbors. The people in that pioneer country elected David Crockett a justice of the peace. They did not care whether he knew much about common law so long as he was possessed of common sense.

When the Creeks and other Indians in the southern states went on the warpath and murdered hundreds of people, General Jackson, the great man of Tennessee, led thousands of white men to kill all the Indians known to have taken part in that massacre, just as he would have tried to rid the country of dangerous bears or snakes. When Davy Crockett got the word he told his patient little wife, "I'm going to help fight the Indians."

"Oh, Davy," she exclaimed, "what will become of us—hundreds of miles from all my friends? The Indians will come and kill us while you are away."

But Davy Crockett could not stay. "I've got to go," he said. "My country needs me, and if we don't fight and kill the Indians they will come and kill us all, that's sure."

Even when fighting in General Jackson's army, Davy Crockett was "a law unto himself." The officers decided to let him do as he liked, for he seemed to wish to do the right thing by them all. He would be missing for hours,{262} and then come back with some game, big or little, to feast the company. Food was very scarce on the long march. When they got to fighting the Indians, Crockett knew exactly what to do. His aim was as sure then as it was when hunting bear or deer. Many a time when a big brave had his tomahawk raised to kill a fallen white man, the savage suddenly dropped dead where he stood. The astonished soldier would rise, look around, and mutter, "Davy Crockett must be somewhere around." Davy's bear-hunting, sharpshooting, and Indian fighting were so remarkable that his life was a strong proof of the saying, "Truth is stranger than fiction."

After General Jackson had put all the hostile savages out of the way and made it safe to live in those western states, the people were so grateful to Davy Crockett for his part in it that they put him up for election to Congress. Rival candidates, who felt much more fitted to go to Washington, made all manner of fun of Davy Crockett, and said the people ought to be ashamed to send a man like that to represent them in Congress. But the people said, "Davy Crockett ain't much on book-l'arnin' an' spoutin' poetry, but neither are we. He knows our life and just what we want. He ain't much of a lawyer, but he's got good sense, an' he can represent us better'n a dozen lawyers."

Those people knew what they were doing. Though Davy Crockett did not know much about books, he was not ignorant, for he was well-educated in the real life of that western frontier. So the people elected him three times to Congress, and he came to be loved and admired there for his homely wisdom and his quaint way of making others understand just what he meant. While he was a member of Congress he traveled up and down the eastern{263} states. Wherever he went he was cheered and feasted. In Philadelphia, the home of American independence, the people presented him with a beautiful rifle and a hunting-knife and tomahawk of razor steel. He told the people he would love and cherish that rifle as he would a daughter. Then and there he named the gun "Betsy."

While he was away in Congress and the east, Crockett's enemies worked against him, and he was defeated in the fourth election. The boyish longing for home came over him then, and he wrote:

"In a short time I set out for my own home; yes, my own home, my own soil, and my own humble dwelling; my own family, my own hearts, my own ocean of love and

109

affection which nothing else nor time can dry up. Here, like the wearied bird, let me settle down for a while and shut out the world."

Yet, much as Davy Crockett loved his home, he loved his country more. With this spirit he had also such reckless love of adventure that he could not bear to live at ease when his country needed him.

The American settlers were having terrible times down in Texas. Thousands of Americans in that country were struggling with the Mexicans, to decide who should control and own the Texas territory. General Santa Anna, the President of Mexico, had sent thousands of soldiers into that region, captured a brave little army of Americans, and, when these had been disarmed, coolly shot them down as if they had been cattle in a slaughter-house.

All these things were more than Davy Crockett's flesh and blood could bear. In his opinion "such cattle as those Mexicans" should be treated like bears or murderous Indians. Armed with "Betsy," his new rifle, "to use if need be for his country's glory," he was ready to leave for{264} Texas. He was now fifty-four years old, but his heart was young. When his friends tried to convince him that the trouble in Texas was no affair of his, Crockett replied that the news from those struggling heroes down there wrung his heart. "Sorrow will make even an oyster feel poetical," and Davy left behind him a farewell poem, of which this is a small part:

"The home I forsake where my offspring arose;
The graves I forsake where my children repose;
The home I redeemed from the savage and wild;
The home I have loved as a father his child;
The corn that I planted, the fields that I cleared,
The flocks that I raised, and the cabin I reared;
The wife of my bosom—Farewell to ye all!
In the land of the stranger I rise or I fall."

When Davy Crockett arrived at San Antonio, Colonel Travis, the commander of the Americans, had turned an old Spanish mission called the Alamo into a fort. Santa Anna was near at hand with a large army to capture the one hundred and eighty men who were waiting in the Alamo.

It would have made the hearts of that brave garrison glad if they could have looked into the future far enough to see that General Sam Houston would soon come there and drive the Mexicans out of the country; and that with the war-cry, "Remember the Alamo!" American soldiers would free Texas from Mexico's cruel rule, and finally add the vast territory of Texas, New Mexico, and California to the United States. But they only knew that Santa Anna was near with five thousand Mexican soldiers and that there was no hope of relief.

When Santa Anna and his army had arrived and surrounded the flimsy Spanish convent-fort, he called on Colonel Travis to surrender. The American answer was a{265} cannon-shot. Then the Mexicans raised a red flag as a signal that "no quarter" would be given; that is, that no American could expect anything but death at their hands.

Then the battle began. The walls of the Alamo were not strong, for the convent was not built for a fort. Yet it took that great Mexican army eleven days to capture it. Among the Americans were thirteen backwoods hunters like David Crockett and Colonel James Bowie, the inventor of the famous Bowie knife then much used in frontier fighting. Bowie was ill, but he fought like a hero, as did each of the others, to sell his life as dearly as possible. On the last day Colonel Travis offered to let the few men who were left go out with a white flag and ask the Mexicans to spare their lives, but not a man would go.

At last the walls of their frail fortress were battered down and four thousand Mexicans came rushing in. They found Crockett with only five men left—their backs to the wall fighting to the bitter end. It is said that Crockett was the last to fall. When beset by too many Mexicans to reload and fire "Betsy," he took his gun by the barrel and clubbed several Mexicans to death before they shot him down.

The Alamo fell on the 6th of March, 1836.

When they found the journal Davy Crockett had kept during the fight, they read his last words in it, written late the night before:

"March 5. Pop, pop, pop! Bom, bom, bom!—throughout the day. No time for memorandums now. Go ahead! Liberty and independence forever!"

{266}

FAMOUS INVENTORS

HOW ELI WHITNEY MADE COTTON KING

ELI WHITNEY began to make things when he was a small boy. He was called a genius because he was so ingenious. But he was not satisfied with doing things with his hands. He had a strong desire to make the most of his mind. So he went to Yale College and studied philosophy. One day the professor said he could not show a certain method to the class because the machine he kept for the purpose was broken. He could not teach that lesson until a new apparatus could be brought from England or France. But the ingenious student looked at the machine, and said, "Let me fix it." The professor thought it could do no harm to let him try. Eli made the fine machine work just as well as it did when it was new.

One of the bravest officers in the Revolutionary War, which ended a few years before this time, was General Nathanael Greene. After the war General Greene lived on a beautiful estate near Savannah, Georgia, and died there. When young Whitney finished his college course, he was engaged to teach a school in Savannah; but when he went down there he found that the school was not what he expected. So he acted as tutor in the family of General Greene's widow.

While he was tutor, Whitney made playthings for the children, and fixed many handy things for Mrs. Greene to use about the house. She told him he ought to make a{267} machine that would take the seeds out of the bolls, or fluffy heads, of the cotton plant. Great machines had been contrived for spinning and weaving cotton, but it took a man or a woman all day to pick the seeds out of a pound of cotton wool.

Eli Whitney, inventor of the cotton gin.
Eli Whitney, inventor of the cotton gin.

Eli Whitney went to work to make something that would do what in those days seemed impossible. He not only had to invent a cotton-gin, as the new machine was called, but he was obliged to make tools for making the machine itself, and even tools for making the other tools. But within a short time he had invented and built a machine which worked quite well. Still he was not satisfied. He locked himself up in a room and worked day and night until he had built a perfect cotton-gin which would work very fast and would clear out all the fine cotton seeds. This was in 1793, while Washington was President, and Philadelphia was the capital of the United States.

Whitney would not let any one but Mrs. Greene and a friend named Miller see the model, or pattern, of his cotton-gin until he could take out a patent for it. But before

111

he{268} could get money enough to have his gin patented, someone broke into his little shop and carried off his precious model.

Then the poor inventor had to begin again and make another machine, to prove to the officials in the Patent Office that the cotton-gin was his invention, before they could make out for him the patent right, which said he was the only person allowed to make and sell that machine in the United States. Before he could get this patent he found that others were making, selling, and trying to get a patent for machines made like the stolen pattern.

Whitney's first cotton gin.
Whitney's first cotton gin.

Young Whitney's friend Miller furnished him money, not only to secure his patent rights and make the machines, but to go into the courts and fight those who were trying to steal his rights as they had stolen his model. These people made him so much trouble and expense that it took thirteen years to beat them by lawsuits. A patent protected an inventor, by keeping others from making and selling that machine, for only fourteen years. When his rivals were beaten, Whitney had but one year left in which he and his friends could sell the machine so as to pay for all his time, labor, and expense. In that year he just made his cotton-gin pay for itself. But he had the great{269} satisfaction of making the land in the southern states known as the cotton belt (because cotton could be grown in those states) worth hundreds of millions of dollars more than before. The raising of cotton grew to be such a great industry that negro slavery became more and more necessary in the cotton-growing states. So, without knowing it, Eli Whitney, by increasing the production of cotton, increased the number of black slaves in the south, and helped to cause the struggle for and against slavery, many years later. But as the inventor did not know that his cotton-gin would make slavery a curse to the United States, he was not to blame.

After his patent had run out and he could make no more money by selling his cotton-gins, Whitney got a government contract for the making of guns. He invented new machinery to make the parts of his guns and was the first to have each part made by a different man according to an exact pattern. When the parts were put together to make a complete gun no special fitting was necessary because each piece was exactly like every other piece for that same part. If a part of the gun was broken it could be replaced with a new one without any difficulty. Before that when one man made an entire gun all the parts were specially fitted and if one got broken a new one had to be made and fitted by hand, which took a long time and made repairs very expensive. His factories and the homes of his workmen formed a suburb of New Haven called Whitneyville.

Eli Whitney furnished hundreds of thousands of men with the weapons they used in putting down the slavery which his cotton-gin had been made the innocent cause of increasing.{270}

"FULTON'S FOLLY"

ROBERT FULTON was a Pennsylvania boy. His father, a Quaker, died when Robert was a baby. His mother was a beautiful Irish lady, whose mind was as lovely as her face. She taught little Robert, and he knew much that was worth while before he began to go to school at the age of eight years.

In those days school teachers were often strict and harsh with young children. Parents seemed to think their children would not learn fast unless they were whipped or

112

beaten with a ruler. Though little Robert was not a bad boy in school, he sometimes seemed to be idle because he was thinking of something else. So his strict Quaker teacher punished him one day by striking his hands with a ferule. Robert's boyish sense of fairness rose up within him, and he exclaimed, "I came here, sir, to have something beaten into my head—not my hands!"

Robert Fulton, inventor of the steamboat.
Robert Fulton, inventor of the steamboat.
One of the pupils brought some artist's brushes and paints to school, and Robert, who already showed real talent for drawing, was allowed to use them. He made such fine pictures that the other boy gave him the paints. This was the beginning of young Fulton's career as a painter. But Robert was not content with painting pictures. He was always trying to make things, or to find ways of doing things more easily.{271}

Robert was eleven when the American colonies went into the War for Independence. During this war, when candles were scarce, people were warned not to waste them in lighting up for the Fourth of July. It was to be a saving rather than a safe and sane holiday. The Fulton boy made up his mind to celebrate the day. So he got some gunpowder and pasteboard and made little tubes with a stick pointing out at one end of each. The neighbors were astonished on the night of the Fourth of July to see these tubes, one after another, go whizzing up in the sky, leaving a trail of sparks behind them. They said to one another, "That Fulton boy's a genius!" Robert had made the first skyrockets these Americans had ever seen.

Robert Fulton afterward became acquainted with Dr. Benjamin Franklin and learned much from the kind old inventor. When Fulton was a young man he went to London and studied painting with Benjamin West, the greatest American painter up to that time. He went also to France to study art. Meantime he kept on inventing things. The French were at war with many of the countries of Europe at that time. Fulton had always been interested in boats; and we have seen that he knew how to use gunpowder. He planned a new kind of boat, which he thought would help the French in their war. It was a submarine, and was provided with torpedoes which could be shot under water. They would have pierced the wooden sides of the best ships built in those days. Fulton's diving boat was shown to the French minister of war, but the government experts could not understand its great value in war and refused to make use of it in the war. Shortly after, a British officer remarked that Napoleon's loss of Fulton's diving boat was the most important event of the century.{272}

Napoleon, who was then emperor of the French, wrote to one of his own advisers: "I have just received the project of Citizen Fulton, which you have sent me too late—since it may change the face of the world!"

But, harmful as Fulton's submarine might have proven to Napoleon's enemies, the chance which Napoleon missed was not important compared with the results of Robert Fulton's next invention.

Robert Fulton had, as a lad, gone fishing with some neighbors on a flatboat in the river. This craft they had to push along with poles, which was very slow, hard work. Bob began at once to try to fix something which would make the boat go faster and more easily. He arranged paddles at the stern which worked quite well. Then he improved this by making paddle wheels. After that he attached the wheels to an engine. He went on working with engines and wheels until at last, while he was in Paris, he succeeded in building a boat with a steam-engine to make it go. He tried it on the River Seine, which flows through Paris. The boat did go a little; but the engine was too heavy, and the watching crowds saw Fulton's queer boat sink to the bottom.

After he returned to America, Fulton went on improving his steamboat until he had built one which he thought would run up the Hudson River from New York City to Albany. He named this odd-looking craft the Clermont, and invited a few of his friends to make the trial trip. A great crowd came down to the wharf in New York City to have a little fun watching "Fulton's Folly," as they called the steamboat. People laughed at the idea that a heavy iron engine could make a boat go anywhere but to the bottom.{273}

Even Fulton's friends, waiting on the deck of the queer-looking vessel, felt foolish and looked anxious. The boat, however, started off, and the people on the shore began to cheer. Out in the river it stopped like a balky horse, and the cheers were turned to jeers. Fulton looked hurriedly at the engine, found out what was the trouble, and soon fixed it. Then the boat went puffing away up the river against the current at the rate of six miles an hour, and the friends on deck thought they were going very fast, as there were no railroads then and this was faster than a sailboat could go. Fulton kept on improving his boats so that within a few years there were steamboats on other rivers of the country. Within a century "ocean greyhounds" were racing across the Atlantic, and "superdreadnoughts," the largest battleships, were being built for the great navies of the world. Submarines were used by many nations in the World War, but their invention, important as it was, could not well be called the greatest event of the century. It was the sailing of "Fulton's Folly" which might have been said to change the face of the world, because it was the first step on the way to the wonderful steamships of to-day.

Just as that ingenious little boy tried to help his friends by making their flatboat run faster so Robert Fulton, as a man, had made the people of the world richer, happier, and better for all the ages to come.

The "Clermont," Fulton's first steamboat.
The "Clermont," Fulton's first steamboat.
{274}
HOW MORSE SENT LETTERS BY LIGHTNING

INTO the family of Doctor Morse, a much respected minister living on the side of the hill on which the battle of Bunker Hill was fought, there came a little baby boy. They named him Samuel Finley for his great-grandfather, a president of Princeton College. To this was added Breese, the maiden name of the boy's mother. When this baby grew up, he was known all over the world as S. F. B. Morse.

This Morse boy had the best kind of schooling at home. His father was a teacher as well as a preacher, and wrote the Morse geographies which were used in the schools of that day. Finley, as he was called at home, showed real talent as a boy for drawing and painting. One of his first pictures showed the Morse family around a table, with the father teaching them from a large globe showing all the countries of the world.

Finley Morse was sent to Yale College, where he was much interested in science and philosophy. But he kept at his drawing and coloring, and became a successful painter. That was years before any one knew how to take photographs; so Mr. Morse painted a great many portraits and did such good work that he received high prices for them. Believing that the artists of America could help one another, he influenced some of them to organize the National Academy of the Arts of Design, and they elected him their first president. When Lafayette, who had been a young officer on General Washington's staff nearly fifty years before, came to America again as an old man, the people of America wished to have the best portrait that could be painted of the Frenchman who had helped the Americans in the War{275}

S. F. B. Morse, inventor of the telegraph.
S. F. B. Morse, inventor of the telegraph.
{276}
for Independence. Finley Morse was chosen to paint this picture of General Lafayette.

While Mr. Morse was in Washington at work on this picture, he received word from his home in New Haven that his young wife had died suddenly of heart disease. Before he could receive the letter she was buried. People in those days traveled by stage-coach, and it took at least a week for a letter to go from Boston to Washington. When the sorrowing father went home to arrange for the care of his three motherless children, he spoke of the slowness of sending word from place to place, and said he hoped the time would come when news could be sent long distances in an instant. But of course he had no idea then that he would have anything to do with bringing that blessing to mankind.

When Morse was returning from one of his visits to Europe to study art, several of his friends on the ship were talking at the table about what someone had done by way of sending signals like lightning by means of electricity. "If they can do that," said Mr. Morse, "why could we not write letters in a second or two from New York to Charleston with it?" The others laughed at the idea.

"Why not?" kept ringing in Mr. Morse's ears. He stayed in his stateroom to study and think. He remembered what he had learned from his professors in college about electricity. With such materials as he could get together on shipboard, he made magnets and electrical appliances. By the time the ship sailed up New York harbor, Mr. Morse had not only a good idea of the way to go to work to make a telegraph apparatus, but he had made up the "dot-and-dash code," now in use in telegraphy.

The idea took such a hold on his mind that he could no{277} longer paint pictures. But when he talked to others about it, it all seemed impossible—"too good to be true"—and he could not find wealthy men who would lend money enough to enable him to prove that a message could be sent a long distance in a moment of time by telegraph.

While Mr. Morse was waiting and struggling to start "the electro-magnetic telegraph" he made a bare living by taking the first photographic likenesses, called daguerreotypes, in America.

After eleven years of hard work and poverty so keen that he had to go hungry sometimes, Mr. Morse's friends in Congress passed a bill in the House to furnish him government money enough for a trial line forty miles long. But on the last day of the session, which was to end at midnight, there were over a hundred bills ahead of his in the Senate. Mr. Morse went home that night utterly discouraged.

In the morning Annie Ellsworth, the young daughter of the Commissioner of Patents, came to congratulate him. His bill had been passed just before midnight and the President had signed it, giving Mr. Morse all the money he needed to show how he could "send letters by lightning."

Morse's first telegraph sounder
Morse's first telegraph sounder

{278}

The overjoyed inventor told Miss Ellsworth that when his line was all ready she should send the first message over it.

It was decided that the trial line should be put up between Washington and Baltimore. It was completed before the 24th of May, 1844. One end of it was in the Capitol at Washington and the other at Baltimore. Miss Ellsworth's first message, flashed by S. F. B. Morse to his partner, Mr. Vail, in Baltimore, was this text of Scripture: "What hath God wrought!"

The first news sent out to the whole country was that of James K. Polk's nomination at the Convention in Baltimore as the Democratic candidate for President of the United States.

Mr. Morse's struggles were now over. The telegraph became a wonderful success and he was honored by presidents, kings, and princes with medals, stars, crosses, and other decorations. The inventor now turned his attention to running telegraph lines under water, and laid a cable under New York harbor. About twenty years later another man, Cyrus W. Field, succeeded in connecting America with Europe by laying a cable beneath the Atlantic Ocean.

So S. F. B. Morse's words were realized: "If I can make the telegraph work ten miles, I can make it go around the globe." He really made true these words of Puck, one of Shakespeare's fairies:

"I'll put a girdle round about the earth
In forty minutes."

Men soon began trying to talk without connecting wires. Marconi invented the radio-telegraph in 1896 and the radio-phone followed. Now it is possible to send wireless messages almost around the world.{279}

CYRUS H. M'CORMICK AND THE STORY OF THE REAPER

WHEN little Abraham Lincoln was three days old in Kentucky, Cyrus H. McCormick was born in Virginia. When the McCormick boy was seven he used to go out to a shed and watch his father working at a machine to take the place of the scythe which was then used in cutting grain. Father McCormick was never satisfied, the neighbors said. He was "always fussing and trying to invent and improve something."

After working for years to make a machine to harvest grain, Farmer McCormick gave it up, saying that it could not be done. Meanwhile young Cyrus, who had inherited his father's inventive turn of mind, went to the fields to work with the men. He found it very hard to keep up with them, so he invented a cradle, or improved scythe, which made his work so much easier that he was able to do as much as a grown man. When he was twenty-two, Cyrus McCormick had invented a plough that would throw up a furrow on whichever side the farmer desired. Two years later he made the first self-sharpening plough.

Although the neighbors had laughed at his father for being so foolish as to wish to invent a labor-saving machine for harvesting, and in spite of his father's warnings that such a thing could never be made, the idea of a reaper haunted the young man's mind. He began to work at it as a boy and kept it up until he was a grown man. He had improved the cradle and his two ploughs without much difficulty, but the reaping machine was a hard problem. It was more difficult because the grain is often lodged, or matted down, and it is necessary not only to cut it but to{280} lay it in even rows, so that it can be bound in sheaves ready for threshing.

116

But in 1831, the same year in which he made his double-furrow plough, McCormick built a machine that would reap quite well. He had made every part of it by hand. This machine had vibrating blades which cut against each other in about the same manner as shears. It also had a reel to draw the standing grain within reach of the moving blades, and a platform to catch the grain as fast as it was cut. He first tried the machine by reaping several acres of oats. The next year he harvested seventy-five acres of wheat, to the great astonishment of the neighboring farmers, and his father's pride.

Cyrus McCormick was not satisfied to let well enough alone. He spent nine more years in making his reaper do everything just right before he was willing to sell it. The farmers admired the clever machine, but they were not ready to buy it, because they thought it would take work from many laborers. The money panic of 1837 occurred during this time, and young McCormick went into the iron-smelting business to make a living during the hard times.

Cyrus H. McCormick, inventor of the reaper.
Cyrus H. McCormick, inventor of the reaper.
{281}

McCormick's first reaper.

From a model
McCormick's first reaper.
From a model
In 1840 he had put his reaper into more perfect shape and now began to manufacture it, first in Cincinnati, then in Chicago. The farmers in the western prairies could not hire laborers enough to harvest their great fields of grain by hand. So the McCormick reaper began to be used in that part of the country. Cyrus H. McCormick, unlike most inventors, was a successful business man. He had to enlarge his factories. To his harvester he kept adding devices until it gathered the grain into sheaves, bound the sheaves with twine, and tossed them out sideways on the ground. He made them so that they would mow grass also.{282}

After his reapers and mowers became well known in America, the successful inventor and manufacturer went abroad to introduce them in Europe. He showed the machine at the first World's Fair in London, in 1851. People in England laughed, and the London Times reported that the reaper was a "cross between a chariot, a wheelbarrow, and a flying machine."

But when the object of their laughter was taken out harvesting in England, the joke was on the men who had made fun of a machine they could not understand. The newspapers then began to praise the inventor they had ridiculed, and Cyrus H. McCormick awoke one morning and found himself famous. He not only received the Great Medal from the World's Fair, but was elected an officer of the Legion of Honor in Paris, and received the high honor of being made a member of the French Academy of Science.

So the McCormick boy, who did not mind being laughed at and was never content with doing less than his very best, became not only one of the wealthiest men in America, but added many hundreds of millions of dollars to the wealth of his country, and gave an immense benefit to the world.

117

ELIAS HOWE was the son of a poor miller. He had to go to work when he was six years old. He was a lame, sickly boy and could never do heavy work. When he was old enough he went away to work in the mills. But as he grew up, his health was still so poor that he had to go back and live with his father.{283}

Elias married when he was twenty-one and, within a few years, he had a wife and three children to support. Once when he was ill, his wife took in sewing to support their little family. As the young father lay on the bed watching his wife slowly plying her needle, he thought what a blessing it would be if a machine could be invented to sew much faster and better than by hand. The idea seemed to fill his mind, for he was an ingenious man. He said to himself, "I can't do heavy work, but perhaps I can invent that machine." At first he said nothing about it to his wife, but he watched her taking stitch after stitch for hours at a stretch.

Elias Howe.
Elias Howe.
When he was out of bed he made a model of the machine which he had been planning. In this rude affair he first had the needle with an eye in the middle. This needle was pointed at both ends, and worked sideways through the cloth, which was held upright. The stitches on this first machine were made like a chain, and the thread raveled out too easily.

Howe kept patiently at work until he hit upon the idea of laying the cloth to be sewed on a small table, and making the needle go up and down through it. He thought of a way to have the cloth pulled along as it was sewn. But the trouble was to get a stitch that would not rip or pull out.{284} At last he tried a shuttle, which looped another thread with that in the needle so that the two made a lock-stitch. When he had done this, he had invented the sewing machine.

Like most inventors, Elias Howe was poor. He found a coal dealer named Fisher, who agreed to keep Howe and his family, and furnish five hundred dollars to pay for the first machines and have them patented. For this Fisher was to receive a half interest in the patents, and the sewing machine business afterward.

At first no one would buy the machine. Tailors thought it would throw too many men out of work. Mr. Fisher grew tired of his bargain and the Howes had to leave his house. There seemed to be a better chance to sell sewing machines in England; so the family went across the sea to London. But the inventor was again disappointed. He was glad to come back to his father's house in America with his sick wife and his small children.

Howe's first sewing machine.

Photo. Brown Bros., N. Y.
Howe's first sewing machine.
Photo. Brown Bros., N. Y.
The wife died soon after their return and the inventor had to do something to support his motherless children. He hired out to help an engineer on one of the first railroads in the United States. While he was working at that, a{285} friend offered to see

what he could do in selling sewing-machines in New York City. They found that others were making and selling machines very much like Howe's.

Money was furnished to sue those dealers. Howe's rights to his patents were confirmed by the courts in 1846, and all other makers of sewing machines were made to pay him a certain amount, called a royalty, on every machine they sold. In this way Elias Howe soon became a very wealthy man.

After the Civil War broke out, Howe enlisted as a private, and when the government was slow in paying the soldiers' wages, he lent the money himself for the men in his company. He died before he was fifty years old with medals and honors from many countries. He had brought a great blessing to the women of the world, just as he had wished to do when he lay on his bed watching his tired wife sewing, hour after hour, to support him and their three little children.

EDISON, THE WIZARD OF MANY INVENTIONS

THOMAS ALVA EDISON was born in the little village of Milan, Ohio. His father was a mechanic, who could turn his hand to anything. While Alva, as they called him at home, was a small boy, the family moved to Port Huron. Here the lad was sent to school, but he asked so many questions that the teacher sent him home.

Then Alva's mother, who had been a school teacher, tried to educate him. She had great patience with his questions, but there were so many that neither she nor his father could answer that he took to reading books. He had{286} the same desire to "know the why" of everything that other great men have shown when they were boys.

Though the Edison boy had no taste for school, he was fond of reading. When he learned how much he could find out from books, he started in, boy-like, to read all the books in a public library. He had worried through several great sets of volumes when he discovered that not all books were of interest to him. After that he chose only those on subjects he liked to read about.

His father was a poor man, and as Alva was not in school he wanted to do his part toward making a living for the family. He began by selling papers around home. Then he had a chance to be train boy on the old Grand Trunk railroad between Port Huron and Detroit. His mother was afraid to have him run on trains and be away from home, but he showed that he could take care of himself. It was during this time that he began taking books from the Detroit Public Library.

He was such a wide-awake, good-natured lad that the trainmen liked him. He found that he had a good deal of time to spare; so he got some old type from a printer and, in a corner of the baggage car, began to print a four-page newspaper about the size of a small handkerchief, which he named The Grand Trunk Herald. The trainmen and their families and friends liked this young Edison's news. Soon he had about five hundred subscribers, so he made about ten dollars a week from his little paper.

Meanwhile he attended strictly to business. During the Civil War he would find out when there had been a battle and have the telegraph operator send word of the event ahead of the train to the towns where the trains would stop. This brought hundreds of people down to the stations at{287}

Thomas A. Edison and one of his early dynamos.
Thomas A. Edison and one of his early dynamos.
{288}

train-time to learn the news of the battle. Young Edison would sell hundreds—once he sold a thousand—newspapers at ten to twenty-five cents apiece.

He was always trying to do something new. After his little paper became well known, he began to buy chemicals and keep them in bottles in his printing office in the car. One day the phosphorus jar fell off the shelf and broke. This set fire to the floor of the car. While Alva was putting out the fire the conductor came through. It made him so angry to have a boy around who might burn up the train with his experiments, that he threw out bottles, printing-press, and type, and pushed the boy after them.

Alva did not hold a grudge against that conductor. He only wondered that the trainmen had stood that sort of thing so long. He saved all he could out of the ruins and set up his printing plant in the cellar of his father's house. He went back to work as though nothing had happened, and attended only to selling papers. One day while waiting on the platform of a station he saw the station agent's child on the tracks and an express train coming. Throwing down his newspapers he jumped, seized the child, and sprang across the track just in time to save its life and his own.

The station man wept as he seized the heroic newsboy's hand. "I am a poor man," he said, "so I can't repay you for saving my child's life; but I can teach you telegraphy."

Edison was delighted. He stopped at that station several times a week and learned very soon to send and receive messages. It is harder to take than to send telegraph dispatches. Young Edison invented a machine which would run more slowly than the telegraph and which gave him time to write out the words while the "dots and dashes" of the telegraph alphabet were clicking away. But sometimes {289} it is impossible to attach this appliance; so young Edison practised till he could receive the fastest news story.

He knocked about the country, hiring out as telegraph operator, but he was always trying to make new machines and improvements. This was more interesting to him than telegraphing. After living in several western cities the young telegrapher and inventor applied for a job in the Western Union office in Boston. Here is Mr. Edison's own account of his first experience there:

"I had been four days and nights on the road, and, having had very little sleep, I did not present a very fresh or stylish appearance. The manager asked me when I was ready to go to work. 'Now,' I replied. I was then told to return at 5.30 P.M., and punctually at that hour I entered the main room and was introduced to the night manager. My appearance caused much mirth, and, as I afterwards learned, the night operators consulted together how they might put up a job on the jay from the woolly West. I was assigned to New York No. 1 wire.

"After waiting upwards of one hour I was told to come over to a certain table and take a special report for the Boston Herald, the conspirators having arranged to have one of the fastest senders in New York send the dispatch and 'salt' the new man. I sat down without suspecting and the New York man started slowly. I had perfected myself in a simple and rapid style of handwriting, without flourishes, which could be increased from forty-five to fifty-four words a minute by reducing the size of the lettering. This was several words faster than any other operator in the United States could write.

"Soon the New York man increased his speed and I easily adapted my pace to his. This put my rival on his mettle, and he was soon doing his fastest work. At this point I happened to look up, and saw the operators all looking over my shoulder with their faces shining with fun and excitement. I knew then that they were trying to put a job on me, but I kept my own counsel and went on placidly with my work—even sharpening a pencil now and then, as an extra aggravation.

"The New York man then commenced to slur over his words, running them together, and sticking the signals; but I had been{290} used to this style of telegraphy in taking reports and was not in the least discomfited. At last, when I thought the fun had gone far enough, I opened the key and clicked back to him: 'Say, young man, change off and send with the other foot!' This broke the New York man all up, and he turned the job over to another man to finish."

Young Edison got the greatest benefit he could from the Boston Public Library. The following year he went to New York and found work with the Gold Reporting Telegraph Company, where he invented the "ticker" now so common in stockbrokers' offices. He was employed at a salary of three hundred dollars a month. He now began to devote all his time to inventing. In a short time he had devised and constructed several machines and improvements for which he was offered forty thousand dollars. This enabled him to begin inventing and manufacturing on a large scale. He built a factory and employed three hundred men to carry out his fast-increasing ideas and make the necessary machines and drawings for securing his patents.

He improved the telegraph so that six messages could be sent at once over the same wire. He made improvements in electric and other motor cars, as well as in the telephone. He also made a delicate instrument to measure the heat of the stars, which he called the tasimeter. Out of more than fourteen hundred different inventions, any one of which would have made him famous, the best known are the incandescent electric light, the phonograph and the moving-picture machine.

Thomas A. Edison is the greatest inventor that ever lived. He has done more for the world's wealth, comfort, and happiness than any other man save, perhaps, Dr. Benjamin Franklin. Yet he is one of the most modest of{291} men. When he was invited to a dinner at which several distinguished men wished to pay him some of the high honors due him, he said:

"I would not sit and listen to an hour of such talk for a hundred thousand dollars!" When asked how he gained his great success, Mr. Edison replied:

"By not looking at the clock."{292}

THE GREATEST AMERICANS

BENJAMIN FRANKLIN, THE BOY WHO WAS DILIGENT IN BUSINESS

WHEN Benjamin Franklin was a little boy he lived in Boston, where his father was a maker of soap and candles. Little Ben was only ten years old when his father took him out of school and set him at work in his shop. Dipping candles all day long is hard, disagreeable work and Ben, who loved books, often wished that he was back in school. His uncle Benjamin sometimes tried to cheer the lad at his tiresome toil by telling him: "It is not so much what you do in life as how you do it."

One day Ben's uncle brought a Bible into the smoky soapfat room and read from it: "Seest thou a man diligent in his business? He shall stand before kings."

Ben Franklin was a thoughtful boy. While he was bending over the little vat of hot tallow all that long day, he could not help thinking of what his uncle had read to him. Half smothered by the burning grease he whispered to himself: " 'Stand before kings?' I'm so tired, and my back is so lame when night comes that I can hardly stand at all!"

After Ben had worked at home for two long years, his father said to him,

"My son, you have been so faithful that I cannot bear to let you dip candles all your life. You are fit for something better. What trade would you like to learn?"{293}

121

Ben was delighted. He was so fond of books that he felt sure he would like to learn how to make them. He answered his father's question by saying, "I would like to be a printer."

When a boy went to learn a trade in those days, he had to serve as an apprentice. That is, he was bound out by law to work for a master until he was twenty-one. At first he received nothing for his work but his board and clothes, and when he was nineteen or twenty he was given very small wages. At that time James Franklin, Ben's older brother, had a printing office in Boston. It was soon arranged that Ben should be his brother James's apprentice, and work for nine years to learn the printing business.

Ben was clever and willing. The work of a printing office boy was very hard. More than this, James Franklin was a hard master. He sometimes boxed Ben's ears and treated him very unkindly. The more the young brother tried to please, the crosser James seemed to be.

Ben bore this abuse for five years. He soon learned to set type well, and to run the "hand"—or foot—press, which was hard even for a man to do. James was so mean to him at home that the boy asked for just half the money it cost his brother to feed him, so that he might board himself. Of course, James was pleased with such a bargain.

The boy was so eager to learn that he saved half of that small sum to buy books. He ate no meat—only bread and a few plain vegetables. Instead of going out, as the men and the other apprentices did, to get a good dinner, he stayed in the shop at noon to eat his dry bread and read. Benjamin Franklin liked books, which other boys thought too dry, even better than good things to eat.

Besides being studious, Ben was ingenious. He had the knack of finding out what was wrong with things and making{294} them right. When the printing press would not work, he fixed it and set it going again. He soon wrote pieces for his brother's newspaper. He was so bright, willing, and useful that every one praised him—except his brother, who, instead of being proud of Ben, was jealous, and treated him worse than ever.

So Ben had to run away—not to sea, but to Philadelphia, where he could get printing work to do. He quickly found a place there and worked with a royal will. If ever a young man was "diligent in his business," it was Benjamin Franklin. When he was about twenty-one, he became the owner of the largest printing business in America. He was soon editing and publishing the best newspaper in the country. Before long he also started "Poor Richard's Almanac," a sort of yearly magazine containing Franklin's maxims, or short, wise sayings. These have been translated into many languages and are quoted all over the world.

Franklin founded the first library in Philadelphia, and started the University of Pennsylvania. He kept on improving and inventing useful things. He made printers' type and presses better than they were before. One night his whale-oil lamp smoked. He went to work to fix it. To do this he had to find out what made it smoke like that. Before he finished he had invented the best lamp in the world. With his new knowledge of the action of drafts, he went on and invented a stove, to take the place of the fireplace, which before this time was generally used for heating and cooking.

Many people thought the most striking thing that Franklin did was to make a silk kite with a steel wire projecting from the end of the long cross-stick to fly in the clouds during a thunderstorm. When the lightning struck the{295} steel wire, it ran down the kite string to a big iron key which Franklin had hung there for that purpose. He then put the key into a big, wide-mouthed glass jar. This was like catching the lightning in a trap. In this simple way, Benjamin Franklin proved that lightning is nothing but electricity flashing up in the clouds.

Thus, by studying into things every chance he had, Benjamin Franklin became not only one of the most learned men in the world, but the greatest inventor of his time. He was honored with the title of Doctor of Philosophy by the greatest universities in Europe. Better than this, he was known and loved by the people all over the world.

While the War for Independence was under way, the leaders of the new nation, called the United States of America, came to Doctor Franklin and urged him to go to France and persuade the king and the people to help the United States. Doctor Franklin said he would see what could be done. When he reached Paris he received a more wonderful welcome than was ever given to a king. "The good Doctor Franklin's" portrait and his stove were seen in nearly every home in France. He became "the fashion" in Paris, "the city of fashion." Storekeepers were selling "Franklin" hats, "Franklin" canes, "Franklin" snuffboxes and so on. While he was entertained by the king of France, the kings of four other nations came to see him. Not only did he "stand before kings," but he sat at table with the rulers of five great nations of Europe. The French government supplied him with money, men, and ships to help to win the independence of the United States. Then he stayed in France and signed the treaty of peace, which he brought home to America.

He arrived at the old wharf in Philadelphia where he had{296} landed many years before—a poor, hungry lad of seventeen, running away from his cruel brother. This time he was welcomed by thousands of people, cheering. Cannon were booming. The bells of the city were ringing. Above them all tolled the great Liberty Bell of Independence Hall. The happy people shouted to one another—

"Hurrah for Doctor Franklin! Hurrah for peace!"

And Benjamin Franklin told some of them about the words his uncle had read to him when he was a boy:

"Seest thou a man diligent in his business? He shall stand before kings."

GEORGE WASHINGTON AND HIS MOTHER

WHEN George Washington was a little boy there was no such country as the United States. The part of America where he was born was called Virginia, but it was not a state then. It was a colony, or new country, settled by people from England.

These colonists lived along the eastern shore. Back from the sea coast were beautiful valleys and high hills covered with woods. That region was called a "howling wilderness," because there were tribes of Indians roaming through its forests, hunting bears and wolves, war-whooping, and killing and scalping one another. Sometimes they stole up to a lone cabin or settlement to murder a few white people who were brave enough to try to live there, and set fire to their little home.

The wealthy Virginia colonists built handsome houses on their large estates. "The First Families of Virginia," as they came to be called, owned negroes that had been stolen{297} from the jungles of Africa and sold to the planters. These slaves worked in the tobacco fields and did other work on the farms. Then there were also white men who had broken the laws in England, and were condemned to hard labor in the fields of Virginia instead of being shut up in the prisons of England. As most of the labor on their farms and plantations was done by black slaves and white convicts, the young gentlemen of the colony thought all that kind of work was too low for them to do. So, instead of laboring to improve their new country, as men did in other colonies, the strong young men of Virginia led lives of ease—drinking, carousing, gambling, and horse racing.

Little George Washington's father was a wealthy planter who owned three plantations. He was a member of a great English company buying up vast tracts of land in the new country. He also owned a big interest in some iron mines. And besides all these, he was owner and master of a ship which took his tobacco and iron to London and brought back cargoes of silks, furniture, tea, coffee, and many other things not then made or raised in Virginia. Mr. Washington sometimes sailed to England on his ship and commanded his crew. From this he was called "Captain."

Captain Washington's oldest son, Lawrence, fourteen years older than George, had enlisted in the army while at school in England, and was now a captain fighting the Spaniards under Admiral Vernon.

When George was seven years old the Washington house was burned down, and the family had to move about fifty miles in a sailboat to another estate named "Ferry Farm," on the Rappahannock River. From there George went to school, riding several miles a day on his own pony.

The schoolhouse was a mere shed in the center of a wornout{298} tobacco field. George did not learn much there, but he did have a great time playing soldier. Small as he was, he was captain of the "white men." The other "men" were Spaniards, French, or Indians, for England was at war with all these people most of the time. So, just then, there were three "captains" in the Washington family—Augustine, the father, Lawrence, the soldier son, and George, the school leader.

When George was eleven his father died, leaving the best part of his wealth to Lawrence. By English law the most of the property went to the eldest son; so the people of Virginia felt that this was the right thing to do. But George's mother thought it was all wrong, when the oldest son of her husband's first wife was made a rich man and her oldest son was left a poor boy by their father's will. As for George, he believed it must be right because his father had willed it so. Instead of being jealous or grudging his half-brother such good fortune, George began to plan how to earn his own living. In this way the boy George Washington was preparing for the great War for Independence.

To keep his little brother from going to work, Lawrence persuaded his stepmother to let him find George a good place where he might become an officer in the English navy. He could do so through Admiral Vernon, for whom Lawrence had named the mansion he had built where his father's house had burned down. But when the time came for parting with her oldest son and stand-by, stern, dignified Mary Washington broke down and cried, pleading with George not to leave his mother alone in her widowhood and poverty. It was so hard for George to give up what he thought was his only chance in life, that his face turned white. But for his mother's sake, he gave it all up. Taking{299}

Washington's farewell to his mother.
Washington's farewell to his mother.
{300}
off his bright "middy" uniform, he folded it away in his new sailor chest, never to be worn again. When he saw the warship, which had been anchored below Mount Vernon, sailing away in the morning sunshine, young George Washington's future looked as dark as ever it could to a heartbroken lad of fifteen. But who would have led the colonists in their rebellion against England if George Washington had entered the English navy then, and had later become a British admiral instead of commanding general of the American army?

By the time George was twenty-one his brother Lawrence was dead and, as his father had willed it, most of the property, including "Mount Vernon," belonged to the oldest son of the second wife. George at once provided for his mother against worry or want in future. But he had to tell her that he was a man now and that his devotion to country must come first—even before his duty to his mother.

The English governor of Virginia sent him, still little more than a boy, as messenger of the British government to the French and Indian commanders in the distant Ohio region. This was a lonely journey of many hundred miles through frozen and pathless forests full of cruel savages. George had several hairbreadth escapes, once from drowning in an icy river, and once from being shot by a treacherous Indian guide. A great writer says of his wonderful success on this difficult and dangerous errand through that western wilderness: "He went in a schoolboy, he came out the first soldier in the colonies."

The brave youth was appointed Major Washington, and given command of a little army to fight the French and Indians. He soon gained a victory which was called "the{301} first blow" in a war which lasted, in America and Europe, more than fifty years. As a member of General Braddock's staff young Washington saved the remaining part of the British army at Fort Duquesne.

He was Colonel Washington when he was sent to the Congress which adopted the Declaration of Independence. While there he was made commander-in-chief of the Continental Army in the War for Independence. His faith and courage and patience endeared him so to the country that no other man could be thought of for the first President of the United States except the "Father of his Country."

ALEXANDER HAMILTON, THE ORPHAN BOY FROM THE WEST INDIES

ON the little island of Nevis, in the West Indies, lived a small boy who had lost his mother, a bright young woman from France. His father, James Hamilton, who was a Scotch planter, soon left the island, and the boy, Alexander, heard little of him after that. No one knows to-day what became of the father of Alexander Hamilton, but his grandfather was a Scottish laird, or lord.

The next that is known of Alexander is that he was a clerk in the store of a merchant on Santa Cruz, a smaller island, and that the lad was not contented there. When he was twelve he wrote back to a friend in Nevis, "I would be willing to risk my life, but not my character, to exalt my station."

Alexander studied with a minister of Santa Cruz who did all he could to help the boy to improve his position in life.{302} As Alexander was a devout lad it is believed that the good man was trying to fit him to be a minister.

The first thing young Hamilton did to win credit was to write a wonderful description of a hurricane, or violent wind storm, that did great damage on the island. The article was printed in a London newspaper. When the people who knew the lad read his account, they could hardly believe that one so young could have written it and several wealthy planters decided to give such a bright boy a chance "to exalt his station" by sending him to school in America.

Soon the little Scotch lad who could speak French and write splendid stories in English was on his way to Boston in a British packet boat. It is stated that on that voyage he first heard of George Washington. When Alexander Hamilton reached Boston, he found the people up in arms because the British government had sent soldiers to keep order in that rebellious city; but the boy had been brought up to think that the king and the great men of England were always right.

The little Britisher from the West Indies was first sent to a grammar school not far from New York to prepare for college. He was so keen and studied so hard that he was fitted to enter King's College in New York City at the age of sixteen. After the war against the king the name of the college was changed from King's to Columbia.

After a year in college, the British-bred youth went to Boston again. This was about the time when the "Sons of Liberty" dressed up as Indians and threw the taxed tea overboard into Boston harbor. This act was intended to show the king and the English statesmen that the Americans would not pay taxes when they had nothing to say in the {303} government as to what taxes they should pay. No doubt Alexander, while studying for college, had learned something of the history and the spirit of the people in America, so that he did not feel so sure that all the king did was right. After he returned to New York, there was a great mass meeting in "the Fields" to talk about the unjust acts of the king of England. In the city were many Tories, loyal to the king. Young Hamilton went down from college to hear the discussion, and it was not long before he was answering a rich Tory in a sharp, vigorous way. The people shouted to him to go up on the platform, and the brilliant West Indian youth of seventeen made a strong speech that became the talk of New York City.

A little while after this the students called on the president of King's College. He was a Tory, and very bitter against the people who were fighting for their rights as British subjects. He scolded the students roundly, calling them traitors, rascals, and other hard names. This made the young men so angry that it might have gone hard with the old gentleman if young Hamilton had not jumped up on the porch and spoken earnestly in his defense. The president, seeing who was speaking, and thinking that the youth was talking against the Tories again, put his angry red face out of an upper window and shouted: "It's a lie! Don't believe a word that rogue says. He's crazy!"

As Hamilton was really taking their foolish president's part, this made the students shout and laugh. The young orator, taking advantage of this, kept on talking till the old Tory made his escape by a back way to a British man-of-war in the river near by. After this Hamilton wrote pamphlets and newspaper articles about the rights of the people. Events began to happen thick and fast. Washington {304} was elected commander-in-chief of the Continental Army and drove the British soldiers out of Boston. Then the Americans decided to separate from England; so the Declaration of Independence was written and signed. Young Hamilton was soon in the midst of the fight—in command of an artillery company. When Washington and his ragged Continentals were retreating from New York, he saw a youth in charge of a battery keeping the red-coats from crossing a wide river, so that the American commander-in-chief and his little army could keep on their way to Philadelphia.

"Who is that young man?" asked Washington.

"That, your Excellency, is Alexander Hamilton."

The great general was so pleased with the skill and courage of the young officer that he soon invited him to become his aide and secretary, with the rank of lieutenant-colonel. The commander-in-chief liked to have bright young men around him. Colonel Hamilton was now twenty. Colonel Aaron Burr was a year older. "Light-Horse Harry" Lee was about the same age; and General Lafayette, who was added to General Washington's staff that summer, was only nineteen. Colonel Hamilton was such a discreet and faithful secretary that it was said, "The pen of the army is held by Hamilton." In some ways Hamilton's pen was mightier than his sword.

At Brandywine, where Lafayette was wounded, Hamilton's horse was shot under him; but he kept at the head of his regiment, on foot. At Valley Forge young Hamilton had occasion to remember the language his mother used in talking with him when he was

a baby on the island of Nevis, for he often spoke French with young Marquis de Lafayette. The West Indian colonel was welcome wherever{305}
{306}

The first meeting between Washington and Hamilton.

{306}From an old print
The first meeting between Washington and Hamilton.
From an old print
he went. He was thoughtful and kind to the sick, writing beautiful letters home for disabled and dying soldiers.

One day when the young staff officer was hurrying to meet his chief, Lafayette detained him. Finally breaking away from the friendly young Frenchman, Hamilton found Washington waiting for him. The commander-in-chief said, "Colonel Hamilton, you have kept me waiting these ten minutes! I must tell you, sir, that you treat me with disrespect."

The young aide flushed scarlet and replied: "I am not conscious of it, sir; but since you have thought it necessary to tell me so, we part."

"Very well, sir, if it be your choice," said Washington.

With face still aflame, Hamilton turned and left the commander-in-chief. Within an hour the general was sorry he had been so severe with "my boy" as he called his aide, and sent for him, asking that their too hasty words might be forgotten. But even then Hamilton could not quite forgive his chief for reproving him. So Alexander Hamilton was placed in command of a detachment in the south, where "Light-Horse Harry" and Lafayette were officers also. At Yorktown, the last battle in the War for Independence, Colonel Hamilton was the first man of the American army to mount the wall before the town, where he was quickly followed by his devoted men. Within a very few minutes the American flag was floating over Yorktown.

After the war, Hamilton returned to New York City to practise law. He had married the daughter of General Schuyler, one of the richest men in that state. Attorney Hamilton soon became successful and prosperous. When the time came to frame the Constitution which was to{307} bind the thirteen states into one Union and make them true to their name, the United States, Alexander Hamilton was one of the leaders in that great undertaking.

After that, his former chief was elected the first President. One of the first acts of President Washington was to send for Alexander Hamilton to be the first Secretary of the Treasury. The young Secretary had to create success for the new nation, like making "bricks without straw." There was no national treasury. Continental money was without value, so that when anything was considered worthless it was said to be—"not worth a continental."

Rival states had been jealous of one another, and as there was no head, nothing was owned in common by the whole country—but debts. Money had been borrowed of other nations, and of patriotic people in America, to carry on the War for Independence. Many good people thought it would be impossible for the new government, just starting, to pay its debts, besides building up a new government and meeting the running expenses. But Alexander Hamilton, still a young man, saw that a country in debt could never be independent, and that if the government of the United States did not pay all it owed, it could not go on, any more than a bankrupt business which could not pay its bills. The only way to secure credit was to pay every dollar it owed.

Hamilton devised ways and means to do all this with such success that, in the street parades which the people arranged in different cities to celebrate the new Constitution, wherever a float represented the Constitution, the only man's name on the ship of state was "Hamilton." The plans of the young Secretary of the Treasury worked like magic, and the new government was soon on a solid foundation.{308}

Daniel Webster, the greatest orator who ever lived in America, in speaking of Hamilton's work, compared it to two miracles told of in the Bible; one, that of Moses when he drew water from a rock for the thirsty Israelites in the wilderness; the other, the raising of a dead man to life by Elijah. These are Webster's words:

"Hamilton smote the rock of the national resources and abundant streams of revenue gushed forth. He touched the dead corpse of public credit, and it sprang upon its feet."

Alexander Hamilton continued to act as the first President's private secretary. It is generally believed that it was he who wrote out Washington's immortal "Farewell Address." When he gave up the office of Secretary of the Treasury, Hamilton returned to the practise of law. He had gladly given up a large income and served his country for about one-third the amount of money he had been receiving from his law business.

In New York Hamilton's chief rival was Aaron Burr, whom Washington had disliked and allowed to retire from his military staff. But Colonel Burr was a brilliant lawyer and a popular politician. When Thomas Jefferson was elected President of the United States by the House of Representatives, Aaron Burr might have been chosen President if three men had voted the other way. Burr was bitterly disappointed, and blamed Hamilton for his defeat. Nursing revenge in his heart Burr practised shooting. As Hamilton continued to oppose Burr's schemes, Burr easily found an excuse to challenge him to fight a duel.

Dueling was still a common means of deciding questions of honor. Hamilton's eldest son had been killed in that way. As a man was called a coward if he did not fight,{309} Hamilton accepted Burr's challenge, though he felt sure it would mean death to himself. The place chosen for the shooting was the spot where Hamilton's son had lately been killed. When the signal was given, Alexander Hamilton pointed his pistol upward and fired into a tree to avoid hitting Burr, whose aim was as true as when shooting at a target. Hamilton fell, face downward, and died next day, declaring that he forgave the enemy who had planned and practised to kill him.

This duel did more than anything else to show the wickedness of the duel as a way of settling disputes. Aaron Burr later was accused of being a traitor to the country which Hamilton had given his great and noble life to place upon a firm foundation. What is true of dueling is also true of war—the unworthy party may succeed by wicked means. But America remembers Aaron Burr as a curse, and Alexander Hamilton as a blessing to his country.

THOMAS JEFFERSON, THE FATHER OF DEMOCRACY

THOMAS JEFFERSON was born on his father's many-thousand-acre farm near Charlottesville, Virginia, on the banks of River Anna, whose name was shortened to "Rivanna." Thomas's father, Colonel Peter Jefferson, had come over the sea from Wales, and his mother was Jane Randolph, a daughter of one of the "F. F. V.'s," or First Families of Virginia.

The Jefferson boy grew up tall, thin, awkward, freckled and red-haired. His father, like George Washington's, was a wealthy planter, who died while Thomas was yet a lad. But young Jefferson's mother was not left poor like Washington{310}'s; she was able to send her son to William and Mary College. Though Thomas was always reading and studying, he was very fond of playing the violin. Several stories are told about Jefferson and his "fiddle," as they called it then. One is that he played duets with Patrick Henry; another is that he once performed with George Washington, who played quite well on the flute.

Thomas was so eager to learn and so afraid of wasting time in college that he took the four years' course in two years, graduating at nineteen. Besides the regular college branches, he studied architecture, and after graduating devoted some time to that profession before fully deciding to study law.

Young Jefferson was not admitted to practise law until five years after finishing his college course. This was because he was not content merely with "reading law," but he read many books on other subjects and continued his study of music.

While he was attending court at Charlottesville, his home at Shadwell was burned to the ground. An old negro house-servant came to tell the young master all about the fire. Lawyer Jefferson thought first of his large library and asked if his precious books had been saved.

"No, massa," said the old slave. "Dem books is all burnt up, but de fire didn't cotch your dear old fiddle. I carried dat out, myse'f, I did."

Perhaps the best story of all that are still told of Jefferson and his fiddle is that about two young men admirers of the young and beautiful widow Skelton. They called on her one evening and found "Tom" Jefferson there already. He was playing his violin while she accompanied him on her spinet—an old-fashioned piano. They listened a{311} moment and laughed. "We won't play 'second fiddle' or break up their duet," said one of the callers. So they went away without leaving their names. It was not long before Thomas Jefferson, like George Washington, married a wealthy widow and brought her to live on one of the largest and finest estates in old Virginia.

Thomas Jefferson had planned and built a new house in place of the one which had been burned down. He chose a high hill on the plantation, from which, across the surrounding country, the town of Charlottesville could be seen miles away. He named the estate "Monticello," the Italian word for "little mountain."

About the time the Jeffersons were married the whole country was stirred by the Stamp Act and other taxes demanded by England of the American colonies. These taxes seemed unjust, because the people were not allowed the right to send men from America to help make the laws which they had to obey. Jefferson wrote a pamphlet on the subject, which he called "A Summary View of the Rights of British America." In it he said, "The God who gave us life gave us liberty at the same time."

When the people of the colonies in America were fully aroused, they sent men to the Continental Congress at Philadelphia to decide what to do about the unjust acts of the British king and his wrong advisers. George Washington, Thomas Jefferson, and Richard Henry Lee were among the men, called delegates, sent from "Old Virginia."

One day in the Congress, Richard Henry Lee arose and made this motion:

"Resolved, That these United Colonies are, and of right ought to be, free and independent states."

After discussing Lee's resolution for three days, the{312}

The signing of the Declaration of Independence, that historic document of which Jefferson was the author.

The signing of the Declaration of Independence, that historic document of which Jefferson was the author.

{313}

Congress voted to have a statement drawn up to send to King George the Third, declaring that the people of the United Colonies could not stand wrong treatment any longer. Thomas Jefferson was appointed chairman of a committee of five to write this paper, which came to be called the Declaration of Independence. This is one of the four greatest legal papers ever written. In it were these lines, which will be repeated as long as there are people living in the world who love liberty:

"We hold these truths to be self-evident—that all men are created equal; that they are endowed by their Creator with certain unalienable rights; that among these are life, liberty and the pursuit of happiness."

"We mutually pledge to each other our lives, our fortunes and our sacred honor."

When the War for Independence was won, Thomas Jefferson was sent to France to represent the young American republic. Then when Washington was President he was called home to be Secretary of State. After Washington died, Thomas Jefferson was elected the third President of the United States. Instead of being fond of show in using the power given to him by the people, Thomas Jefferson was very simple in his tastes. When he came to be inaugurated President he did not drive through the streets of Washington in a coach with six horses and outriders and escorts, as other Presidents had done, but walked with a few friends from his boarding-house to the new Capitol, then building, where he delivered his Inaugural Address and took the oath of office.

This so-called "Jeffersonian simplicity" seemed strange then, because he was a man of wealth and lived in a beautiful mansion. Many people did not like his simple ways.{314} They thought the President of the United States should show more dignity. The minister from Great Britain was offended because, when he came to present his respects and those of the king of England, President Jefferson received him in a dressing-gown and slippers and heavy yarn socks. But the sensible people thought so much of the man who wrote the Declaration of Independence that they did not mind what kind of stockings Thomas Jefferson wore.

While he was President, Jefferson saw that the country's interests would be hampered while New Orleans, near the mouth of the Mississippi River, belonged to France. It was like having another nation own and control the south door of the United States. So Jefferson sent men to purchase from the French government New Orleans and the right of way out of the Mississippi. Napoleon was then in power, and as he needed money to carry on his war with England, he offered to sell to the United States, for fifteen million dollars, not only New Orleans, but all the western country which France had claimed since the days of La Salle and other explorers. This was a great bargain and the men whom President Jefferson had sent bought the land without waiting to hear from home. This was called the Louisiana Purchase, and the people were more than glad to approve what the President had done.

The expedition of Lewis and Clark was sent out by Jefferson to explore and make maps of the Louisiana Purchase.

So Thomas Jefferson not only wrote the Declaration of Independence but he was the means of doubling the size and wealth of the country, making it extend from the Great Lakes to the Gulf of Mexico and from the Atlantic to the Pacific Ocean.{315}

ANDREW JACKSON, AMERICA'S MOST POPULAR HERO

ABOUT ten years before the signing of the Declaration of Independence, two Irish linen weavers, Andrew and Elizabeth Jackson, came across the Atlantic to a backwoods settlement in North Carolina. There the young settlers built a cabin, but before they had lived long in their rude little home, Andrew Jackson died, leaving his wife with two small sons, Hugh and Robert. The young widow went to live with a sick sister a few miles away, and when the third baby boy was born to her here, she named him Andrew for his dead father. The house in which little Andrew Jackson was born was so near the boundary line between North and South Carolina that years afterwards both states claimed him as their son.

Elizabeth Jackson had to keep house for her sister to support herself and her three little boys. Andrew was in his tenth year when the War for Independence broke out in the north. Three years later the British came to fight near the Jacksons' home in the south. Hugh, the oldest, now a lad of seventeen, fought in the battle of Stono, and died, soon after, of heat and exhaustion.

Then the British troops came nearer, and Widow Jackson, with Robert and Andrew, was driven from her poor home. These terrible experiences developed in the tall, red-haired, freckled, thirteen-year-old Scotch-Irish lad a deep hatred of the "red-coats," as the British soldiers were called.

As if Andrew had not already reasons enough for hating his enemies, a squad of dragoons surprised him with his brother Robert and a cousin, Lieutenant Thomas Crawford, at the home of the Crawfords, where they had brought Tom, wounded and ill, for his mother's care. After capturing {316} the young American "soldiers three," the British cavalrymen broke the Crawfords' dishes, tore their clothing, ripped open feather beds, insulted the frightened mother and abused the little children. Then, as if for a crowning insult, the British officer ordered Andy to clean his boots. The young Irish soldier drew himself up and said proudly,

"Sir, I am not a servant, but a prisoner of war, and I claim to be treated as such."

The angry dragoon struck at the youth's head with his saber. Andy threw up his hand and saved his own life by breaking the force of the stroke, but received deep cuts on his forehead and hand. He wore the two scars to his dying day.

Andrew's brother Robert was commanded to perform the same low service and refused with the same proud spirit; he also received a sword-cut on his head which nearly killed him. The two Jackson youths were then taken away to a prison pen at Camden, South Carolina, where American soldiers were treated like beasts and where many were already dying of smallpox.

While the Jackson brothers were in this prison, a battle was fought near by. Young Andrew whittled a hole through a board with an old razor, so that he could watch the battle that was raging around them.

When the poor mother heard that her wounded sons were confined in a filthy prison where they were exposed to smallpox, she walked forty miles to Camden and managed to have them exchanged for some British soldiers the Americans had captured. Begging the use of two horses, she placed Robert on one of them, as he was very ill with smallpox. She rode the other horse to hold her son in his saddle; and young Andrew, "weak and wounded, sick and {317} sore," staggered along behind them on foot. Robert died two days after reaching home, but Andrew recovered after a long and severe illness.

After nursing her only remaining son back to health, that brave, unselfish mother heard that many American soldiers were sick and dying in the British prison ship in the harbor of Charleston, South Carolina. She walked more than one hundred and fifty miles to nurse and help them as she had nursed her own sons. She took the ship fever and died, giving her devoted life for freedom and for country.

So Andrew Jackson, now a tall, thin youth of fourteen with a "shock of sandy hair," was without father, mother, brothers, money, or near friends—but with a bitter grudge against Britain as the cause of all his troubles and sorrows. His life was made better by his deep love of his brave, noble mother's memory. When he grew up and became the most popular man in the United States, Andrew Jackson often said with a smile of pride:

"That I learned from my good old mother!"

Andrew Jackson had but few chances to go to school, and then only a few weeks at a time. He learned the saddler's trade and studied when he could take the time from hard work. Little as he learned from books, he knew more than most of his neighbors. He taught school sometimes to add to what he earned at his trade, so that he could study law. Even North Carolina, wild as that new country was, became too "civilized" for Andrew Jackson, and he crossed the mountains into Tennessee and settled at Nashville, where he began to practise law. In that rough country he soon became a leader. In the midst of the wild life in which the chief "sports" were horse-racing,{318} Indian shooting, fighting duels, and the like, young "Judge" Jackson was "hail-fellow, well met!" He soon was elected to Congress, but he found life at the capital entirely too "genteel" for him. When the southern Indians went on the warpath and massacred white settlers, General Jackson and his troops from Tennessee drove them from place to place and killed nearly all the savage murderers. He was called the Hero of the War of 1812, because he won the Battle of New Orleans, the greatest land victory in that war.

The people loved General Jackson because he was a bluff, warm-hearted man, and because, whether he fought with the Indians or the British, "he thrashed 'em every time!" He was named "Old Hickory" because he was about as tough in fiber and as rough on the outside as the hickory tree. He was probably the most popular hero that ever lived in America, for more boys were named Andrew Jackson than even George Washington or Abraham Lincoln. January eighth, the date of Jackson's victory at New Orleans, is still celebrated as Jackson Day. Jackson was called "the Man of the People," including the "rough and ready" people of the great, new west; Jefferson represented the more educated classes; while Washington was the man of the upper class of people. Still, Jackson stood for the white people only. It was Abraham Lincoln who came thirty years later and stood for all the people, black and white.

General Jackson was elected and carried to the White House by a great wave of popularity. The people were so pleased to have him for their President that they crowded into the White House and stood on the new satin covered furniture in their muddy boots. They broke the china and glassware and spilled punch on the velvet carpets. In their{319}
{320}

General Jackson at the Battle of New Orleans.

{320}From the painting by D. M. Carter
General Jackson at the Battle of New Orleans.
From the painting by D. M. Carter
frantic efforts to shake hands with their hero-president they nearly crushed him to death.

President Jackson treated his political enemies as he did the Indians and the English. He turned thousands of men out of office and appointed his friends in their places. "To the victors belong the spoils," he said, but most people to-day believe the warlike President had the wrong idea in treating public service as "spoils of war." After serving his country as President, Andrew Jackson lived at the Hermitage, a beautiful mansion he had built near Nashville, Tennessee.

When the aged ex-President knew he was dying, he called his friends and slaves around his bed and told them he wanted them all to meet him in heaven. When the simple but grand old hero died, they found his dead wife's miniature close to his heart where he had worn it for many years.

Then they remembered that, rough and violent as he often had been with men, he had never spoken a cross or cruel word to his wife or any of his own household.

"The bravest are the tenderest."

WEBSTER, CLAY, CALHOUN, THREE GREAT CHAMPIONS IN CONGRESS

"THERE were giants in those days," a hundred years ago in the United States of America; not giants in body, but in mind and heart. Besides the Presidents and the generals in the War of 1812 and the Indian wars, the greatest men in America were Webster, Clay, and Calhoun, who were in Congress together. Daniel Webster{321} was the man of New England, Henry Clay of the west, and John C. Calhoun of the south.

Daniel Webster was born among the hills of New Hampshire, the ninth of the ten children of his father. He had a huge head, a high forehead, and great, deep, inquiring eyes. Webster once said that he did not remember when he could not read the Bible. He learned chapter after chapter of it by heart and remembered them all his life.

Clay, Calhoun and Webster, "The Statesmen of the Compromise."

(From left to right.)

From the painting by A. Tholey
Clay, Calhoun and Webster, "The Statesmen of the Compromise."
(From left to right.)
From the painting by A. Tholey

Daniel's father lived on a rocky farm in New Hampshire and had a hard time to educate his growing family. He was called Captain Webster because he had been an officer in the War for Independence. His children used to delight in hearing about General Washington. After Daniel grew{322} to be a great man he was proud to tell how the Father of his Country had trusted his father. Once he said,

"I should rather have it said upon my father's tombstone that he had guarded the person of George Washington and was worthy of such a trust, than to have carved upon it the greatest title that the world could give."

Captain Webster said to his son one day after a gentleman who was riding by had stopped to speak to him:

"Dan, that man beat me by a few votes when I ran against him for Congress, and all because he had a better education. For that reason I intend you shall have a good education, and I hope to see you work your way up to Congress."

Daniel's next older brother's name was Ezekiel. He was larger and stronger than Daniel who, because of his poor health, was not expected to do hard work on the farm.

133

This gave Daniel time to read and improve his mind. Yet he was not allowed to be idle; he was expected to do "chores" and other light work about the place. One day Captain Webster went away, after giving both boys a certain task to do while he was gone. The lads, boy-like, spent the day having a good time, so that when their father came home he found the work not done.

"Zeke," he said sternly, "what have you been doing all day?"

"Nothing," said Zeke sheepishly.

"And what have you been doing, Dan?" asked Captain Webster.

"Helping Zeke!" said the younger boy with a grin.

After that when any one was idle, it was said that he was "helping Zeke."

When the time came for Father Webster to send Daniel{323} away to school, as he had promised, the younger boy said he would not go unless Zeke could have the same chance. So Captain Webster mortgaged the farm to raise the money to educate both boys. Even then the sons had to stay out of school at times to earn money to help themselves through the academy and college.

In mental work Daniel proved stronger and better able to earn money than his older brother. A good story is told of Daniel's coming, after teaching a term of school, to see Ezekiel at college and giving his brother one hundred dollars—nearly all he had earned, keeping only three dollars for himself until he could earn more. That was Daniel Webster's best way of "helping Zeke."

Daniel was the more brilliant of the two, so that he was through college as soon as his brother, though he had not spent so much time there. Their father explained one difference between the two sons:

"Ezekiel could not tell half he knew; but Daniel could tell more than he knew."

By the time Daniel was out of college his father had become a county judge, and was able to offer his youngest son a position as clerk of the court at fifteen hundred dollars a year, which was a large salary for that time and place. But Daniel refused the place, saying: "I intend to be a lawyer myself and not to spend my life jotting down other men's doings."

" 'A bird in the hand is worth two in the bush,' " said Judge Webster, reminding his son that there were already too many lawyers for them all to make a good living.

"There's always room at the top," said young Daniel Webster.

He went to Boston to study law, and his fame as attorney{324} and orator spread far and wide. The two sons soon paid their father's debts, and proud old Judge Webster soon saw his son Daniel not only in Congress, but acknowledged to be the greatest man in the Senate.

Ezekiel Webster did not have so brilliant a career as his younger brother, but Daniel always yielded to "Zeke's" better judgment, even in the greatest public affairs. Ezekiel did not live to see Daniel's highest success, and it was said that a new look of sadness came into the great Webster's face, and never left it, after hearing of "Zeke's" sudden death.

Although Daniel Webster was not six feet tall, his high, full, square brow and dignified bearing made him seem a giant. Carlyle, the great Scottish philosopher, met him in London and said: "Webster is a walking cathedral!"

When Daniel Webster was still a small boy on his father's "rock-ribb'd" farm in New Hampshire, a thin, homely youth of fifteen came into the Court of Chancery in Richmond, Virginia. He was so awkward and bashful and dressed so queerly that the clerks winked at one another and snickered behind his back. That youth, whose name was Henry Clay, had come to Richmond from a low, swampy region called "the Slashes," where he lived with his widowed mother. Because he used to ride a poor old horse to a mill near his home to get a little corn ground, Henry Clay was afterward called "the Mill Boy of the Slashes."

Henry's mother married again and moved out to Kentucky when it was still a western wilderness. Young Clay stayed in Virginia to study law and was soon admired because of his brightness. He improved his time, as well as his appearance, so that when he was eighteen, he was a popular orator and "the bright, particular star" of the Richmond Debating Society. {325}

Then, instead of finding "room higher up" in his home state, Henry went west to be near his mother, and to "grow up with the country." The twenty-one-year-old attorney hung out his sign in the new and growing town of Lexington, Kentucky. He was good-natured and thoughtful. He understood law very well for so young a man. As he was an eloquent speaker, he became a successful attorney. He married and settled down on a 600-acre estate which he named "Ashland." This estate is still known all over the world as "the home of Henry Clay."

The year before the War of 1812 began, Henry Clay was sent to Congress from Kentucky and was elected Speaker of the House of Representatives. He raised his eloquent voice against England and bore a strong part in supporting President Madison in carrying on the war. He was so earnest in this that he was known as a leader of "the War Hawks." When the war was over, Henry Clay was one of five men sent to Europe by the United States to arrange the terms of peace with Great Britain—a peace which has not been broken for more than a hundred years.

Henry Clay was three times a candidate for the presidency. He had done so much for the country that he had made enemies of many whom he had to oppose at different times. So each time he was defeated by a man not nearly so great or powerful, but for whom more people were willing to vote.

While Webster and Clay were leaders in Congress there was great excitement because that body passed a tariff law which the southern people did not like. Many of the southern leaders, especially those of South Carolina, said that Congress had no right to pass such a law and that each state might declare the objectionable law null and void or{326} of no effect within its borders. Such action by a state was called "nullification." There was talk that some of the states would withdraw from the Union if the President tried to enforce the hated law. Such withdrawal on the part of a state was called "secession."

About the time these mutterings of disunion were in the air, Robert Y. Hayne, a great orator from South Carolina, made a strong speech in the Senate of the United States, maintaining the right of his state to "nullify" and withdraw from the Union. Daniel Webster, the champion of the Union, delivered one of the greatest appeals ever made by any orator, in his famous reply to Hayne. It closed with these now familiar words:

"Let my last feeble and lingering glance behold the glorious ensign of the republic, now known and honored throughout the earth, still full high advanced, its arms and trophies streaming in their original luster, not a stripe erased or polluted, not a single star obscured; bearing for its motto no such miserable question as, 'What is all this worth?' or those other words of delusion and folly, 'Liberty first and Union afterwards;' but everywhere, spread all over in characters of living light, blazing in all its ample folds, as they float over the sea and over the land, that other sentiment, dear to every true American heart—Liberty and Union, now and forever, one and inseparable."

The greatest leader in the south and champion of the right of his state, South Carolina, was John C. Calhoun. He also was an eloquent speaker. He declared in the Senate of the United States, in speaking of the tariff law meant to tax goods which people needed, "We look upon it as a dead law, null and void, and will not obey it." South Carolina nullified the tariff law and threatened to secede from the Union.

General Andrew Jackson, the bluff old Indian fighter and hero of the War of 1812, was then President. He declared, "The Union must and shall be preserved!" John C.{327} Calhoun and all others acquainted with "Old Hickory," as the President was nicknamed, knew that he meant just what he said. It seemed that civil war was about to begin when Henry Clay, who loved the Union, averted the danger by proposing a plan of compromise which both sides could accept.

THE KIND HEART OF ABRAHAM LINCOLN

LITTLE Abe Lincoln lived in a log cabin in Kentucky. When he was seven, his family moved across the Ohio River into Indiana, and lived all winter in an open shed called a "half-faced camp," before his father built a better cabin, with bare earth for its floor. Tom Lincoln, Abe's father, was "a mighty hunter." He liked to shoot game better than the hard work of clearing land and farming. He thought Abe was timid because he did not like to kill harmless animals or see them suffer.

During the fourteen years Abe lived in southern Indiana, he went to school a few weeks at a time—less than a year in all. A girl who went to school when he did, used to tell, after she became an old woman, that Abe's first "composition" was against cruelty to animals. She always remembered how he read this sentence in it: "An ant's life is as sweet to it as ours is to us."

One day Abe caught several lads laughing at a turtle as it moved slowly about, showing, as well as a dumb animal could, the misery it was in. For there were burning coals on its back, and the biggest boy stood by with a smoking shingle in his hand. This showed Abe how the hot coals came upon the terrapin's back. Snatching the shingle from the big bully's hand, he brushed them off and began{328}

The boy Lincoln reading by the firelight in the log cabin in which he was born.

The boy Lincoln reading by the firelight in the log cabin in which he was born. {329}

to paddle the cruel boy with it, calling him a cowardly fellow for hurting a helpless turtle.

Just before Abe was twenty-one, Father Lincoln moved to newer country in Illinois. Abe's step-sisters were now married, so there was a big family going west in a lumbering wagon drawn by two yoke of oxen. One of the step-sisters took with her a pet dog. It was in the midst of winter, and some of the rivers they had to cross were covered with ice. One day the little dog strayed away from the wagon and failed to come back until the Lincoln party had forded a shallow stream. After crossing, Abe, who was then driving the oxen, saw the poor little fellow jumping about and whining, afraid of being left behind. It was growing dark and they had to make their camp for the night. All the others were for leaving the "troublesome cur" to its fate. Mr. Lincoln, in telling of their moving to Illinois, said of this:

"But I could not endure the idea of abandoning even a dog. Pulling off shoes and socks, I waded across the stream and triumphantly returned with the shivering animal under my arm. His frantic leaps of joy and other evidences of a dog's gratitude amply repaid me for all the exposure I had undergone."

136

Many other stories are told of Abraham Lincoln's kindness of heart. When he was a country lawyer he had to ride from one county seat to another, attending court. The judge and several attorneys rode from place to place where court was to be held. Lawyer Lincoln was the most popular man of them all, because of his good nature and his ready fund of funny stories.

The Illinois roads were then nearly always very dusty or very muddy. One day their party saw a hog stuck in a deep mudhole, squealing loudly. The party rode by and{330} laughed at the pig's plight, but no one took the trouble to help it out. But those despairing squeals touched the heart of Abraham Lincoln.

He soon fell behind and galloped back to rescue the animal. Taking several rails from the roadside fence, he used one to pry over, and another to lift the pig out. By taking care and plenty of time, he managed to place the end of a rail under the hog without hurting it. The animal was now so weak that this took a long time, and Lawyer Lincoln's clothes were badly smeared with mud.

At last, when the pig realized that it was free, it started off toward the farmhouse where it belonged, flopping its big ears and grunting gratefully. Mr. Lincoln did not catch up with his friends until they had arrived at the tavern in the next town.

When they saw his mud-plastered clothes, they all began to laugh, for Lawyer Lincoln did not often have a new suit of clothes. When they stopped chaffing him about helping his "dear brother" in distress, Lincoln said soberly,

"That farmer's children might have to go barefoot next winter if he lost his hog."

Another day Lincoln was missing. One of the party explained,

"I saw him an hour ago over the fence in a grove with a young bird screaming in each hand, while he was going around hunting for their nest."

It took a long time to find it. Lawyer Lincoln had to let one bird go while he climbed the tree to put the other in its nest. Then he had to climb up again to put the other bird in. So it was after dark when he rejoined his friends at the tavern table. It seemed so absurd for a big man like Lincoln to waste hours on two birds that had fallen out of{331} their nest, that even the judge scolded him. Mr. Lincoln replied with deep feeling,

"Gentlemen, you may laugh, but I could not have slept well to-night if I had not saved those birds. Their cries would have rung in my ears."

The spring after he was twenty-one, Abraham Lincoln helped to build a flatboat and went on it to New Orleans to buy stock for a store in the village. While in the southern city with two companions, he witnessed the sale of a mulatto girl in a slave market. The sight filled his righteous soul with wrath. Clenching his fists, he exclaimed:

"Boys, let's get away from this. If I ever get a chance to hit that thing (slavery) I'll hit it hard!"

So Lawyer Lincoln became the champion of the negro and lifted his voice against slavery. "This country cannot exist half slave and half free," he exclaimed. His ringing words in the famous debates with Senator Douglas pleased the people of the north so much that Lincoln was elected President next time. Within six weeks after he went to live in the White House, the Civil War broke out.

The tender heart of President Lincoln was often hurt when the news of a battle came to Washington with its list of killed and wounded. He tried to keep up his own spirits and the heart of the nation by his constant flow of stories which made the people smile through their tears. To him it was an awful thing for his brothers in the north to be fighting and slaying their brothers down south.

137

When Abraham Lincoln saw that the time was right, he gave out the Emancipation Proclamation—his order to free four million slaves. He now had "a chance to hit that thing," and he did "hit it hard."

Grand as it was to write that great paper and free all the {332} slaves, it was even greater to show the people of the United States and of the whole world how to look on the bright side of the hardest trials, and even to laugh in the face of trouble.

President Lincoln had the supreme joy of seeing the purpose of the war accomplished. His Gettysburg Address—which every boy and girl should know by heart—and the words from the Second Inaugural, "With malice toward none; with charity for all," are ever-living witnesses of the kind heart and unselfish spirit of Abraham Lincoln.

William Cullen Bryant, one of the first of American poets, wrote these lines for the Martyr President's funeral:

"O, slow to smite and swift to spare,
Gentle and merciful and just!
Who in the fear of God didst bear
The sword of power, a nation's trust.
Pure was thy life; its bloody close
Has placed thee with the Sons of Light,
Among the noble hearts of those
Who perished in the cause of Right."

ULYSSES S. GRANT, THE GENERAL WHO HATED WAR

"THIS poor little boy has no name!" exclaimed Miss Simpson, the aunt who was visiting the Grant family at Point Pleasant, overlooking the Ohio River, about twenty miles east of Cincinnati.

The rest of the family agreed that it would be a shame to let the baby go a day longer without a name.

"Let's name him now," said the aunt; "let's vote on it."

The others consented, and each wrote a preferred name on a bit of paper. Then a hat was passed and all put their {333}

General Ulysses S. Grant.
General Ulysses S. Grant.
{334}
slips in it. The aunt took out a ballot which read, "Ulysses." This name was on several slips, because Grandfather Grant had just been reading the story of the siege of Troy. "Hiram" and "Albert" were on two other ballots. At last they decided to call the baby Hiram Ulysses Grant.

When "Baby Lysses," as the family called him, was about a year old, the Grants moved to Georgetown, a village about ten miles farther from Cincinnati, and ten miles back from the Ohio. Here little Ulysses grew and began to go to school, and some of the boys called him "Hug," from his initials, H. U. G. Other boys, just to be funny, called him "Useless."

Ulysses' father was a tanner and leather worker. The boy did not like tanning hides because it was dirty, bad-smelling work; but he did like horses. Besides his tannery, Mr. Grant owned a small farm. So Ulysses, while he was a boy, learned to plow and harrow, and to haul logs to the creek near by, where they were floated to the sawmill to be cut up

138

into boards and timber. The lad found a good way to make a horse do the heavy work of lifting or rolling logs on to the sled, so that he and the horse could do that better than two or three men.

A visitor in Georgetown was astonished one day to see a boy dash by, standing on the back of a horse on the run.

"Circus rider?" the stranger asked.

"No—only 'Useless' Grant," was the reply.

When a circus did come to Georgetown, the Grant boy was there to see the trained horses and the fancy riding. There was a trick pony that had been trained not to allow a man or even a boy to stay on its back. The manager came to the side of the ring and called out that a prize of five dollars in gold would be given to any one who could{335} ride the pony five times around the ring. Some of the men and boys in the crowd shouted, "Lyss Grant can do it. Try it! Oh, go ahead, Lyss!"

Although Ulysses was a bashful lad and hated to make a show of himself, the prize and his desire to see what he could do were too tempting to resist. So he went to the ringside and began to pat the pony. Then he sprang lightly upon its back. The vicious little beast began to rear and tear around to shake or rub the rider off, but Ulysses hung on in spite of all its frantic efforts. He won the prize, but that five dollars was of small value compared with the lesson he learned of trying hard and not giving up anything he attempted.

The Grant boy's mastery of horses and his way of finishing whatever he started out to do made his services valuable to the neighbors. He rode hundreds of miles on important business errands. One time he was driving two young ladies and their baggage on a long journey where they had to ford a swollen stream. The ladies, seeing the horses were swimming and that the wagon was full of water, began to scream and take hold of his arms.

"Keep quiet, please," said Ulysses calmly. "I'll take you through safe." And the Grant lad was as good as his word.

Sometimes he was asked to break a horse to trot or to pace. The wildest animal would soon become tame and gentle and would do whatever he wished. People thought he would be a horse-trainer or jockey, or keep a racing stable, but Ulysses Grant, much as he enjoyed training horses, had a mind above doing that all his life.

He was studious at school and excelled in games and sports. One day, while playing with a neighbor boy, he{336} batted the ball through the window of a neighboring house. Instead of running away or pretending that another boy had done it, Ulysses went at once and knocked at the door of the house, and said to the lady when she came out, "I have broken your window, but I'm going to get a pane of glass and have it put right in."

The woman, who had seen how it happened, told the Grant boy to go back and play, and she would attend to the glass. In telling about the accident, she said Ulysses was no more to blame than the other boy, and ended her story with, "I like Lyss Grant; he's such a square, manly little fellow."

The school at Georgetown was not advanced enough to suit Ulysses' father; so the lad was sent away to a private school at Marysville. When he came home, though he did not like the tannery, he worked faithfully there. He told his father plainly that he would work at tanning hides until he was twenty-one—"but not one day after that!"

"What would you like to do?" his father asked.

"I'd like to be a planter, or a river merchant, or—or—get an education," stammered the boy.

Father Grant smiled and sent his son off to another school. He knew it would be very wrong to expect a real man to work all his life at something he did not like. While Ulysses was away this time, his father obtained an appointment for his son to go to West Point. Ulysses himself has written about this:

"I was attending school at Ripley, only ten miles distant from Georgetown, but spent the Christmas holidays at home. During this vacation my father received a letter from the United States Senator from Ohio. When he read it he said to me, 'Ulysses, I believe you are going to receive the appointment.'

" 'What appointment?' I inquired. {337}

" 'To West Point. I have applied for it.'

" 'But I won't go,' I said.

"He said he thought I would, and I thought so too, if he did!"

Young Grant had such a high idea of the requirements at West Point that he was sure he could never pass the entrance examinations. He began to study algebra and other branches to fit him better, but he said he never gave up hoping something would happen—even that the Military Academy might burn down!—so he would not have to go. He was afraid he would fail. The neighbors also thought his father was making a mistake to send the boy to West Point when he seemed so little fitted for a soldier. But, soon after his seventeenth birthday, the neighbors bade Ulysses good-bye, expecting him to come home because he could not pass.

Ulysses found the West Point buildings still standing when he arrived. He registered, and, to his surprise, was permitted to enter as a cadet. They made a mistake in recording his name, writing it Ulysses S., instead of H. Ulysses Grant. He was tired of being called "Hug," and, as it seemed too much trouble to correct the error, he let it go, accepting the S. for his middle initial. As his mother's maiden name was Simpson, he let them name him Ulysses Simpson Grant, in honor of the U. S. government and his little mother. But even then the boys made fun of his initials, "U. S.," calling him "United States" and "Uncle Sam" Grant. From this he was nicknamed "Sam."

Cadet Ulysses did well enough in his studies, and developed a taste for drawing and painting. He thought he would rather be a water-color artist than a soldier. The idea of shooting at men was shocking to him. The sight of blood made him sick—"Just like a girl!" the fellows said. {338} But there were horses at the Academy, so the young cadet managed to be quite happy. He learned to ride like an Indian and to leap from one horse to the back of another as he met it running in the opposite direction. The one thing for which he was remembered by the other cadets was the great feat of jumping York, a huge horse, over a bar. Every one was afraid the vicious horse, if forced to clear such a height, might kill his rider. "I can't die but once," remarked Cadet Grant coolly, and made the horse jump over the bar without the least harm to horse or rider. The record of "Grant on York," then made, has never been beaten since.

The people of Ulysses' home town had changed their minds about him when he came home after two years, in his mid-course furlough, as a cadet in full uniform with gold lace and gilt buttons. After he had been President of the United States, Ulysses S. Grant said this summer vacation was the happiest time in his whole life, because every one was so kind, and his family were so proud of him.

When he finished his course at the Military Academy and was graduated, it was said of him: "There is 'Sam' Grant. He is a splendid fellow; a good, honest man against whom nothing can be said, and from whom everything may be expected."

Lieutenant Grant went home for a while, and then entered military service near St. Louis. Here he became acquainted with Miss Julia Dent, who afterward became Mrs.

Grant, wife of the great general and President of the United States. He had the usual experiences of young army officers in the southwest, with wild beasts and savage Indians. He tells of being wakened early one morning by hearing shots near at hand. Getting up, he learned that two men had been fighting a duel. He afterward wrote:{339}

"I don't believe I ever could have the courage to fight a duel. If I should do another man such a wrong as to justify him in killing me, I would make any reasonable amends in my power, if convinced of the wrong done. I place my opposition to dueling on higher grounds. No doubt, most of the duels have been fought for want of moral courage, on the part of those engaged, to decline."

Lieutenant Grant's friends thought it strange for the bravest man they ever met to say, "I don't believe I ever could have the courage to fight a duel." But some things that seemed heroic to others did not seem so to Ulysses S. Grant. He spoke almost with scorn of mere physical courage. It is moral courage that counts—the heroism that will face a sneer and bravely say, "That is not right and I will not do it." He had shown this kind of courage as a boy, when other lads dared him to come out with them at night and disobey his little mother.

In the Mexican War, while fighting desperately in Monterey, the Americans ran short of powder. Who would dare to go back through the streets of the town held by the enemy, and carry the request for more ammunition and reinforcements? "Sam" Grant volunteered, and rode, Indian fashion, keeping his horse between him and the Mexicans' bullets. He made the dangerous run with both his horse and himself unhurt, relieved the Americans, and thus helped to save the day at Monterey.

When the Civil War broke out, Captain Grant was in business. He had withdrawn from the army, and had been mentioned as a "military dead beat," working in his father's leather store at fifty dollars a month. He at once enlisted as a volunteer, and was sent to command a brigade in Missouri. Within a year the name of General U. S. Grant was on every tongue. He had won the battles of Fort Donelson and Fort Henry, and had made his famous demand{340} of "Unconditional Surrender," words which meant that they were to yield without asking any favors. After that, people said his initials, U. S., stood for "Unconditional Surrender" Grant. He went from one triumph to another until his enemies in the west were beaten. Then President Lincoln called him to end the war in the east, a thing which five northern generals before him had failed to do.

Though he won great victories for his country and became the most successful general of his day, the greatest thing General Grant ever said was, "Let us have peace," When Richmond was captured he refused to enter the city as its conqueror. When General Lee surrendered, the northern commander treated the enemy general as a friend and a brother.

A grateful nation elected General Grant twice to the presidency of the United States. After he left the White House, he and Mrs. Grant made a trip around the world and became the guests of kings, queens, princes, prime ministers, and peoples.

Wherever General Grant went, he went as a man of peace. When he visited Prince Bismarck, "the man of blood and iron" who taught the Germans that everything they did would be right if they only had the power to do it, General Grant apologized for his record as a soldier. In this way, the greatest living general became the foremost man in the world for peace. He had learned to regard war as a duel between nations. He thought that was quite as wrong as dueling between men, and that war was due to moral cowardice rather than to courage.

General Grant gave this as his belief:

141

"Though I have been trained as a soldier and have taken part in many battles, there never has been a time when, in my opinion, some way could not have been found to prevent the drawing of the sword."

{341}

THE NOBLE SOUL OF ROBERT E. LEE

ROBERT E. LEE'S father, Colonel Henry Lee, was a hero of the Revolutionary War. He was commander of the famous company known as "Lee's Legion." He was called "Light-Horse Harry" because he was so ready and alert with his cavalry regiment. He was such a friend of the commander-in-chief that it was said: "General Washington loves Harry Lee as if he were his own son."

Therefore, when the Father of his Country died, Robert E. Lee's father was chosen by Congress to deliver the great oration in his memory. It was in this brilliant address that Colonel Henry Lee used the now familiar words describing Washington as "First in war, first in peace, and first in the hearts of his countrymen."

Like George Washington, Robert Lee was born in Virginia, near the Potomac River, in a huge brick house which looked like a mansion, a castle, and a fort, all in one. When Robert was four, his father moved to Alexandria, near the new city of Washington, to send the boy, with his brothers and sisters, to school.

The next year the War of 1812, often called the Second War for Independence, was declared. The father's rank was raised at once from Colonel to General Henry Lee. But General Lee was badly hurt while defending a friend from a mob in Baltimore. It was very hard for a brave man like "Light-Horse Harry" to be sent away for his health instead of leading in another fight for his country's liberties. The general did not become better and, after five years of absence and longing, he started home to die. But the end came while he was on his way, and the Lee children were told, one sad day, that they would never see the dear father's face again. {342}

Robert was now eleven, the same age as George Washington when he lost his father. Mrs. Lee was not left so poor as Washington's mother, but she was an invalid.

The oldest Lee son was in Harvard College, and the next was a midshipman in the Naval Academy at Annapolis. So Robert was left at home to take care of his mother. He nursed her

"With a hand as gentle as woman's,"

yet in his strong, manly arms he carried her out to the family coach, when she was well enough to go for a drive. No mother ever had more reason to be proud of her tall, handsome son than the widow of Henry Lee. Feeling that his mother could not afford to send him to college, young Robert studied hard to enter West Point Military Academy. Because the country was still new and settlers had to defend their homes and lives from Indians, and also because the nations were always at war, such boys as George Washington and Robert Lee said to themselves, "When I'm a man I'll be a soldier."

When Robert was eighteen he became a West Point cadet. After he left home his brave little mother exclaimed, "How can I do without Robert? He is both son and daughter to me!"

Cadet Lee's life was without doubt the bravest any young man ever led at West Point. Young Jefferson Davis, who was there at the same time, fell off a cliff and nearly lost his life while breaking the rules of the Academy. Young Ulysses Grant wrote home ten years later that it was impossible to get through at West Point without demerits. But Robert E. Lee went through the whole four years without a single "black mark"! More than this, he did{343}

Lee's invasion of the North.

From the painting by J. Steeple Davis, © 1897, by The Woolfall Co
Lee's invasion of the North.
From the painting by J. Steeple Davis, © 1897, by The Woolfall Co
not drink, though young gentlemen of that day thought the serving of wine necessary in polite society. He did not even smoke.

It was a wonder that the other cadets did not hate a young man who seemed to feel that he must behave better than the rest of them. What kept them all from calling him a "goody-goody boy," a snob or a prig? It was the love of his kind heart, which they could see shining through his strange courage. Robert Lee fully realized that he had come to West Point to learn, at his country's expense, how to be a soldier, and that the first duty of a soldier is to obey. If he had left his post and sneaked off the Academy grounds to drink, or gamble, or break some other rule, he would have been a deserter who, in real army life, would have deserved to be shot. But he never acted as if he felt above the rest, and so his fellow cadets did not sneer at Robert E. Lee. One of them said of him afterward:

"He was the only one of all the men I have known who could laugh at the faults and follies of others without losing their affection."

At graduation, Lieutenant Lee was the most popular man at West Point; he ranked second in his class, and received the highest military honor in the course.

The physical courage of Robert E. Lee was put to the supreme test in the Mexican War. On a dark night he found the way across a dangerous lava field cracked in all directions by deep crevices—"without light, without a companion or guide, where scarcely a step could be taken without fear of death." General Scott, then chief in command, reported this act to be "the greatest feat of physical and moral courage performed by any one in the campaign." In his official statement about the whole war,{345} this general stated that the United States' "success in Mexico was largely due to the skill, valor, and courage of Robert E. Lee, the greatest military genius in America."

Colonel Lee's high military reputation made it natural for President Lincoln to offer him the highest command of the United States army when the Civil War broke out. But Colonel Lee did not accept the honor. He did not believe in slavery, and did not think it was right for any of the states to secede, or leave the Union. But he was a Virginian, and he could not bring himself to lead an army to burn his own home or to kill or drive out his relatives, friends, and neighbors. He had heard his father, who was once governor of the state, say with deepest feeling, "Virginia is my country; her will I obey, no matter how sad my fate may be." So, when his native state went out of the Union, Robert E. Lee resigned as colonel in the United States army and went with her.

The southern people soon made Lee their general and it became, as he thought, his duty to defend the homes and lives of the people not only of Virginia, but also of the other states of the south.

General Lee soon proved that he was, as General Scott had said, "the greatest military genius in America." With smaller armies and poorer supplies and weapons than those of the north, he gained great victories—the second battle of Manassas, or Bull Run, Fredericksburg, and Chancellorsville. He defeated five northern generals, one after another. It took Grant, the sixth general sent against him, a whole year to "hammer" and surround Lee's ragged, starving heroes, and capture them at last, when they were almost as helpless as a little flock of shorn sheep. And so noble and dignified was his character that he was honored and admired by north and south alike.{346}

The motto of West Point Military Academy is "Duty, Honor, Country." All through his life, in all that he did, Robert E. Lee showed that he respected Honor, loved his Country, and almost worshiped Duty. He expressed this thought when he wrote, "Duty is the sublimest word in our language."

DAVY FARRAGUT, THE HERO OF MOBILE BAY

AFTER the War of Independence, there lived in a cabin among the mountains of Tennessee a Spaniard named Farragut, who had come to America to help the people in their fight for liberty. He had married a brave little Scotch woman. While her husband was away one day several skulking Indians hung around and watched for a chance to get into the cabin. The mother had seen them and sent her two little boys up under the roof, while she stood inside the door for hours, with an ax in her small hands, to kill the first Indian who tried to enter. After a long watch, the red men stole away, as much afraid of the fire in that little woman's eye as of the ax in her hands. One of the two boys who crouched in almost breathless silence up in the cabin loft was Davy Farragut.

When this lad was seven his father was appointed sailing master in the navy, and moved with his family to live by the large lake near New Orleans. When off duty, Farragut took his boys sailing on the lake. One day when he was out fishing he found an old man lying in the bottom of a rowboat, alone and unconscious. Farragut took the sick man home for his wife to nurse. In a few days the stranger died of yellow fever. The good wife caught the dread disease and died, too. The poor father was left to care for five motherless children under ten years of age.{347}

It turned out that Captain David Porter, who was then in command of the naval station at New Orleans, was the dead man's son. In gratitude for the care of his dying father, Captain Porter offered to adopt one of the Farragut boys. David was chosen, and the naval officer took the sturdy little lad to his home in New Orleans, and afterward to Washington, where he was sent to a good school.

In Washington the Secretary of the Navy saw what a bright, honest, pleasant-faced lad Davy Farragut was and, when he was ten years old, appointed him a midshipman on his adopted father's ship. This was early in the War of 1812. After Porter's warship, the Essex, had captured a British ship, the Alert, Middy Davy, lying awake in his hammock, saw a sailor of the Alert standing near, with a cocked pistol in his hand. Davy pretended to be asleep and the man passed on. The boy got up, crept into Captain Porter's cabin, and whispered to him what he had just seen.

"Fire! Fire!" shouted the captain, and the sailors of the Essex came scrambling up on deck. Porter ordered them down to capture the imprisoned sailors of the Alert, who were preparing to kill the American crew and take the ship to England. Before any damage was done, the astonished Britishers were all in irons, thanks to the wide-awake shrewdness of eleven-year-old Midshipman Farragut.

Captain Porter was ordered to sail around South America into the Pacific Ocean to warn American crews that there was a war going on between the United States and Great Britain. He was also to capture British ships as prizes. Over one of these ships he placed in command David Farragut—then a boy of twelve. When Davy ordered the British sailors to "fill away the maintopsail," the former captain of the ship was angry. It was bad enough to be{348} captured and have his ship taken into a South American port as a

144

prize; but to have his crew ordered about by an American boy of twelve seemed too much for an English captain to bear.

Shouting that he would shoot any Englishman who dared to touch a rope without his orders, the former captain went below to get his pistols to carry out his threat. Captain Farragut sent one of his men to follow the swearing captain down and tell him that if he came back on deck with a pistol in his hand he would himself be shot and pitched overboard. The man decided not to come back. Young David brought the British ship into port and reported to his proud foster-father what he had done.

The Essex fought a great battle with two British warships, and Farragut himself has left a description of the sights in his first great sea fight:

"I shall never forget the horrid impression made upon me at the sight of the first man I had ever seen killed. It staggered me at first, but they soon began to fall so fast that it all appeared like a dream, and produced no effect on my nerves.

"Some gun-primers [for loading the cannon] were wanted and I was sent after them. In going below, while I was on the ward-room ladder, the captain of the gun directly opposite the hatchway was struck full in the face by an eighteen-pound shot, and fell back on me. We tumbled down the hatch together.

"I lay for some moments stunned by the blow, but soon recovered consciousness enough to rush up on deck. The captain, seeing me covered with blood, asked if I were wounded; to which I replied, 'I believe not, sir.'

" 'Then,' said he, 'where are the primers?' This brought me to my senses, and I ran below again and brought up the primers."

After being powder boy and doing all sorts of service on a man-of-war, the little middy was taken prisoner, but was released at the close of the war.{349}

When Farragut was fifteen he went on a cruise in the Washington to watch for pirates in the Mediterranean Sea. While anchored off Naples he witnessed an eruption of the great volcano, Vesuvius. A naval chaplain, then American consul at Tunis, begged to have the Farragut youth stay with him, and study French, Italian, literature, and mathematics. While on a horseback journey to the Desert of Sahara, David suffered a sunstroke, which hurt his eyes so that he was unable to read much afterwards.

On his return home, Farragut passed the necessary examinations and at eighteen received the rank of lieutenant in the navy. Then he went to New Orleans and found that his father was dead and that his own sister did not know him. Here he was exposed to yellow fever and was very ill of it in a hospital after his return to Washington.

Lieutenant Farragut was married, soon after his recovery, and spent most of his time on shore until the breaking out of the Civil War. At that time he was living in Norfolk, Virginia. He did not, however, approve of the act of Virginia in withdrawing from the Union. People told him, that if he thought that, it would not be safe for him to live in Virginia. He replied coolly, "Well then, I can live somewhere else"; and he and his wife packed up and went to live on the Hudson River above New York City.

Though born and bred in the South, Farragut was a Union man and offered his services to his country. He was appointed to take New Orleans. It was the largest city in the South, and an important seaport. Its capture would cut short the war by preventing the South from selling cotton. Also, it would open the Mississippi, so that the western states could have that outlet to the sea. It was a dangerous undertaking, but Farragut was glad of the chance to risk{350} his life for his country. He said as he started out, "If I die in the attempt, it will only be what every officer has to expect."

Captain Farragut now commanded a fleet of forty-eight ships, carrying over two hundred guns. In six days and nights his mortars threw nearly six thousand shells on the two forts barring his way, one on each side of the Mississippi. The enemy sent five blazing rafts to set fire to his fleet, but Farragut's men either dodged the burning craft or towed them out of the way. One heroic deed was the cutting, under fire from the forts, of the great chain which had been stretched across the Mississippi to keep the ships from coming up to New Orleans.

This was one of the greatest naval battles in the war; for, with a few wooden ships, Farragut ran against the current and past the two forts, meeting fire-rafts and fighting with a large fleet above the forts. Two of the enemy's warships were ironclads. He finally captured the city of New Orleans after great loss of life on both sides. The next day the happy victor wrote home:

"My Dearest Wife and Boy:

"I am so agitated that I can scarcely write, and shall only tell you that it pleased Almighty God to preserve my life through a fire such as the world has scarcely known. He has permitted me to make a name for my dear boy's inheritance, as well as for my comfort and that of my family."

"The Hero of New Orleans" was soon made Rear Admiral for this, splendid service to the country. But there was to be still another test of the courage of David Glasgow Farragut. It came two years later in Mobile Bay, which he entered with fourteen ships and four monitors, or small ironclad boats. He saw his monitor, the Tecumseh, sinking with all on board.{351}

Farragut in the rigging at the battle of Mobile Bay
Farragut in the rigging at the battle of Mobile Bay
{352}
"What's the trouble?" came through his speaking trumpet to the men on the monitor nearest the sinking craft.

"Torpedoes!" was the reply.

What was to be done? Should he risk the whole fleet in a harbor filled with lurking mines? The good admiral sought help from above. "O God," he whispered, "direct me what to do."

Farragut heard the answer in his heart. Without an instant's delay he shouted to the captain of his own ship, the Hartford, "Go ahead! give her all the steam you've got."

The Hartford took the lead and became the chief target of forts and batteries on shore as well as of the Southern gunboats in the harbor. As if that was not dangerous enough, the heroic admiral took his place in plain sight high above the deck, where he could better direct the battle; and so that he could still keep his commanding place if struck by a cannon-ball, his devoted men lashed him to the rigging.

That is one of the heroic pictures in the history of patriotism: Admiral Farragut tied up in the rigging of his flagship and borne amid the whizzing of cannon-balls and the bursting of shells, carrying the Stars-and-Stripes through the fire and smoke of battle to one of the grandest victories ever won in naval warfare.

THE STRENUOUS LIFE OF ROOSEVELT

THEODORE ROOSEVELT'S father was a well-to-do business man in New York City. His forefathers were Dutchmen from Holland, who had come over when the country was new. The Roosevelts had been wealthy and well known for two hundred years. Though Theodore{353}'s

146

Theodore Roosevelt as Colonel of the Rough Riders.
Theodore Roosevelt as Colonel of the Rough Riders.
{354}
father was able to give his family everything they needed or desired, he could not give this little son health and strength, for the baby was born frail and weakly. He suffered so with asthma that his anxious parents feared he could not live long. One dark night when Baby Teddy was gasping for breath, they took him driving fifteen miles into the country where he could have pure air.

While yet in his childhood, Theodore Roosevelt began the long, sturdy fight to conquer his weak body and "make the most of himself." He was a "self-made man" even more than if he had been born poor but healthy in a log cabin. As a tiny child he tried to do what he saw well, strong boys do. As soon as he could run about the house he would climb up and perform such daring feats that the neighbors were often frightened. His father fitted up a gymnasium on a porch for him so that he could have fresh air while taking his health exercises.

It was a long, hard fight, but young Theodore's brave spirit won the victory over his frail body. While his body grew big and strong his brave heart seemed to grow larger too, and he showed a broad, unselfish spirit. Thus his big, warm, strong heart conquered his poor, puny body.

Almost in babyhood Teddy began to read. His sister tells how he came to her one day, still wearing a stiff white dress and his curly hair long, dragging a book that was too big to carry in his little arms, to ask her what "foraging ants" were. While learning to walk, ride horseback, and swim, Theodore Roosevelt was reading books and finding out all he could about birds, butterflies, and other insects by watching and catching them. He and several other small boys at Oyster Bay, where the family spent many summers, collected and mounted specimens, and started{355} what the boys called the "Roosevelt Museum of Natural History."

While preparing a butterfly for his "museum," Theodore happened to look at it through a small glass and found that he could not see as well as other boys. His father had spectacles fitted to his eyes, and everything looked so much clearer and brighter that he went about laughing and shouting "I can see!—I can see!"

The year when Theodore was eleven, the family traveled in Europe and Egypt. During their trip up the Nile he made quite a collection of the bright birds of that country for his "museum." His brother scolded because Theodore kept live specimens and mounting materials in the washbowls and pitchers in the rooms of the hotels where they were staying. The boys lived and studied in Germany long enough for Theodore to learn to speak German quite well.

At sixteen, young Roosevelt went to Harvard University. He was a good student, yet he spent much of his time in athletic sports. He would tie his glasses tight to his head and box with the biggest fellows he could find who would fight with him. Of these "misfit matches" the other students said, "Roosevelt has a bad handicap, but what he lacks in size and strength he makes up in pluck."

He spent his college vacations in the backwoods of Maine, and when he was graduated, at twenty-one, he had not only shown himself to be a good student, but he had gained much in health and strength. Also he read much more than was required in his college studies, and had begun to write his first big book, "The History of the Naval War of 1812."

After graduation, Theodore began to study law, and decided to go into politics. Many of the ward headquarters of New York City were in saloons. As he went about with{356} the ward workers, they expected their "silk stocking" candidate, as they called young Roosevelt, to favor the saloons and to use his "roll" (of money) freely. But instead of this, Theodore Roosevelt told them plainly that, if elected, he would fight against them and their bad methods.

He was elected and he kept his word. He began as a reformer, exposing and opposing bribery and other wicked things that were being carried on in politics. As Police Commissioner of New York he found much that was wrong and fought and struggled to make it right. He was Assistant Secretary of the Navy when the war was declared against Spain. He could not rest day or night because he found so much to do in getting ready to carry on the war. It was he who sent the word to Admiral Dewey on the other side of the world which prepared him for battle and helped the United States with the famous victory of Manila Bay. He was so keen and active that President McKinley said to his Cabinet: "Roosevelt has the whole program of the war mapped out." But he resigned from his office to become a colonel of the Rough Riders, and was soon leading his brave company of cowboys and college men up San Juan Hill in the face of a blazing Spanish battery.

Although Colonel Roosevelt was by no means highest in military rank, he became the hero of the United States' war with Spain. When that war was over he was elected governor of New York. All the "bosses" hated this man who would not consent to their robbing or cheating the people. They asked him to run for Vice-President of the United States, thinking that his hands would be tied, for a vice-president has very little to say as to how the government shall be conducted. But in a few months President McKinley, with whom Roosevelt was elected Vice-President,{357} was shot and killed. This made Theodore Roosevelt President of the United States. Four years later he was elected President again. His courageous spirit and true heart, with his active brain and tireless body, made him one of the greatest presidents of the United States.

He had kept himself in good health and spirits by his constant labors and many risks as a cowboy on his own ranches, and by hunting grizzly bears and other big game in the Far West. Even while living in the White House, he showed his friends and fellow-workers in the government what he meant by "the strenuous life."

Many expressions first used by Theodore Roosevelt are now heard in common conversation. This is the first use he made of the words, "the strenuous life":

"I wish to preach, not the doctrine of ignoble ease, but the doctrine of the strenuous life—the life of toil and effort."

The "square deal" was another expression of his, as in this statement:

"The labor unions shall have a square deal, and the corporations shall have a square deal, and, in addition, all private citizens shall have a square deal."

The "big stick," another phrase of Roosevelt's, was not so well understood. He said of this:

"There is a homely old adage which runs, 'Speak softly and carry a big stick and you will go far.' "

Other words of his—such as "mollycoddle," "pussyfoot," "hit the line hard," and "one hundred per cent American"—almost explain their own meanings.

A year after leaving the White House, Colonel Roosevelt went hunting big game—elephants, lions, rhinos, and so forth—through the heart of Africa. On the way back he{358} was the guest of kings, emperors, and important citizens of Europe.

After his return home he went on a dangerous trip of adventure and discovery in South America. From all these hunting trips he brought home many rare specimens for

148

collections called by his name in the finest Natural History museum in the United States. It was even proposed to name the wonderful Panama Canal, which he did most to put through, the "Roosevelt Canal."

His last years were spent in urging the patriotic men and women of America to take the part of human freedom, and force the "square deal" among the nations of Europe. Among his last words were: "He who is not willing to die for his country is not worthy to live in his country."

He believed in preventing war by being fit and prepared to fight. One of the best things he did was to help in arranging the peace treaty between Japan and Russia. Theodore Roosevelt's life motto, as expressed by his actions, was:

"In time of peace prepare for war; and in time of war prepare for peace."

CLARA BARTON, "THE ANGEL OF THE BATTLEFIELD"

MISS CLARA BARTON, a quiet little old lady, used to tell stories of her childhood among the hills of central Massachusetts. She remembered how she was taken to the village school for the first time, and how the teacher, a tall, kind-looking man, put her in the spelling class with the smallest children, to study such words as dog and cat.

"I don't spell there," said little Clara; "I spell in {359}Artichoke." And the small three-year-old showed her contempt for words of three letters by turning the leaves of her spelling book till she came to a page of wide three-syllable columns beginning with "Artichoke." The teacher had to hide his smile from the small girl who could spell such long words.

Clara was very fond of her handsome big brother. "My brother David was very fond of horses," she said, telling about him in later life. "He was the 'Buffalo Bill' of that part of the country. It was his delight to take me, a little girl five years old, to the field, seize a couple of beautiful young horses, and, gathering the reins of both bridles in one hand, throw me on the back of one colt, then spring upon the other himself; catching me by one foot, and bidding me 'cling fast to the mane,' we would go galloping away over field and fen, in and out among the other colts, in wild glee like ourselves.

"They were merry rides we took. This was my riding school. I never had any other, but it served me well. To this day my seat on a saddle or on the bare back of a horse is as secure and tireless as in a rocking-chair—and far more fun!

"Sometimes, in later years, when I found myself suddenly on a strange horse in a trooper's saddle, flying for life or liberty, I blessed my baby lessons and wild gallops among the beautiful colts."

By the words, "riding for life on a strange horse in a trooper's saddle," Miss Barton referred to her life as an army nurse, when she, with the mounted soldiers, sometimes found herself in great danger when the enemy's cavalry was close behind.

At the age of eleven, Clara had her first chance to learn to be a nurse and fit herself for her life work. Her brother{360}

Clara Barton, "The Angel of the Battlefield."
Clara Barton, "The Angel of the Battlefield."
{361}
David, then a young man, fell from the ridgepole of a large barn he was helping to build. The shock of this fall affected his mind, besides making him ill in body. He wanted no one near him but the brave little sister he had taught "to ride like the wind."

149

So Clara stayed with her big brother, day and night, for two long years. She was thirteen when he was well again. Miss Barton told, long afterward, of the strange feeling she had at that time:

"I was again free, my work done, I wondered that my father took me to ride so much, and that my mother hoped she could make me some new clothes now—for in those two years I had not grown an inch!

"My shut-in life had made me the more bashful. I had grown even more timid, shrinking, and sensitive in the presence of others; also I was afraid of giving trouble by making my wants known. Instead of feeling that my freedom gave me time for play, it seemed to me like time wasted, and I looked about, anxious to find something useful to do."

Then the family sent Clara away to school, hoping to conquer her painful shyness. She studied so hard that, at the age of fifteen, she became a teacher. There were not many public schools in those days, twenty-five years before the Civil War; and the few free schools were looked down on by well-to-do people as "charity" schools.

Clara Barton began with one of these schools where she had at first only six poor children to teach. But she was such a good teacher that before long six hundred came there to be pupils under her charge. She tried very hard to help everyone she could; at the end of eighteen years' service as a teacher she had become almost an invalid and had lost her voice.{362}

Still she could not bear to be idle while she had the use of her hands. From early girlhood her handwriting had been plain and neat. This, with her great desire to work, helped her to find a place in the Patent Office in Washington. Clara Barton was one of the first women to hold a position in the employ of the United States government. This gave offense to some of the men in that department. In those days most people thought it improper for a woman to work in an office; so these men stared at the new clerk, making remarks in her hearing about "brazen, strong-minded, 'woman's-rights' women," adding that such a creature was not fit to associate with gentlemen like themselves.

Sensitive and shrinking though she was, Miss Barton kept on. She was soon promoted to a position of trust. It was not long before she found that some of the very men who had insulted her were "patent thieves," guilty of selling government secrets. Her duty to the country, rather than a wish for revenge, obliged her to report the wrongs that these ungallant "gentlemen" had done, and they were promptly dismissed from the service they had betrayed.

During the years of her humdrum life as a government clerk, Miss Barton was thrilled by the stories she read in the newspapers of the noble work of Florence Nightingale, the famous nurse in the Crimean War between Great Britain and Russia. It was said that the English soldiers adored Nurse Nightingale almost as if she were an angel from heaven, and some of them kissed her shadow when it fell upon their pillows as she passed by.

When Fort Sumter was fired on and President Lincoln began calling for soldiers to defend the country, Clara Barton was soon found at the front, in places of great danger. Fitting up a house or even an old barn for a hospital, she{363} went about on the battlefields looking for wounded men, and doing all she could to relieve and help them. She ministered to the dying, writing many a last letter to give comfort to the sorrowing ones at home. Corresponding with newspapers in the north, she did wonders in obtaining medicines, hospital supplies, and comforts for her sick and wounded brothers in the army. She was appointed "lady manager" of all the hospitals at the front in Virginia. Those who knew most about her great work declared that her services to her country were wider reaching even than those of Florence Nightingale, the greatest nurse the world had yet known. Then it was that the grateful soldiers called Clara Barton "the Angel of the Battlefield."

During the last weeks of his life, President Lincoln sent for Miss Barton and asked her to undertake the difficult task of finding out in as many cases as possible what had become of the eighty thousand soldiers reported missing from the Union army. At this memorable meeting the Great Heart of the White House stood face to face with one of the greatest-hearted women in the world of that day.

Clara Barton spent four years more tracing out the fate of thirty thousand missing men. To her great joy she learned that thousands upon thousands of those who had been reported as deserters had bravely given their lives for their country.

Miss Barton then went to Europe to rest awhile and regain the health she had lost by overwork. While there she studied the work of a Swiss who was trying to found a new society for nursing and caring for the sick and wounded soldiers of all nations. Because it had a red cross on a white ground for badge and flag, it was named the Red Cross Society.{364}

When war broke out between France and Prussia, Clara Barton became known as "the Angel of the Battlefields" of France. After her return to the United States she began to organize the American Red Cross Society, which has since become the greatest power in the world for the relief of suffering.

Wherever there was a calamity or a pestilence—the great forest fire in Michigan; the earthquake at Charleston, South Carolina; yellow fever in Florida; the Johnstown flood in Pennsylvania; the Turkish massacres in Armenia—there Clara Barton, though now an old woman, was always "the first to come and the last to go."

Though she was seventy-seven in the year of the war with Spain, she was active in sharing the hardships of the American soldiers in Cuba, nursing Roosevelt's Rough Riders along with the rest of the sick and wounded at the front.

Though she lived to be over ninety, honored and beloved by millions for her constant labors of love and mercy, Clara Barton did not live to see, in the World War, the most wonderful carrying out of all her plans for soldiers on the field and in the hospital. The beautiful woman known as "the World Mother," pictured on the poster displayed to raise money and supplies for the Red Cross work in America, might well have been the portrait of Clara Barton, for no woman in all history has done more to relieve and heal the sufferings of mankind. The millions upon millions of men, women, and children now numbered in the membership of the American Red Cross Society, by giving, knitting, rolling bandages, or buying Red Cross stamps and Christmas seals, are carrying on the work begun by the frail, sickly, bashful little girl whose yearning heart and busy hands gave her the name of the "Angel of the Battlefield."{365}

HENRY W. LONGFELLOW, THE AMERICAN CHILDREN'S POET

LIVING in Portland, Maine, a town of rare beauty, Henry Wadsworth Longfellow could hardly have helped being a poet, even if he had tried. He was born in a big, square, three-story house, close to the edge of Casco Bay, one of the largest and loveliest harbors in the world. Portland stands on several wooded hills, overlooking the bay, which is said to contain three hundred and sixty-five small islands—one for every day in the year. On the blue water the green islands sparkle like emeralds on a shining sea of sapphire.

From the highest point on Great Diamond, one of the larger islands in the harbor, little Henry could see, sometimes, as the sun was setting behind the hills of Portland, the hazy blue and pink outlines of the White Mountains, more than a hundred miles away.

151

Any boy with eyes and heart to take in the deep meaning of it all would have wanted to be a poet. Henry's inner nature throbbed in response to the beauties of Nature without, and because he had the gift of putting his feelings into words, he was a poet long before he or those around him realized it.

Like the boy Benjamin Franklin and the boy George Washington, who lived about a hundred years before him, the Longfellow boy had the best chances to hear the sailors who came into port tell their tales of the sea—of pirates and hairbreadth adventures.

Henry's grandfather—his mother's father—was bluff old General Peleg Wadsworth, a hero of the Revolutionary War. He could tell stories of the struggle for independence that would have fired the soul of any boy.{366}

Henry Wadsworth Longfellow.
Henry Wadsworth Longfellow.
{367}
In the War of 1812, when the little Longfellow lad was only five, a company of American soldiers was stationed in the fort at Portland to defend the town against attacks from British warships. Young as Henry was, he understood what all the excitement meant. When he was in his seventh year, he heard the booming of the cannon in the great sea battle between the American brig Enterprise and the British schooner Boxer. Both commanders were killed and buried on one of the hills of Portland. There was a sensation when the Enterprise towed the Boxer into port as a prize of war. In the poem, "My Lost Youth," nearly fifty years after the battle, Longfellow wrote:
"I remember the sea-fight far away
How it thundered o'er the tide!
And the dead captains as they lay
In their graves o'erlooking the tranquil bay
Where they in battle died."

Out near Hiram, Maine, where the Wadsworth family lived, there was a little lake known as Lovell's Pond. On one of his visits to his grandfather's, young Henry heard the story of a battle which had taken place there during the French and Indian War. When he was thirteen he wrote four stanzas which he named "The Battle of Lovell's Pond." Signing it "Henry," he left it at the office of the Portland Gazette, telling only his sister what he had done. A writer has told a story of the way Henry's first published poem was received:

"In the morning how slowly the father unfolded the damp sheet, and how carefully he dried it at the open fire before he began to read it! And how much foreign news there seemed to be in it!{368}

"At last, Henry and the sister who shared his secret peeped over their parent's shoulder—and the poem was there! They spent most of the day reading it. In the evening they went to play with a son of Judge Mellen, and while the judge was sitting by the fire in the twilight with the young folk and a few older neighbors around him, he said,

"Did you see the piece in to-day's paper? Very stiff, remarkably stiff! Moreover, it is all borrowed—every word of it!"

When Henry was fifteen, his father sent him to Bowdoin College, at Brunswick, Maine, with his older brother, Stephen. Though the father was himself a graduate of Harvard, he was a director of this new college in his own state. Henry was graduated at eighteen and, young though he was, the trustees of the college invited him to come back, a few years later, as their professor of modern languages.

So the young graduate traveled in Europe to gain a speaking knowledge of all the languages he would have to teach. At the age of twenty-two, he became a professor at Bowdoin.

After five years at his own college, Henry Wadsworth Longfellow was chosen Professor of Modern Languages at Harvard. He spent the first year in Europe. The next year he began his work as a Harvard professor. He boarded at the Craigie mansion, which had been General Washington's headquarters during the first year of the War for Independence, sixty years before. Indeed, he slept in the same room occupied by the Father of his Country as a bedroom.

Although he had published several books of poetry, Longfellow's poems did not begin to be popular till "A{369} Psalm of Life" was published, in his thirty-third year. This poem made many people talk about him. Ministers preached about it, and the lines were set to music. Here is one stanza of this famous poem:

"Lives of great men all remind us
We can make our lives sublime,
And, departing, leave behind us
Footprints in the sands of time."

Then such short poems as "Excelsior," "The Village Blacksmith," "The Rainy Day," "The Arrow and the Song," "The Day Is Done," and many others, were recited in schools and sung in thousands of homes.

Of Longfellow's longer poems, "Evangeline" and "The Courtship of Miles Standish" are, perhaps, the most popular. It is said that more people know of the Pilgrim Fathers of Plymouth through the latter poem than by reading the history of the country. It is a story of the lovely Priscilla and her true lover, John Alden, who came to ask her to marry Miles Standish. That little captain was brave enough to fight with savages, but he shrank from the bright eyes of Priscilla Mullens. John Alden was a true soldier and delivered his captain's message, but Priscilla, knowing his loyal heart, only smiled at him and asked: "Why don't you speak for yourself, John?" And one of the great-great-great-grandsons of John Alden and his lovely wife, Priscilla, was the poet Longfellow!

"Hiawatha," the poem about the Indian tribes, is also a great favorite, especially with the children. This is because of its descriptions of Indian customs and legends. It is the life history of the Indian boy, Hiawatha, from the time when he was a funny little papoose till he had grown to sturdy manhood.{370}

When the little Indian boy was old enough he was sent out on a lone hunt through the wilderness to fit himself to become a true Indian brave. Here is what he did and saw and heard at that time:

"Forth into the forest straightway
All alone walked Hiawatha
Proudly, with his bow and arrows;
And the birds sang round him, o'er him:
'Do not shoot us, Hiawatha!'
Sang the robin, the Opeechee,
Sang the bluebird, the Owaissa,
'Do not shoot us, Hiawatha!'
"Up the oak-tree close behind him,
Sprang the squirrel, Adjidaumo,
In and out among the branches,
Coughed and chattered from the oak-tree,
Laughed, and said between his laughing,

153

'Do not shoot me, Hiawatha!' "

Some of the Indian tribes of the Great Northwest were so delighted with "Hiawatha" that they voted to make the poet one of their great chiefs; and after Longfellow himself had gone to the "Happy Hunting Grounds" across the River of Death, the Indians went through a formal service making the poet's daughter Alice a girl chief.

It must have been because he was so fond of children that Longfellow became known as the "Children's Poet." In the hall of quaint old Craigie House, which became the poet's home, stood the stately "Old Clock on the Stairs," solemnly ticking: "Forever, never! Never, forever!" In the early morning the spacious rooms were made bright with the merry laughter of Longfellow's three little daughters, running down to spend an hour with their kindly, white-haired poet father. Of this he wrote in a poem named "The Children's Hour"{371}:

"From my study I see in the lamplight,
Descending the broad hall stair,
Grave Alice, and laughing Allegra,
And Edith with golden hair."

Longfellow's last poem was about "The Bells of San Blas," which appeared in print just a few days before he died. The close of this—the last poetry he ever wrote—were these three lines:

"Out of the shadow of night
The world rolls into light—
It is daybreak everywhere."

Printed in the USA
CPSIA information can be obtained
at www.ICGtesting.com
LVHW010952210224
772436LV00013B/172